YOUR IBM® PC
MADE EASY

Jonathan Sachs

Osborne/McGraw-Hill
Berkeley, California

Published by
Osborne/McGraw-Hill
2600 Tenth Street
Berkeley, California 94710
U.S.A.

For information on translations and book distributors outside of the U.S.A., please write to Osborne/McGraw-Hill at the above address.

Material in Chapter 20, "Error Messages and Other Messages," is reprinted with permission of IBM.

YOUR IBM® PC MADE EASY

1234567890 DODO 89876543
ISBN 0-88134-112-6

Judy Ziajka, Acquisitions Editor
Steven Cook, Technical Reviewer
Jean Stein, Tim Field, Technical Editors
Geta Carlson, Copy Editor
Irene Imfield, Text Design
Yashi Okita, Cover Design
Richard Cash, Photographer

TRADEMARKS

The italicized names are trademarks of the following companies with registered trademarks noted with an ®.

Ashton-Tate	*dBASE II*®
Bell Laboratories	*UNIX*
Corvus Systems	*the Mirror*®
Digital Research	*CP/M-80, CP/M-86*
Dow Jones	*Dow Jones News/Retrieval*®
Information Unlimited Software	*EasySpeller II* *EasyWriter, EasyWriter II*
Lotus Development Corporation	*1-2-3*
Mark of the Unicorn	*The Final Word*
MicroPro International Corp.	*CalcStar, SpellStar, Wordstar*® *MailMerge*®
MicroSoft Corp.	*Multiplan, Xenix*
Phase One Systems	*Oasis*
Sorcim Corp.	*SuperCalc, SpellGuard,* *SuperWriter*
The Source Telecomp Corp.	*The Source* (service mark)
VisiCorp	*VisiPlot*®, *VisiTrend,* *VisiSchedule, VisiCalc*®, *VisiSpell*

ACKNOWLEDGMENTS

Steven Greenberg, of the Marin-Sonoma PC User's Group, gave me practical answers to many technical questions and provided me with a copy of PCDOS Version 2.0 months before it was generally available.

The staff of *PC World* provided incalculable aid, opening doors that I could not have opened myself, and supplying useful pieces of information that I would not have know where to look for.

IBM contributed a complete set of IBM's press releases on the IBM PC.

Many of the manufacturers and software developers that I contacted while compiling the "Guide to Resources" went out of their way to help me procure information I needed, whether or not it related specifically to their products. Of particular note were Ben Hedrick of the Safeco Insurance Companies and Steve Smith of FLC Financial Services.

Ron Lawrence, of Computerland of Oakland in Oakland, California, generously donated the use of his store's hardware and software for the computer graphics illustrations that appear in the "Guide to Hardware" chapter. Toni Thompson, also of Computerland of Oakland, created the graphics images that appear there.

Janet Gilvin gave me the hospitality of the Softwaire Centre International in Concord, California, for the better part of a day. Her assistance was most valuable in collecting information about software and services available for the PC.

J.S.

CONTENTS

INTRODUCTION

If you have just purchased an IBM PC or PC XT for use in your work or if you are considering one, this book is for you. It is written specifically for three different versions of the IBM PC:

- The PC, announced in August 1981.
- The PC XT, announced in March 1983. It has all the features of the PC, plus several features that the PC does not have.
- An updated version of the PC, informally introduced soon after the announcement of the PC XT. It is very similar to the original version but can accommodate more memory on its main circuit board: as many as 256,000 characters (256K), compared to the original PC's 64,000 characters (64K).

These three PCs are the same in most ways, and we will usually refer to them all as "the PC." When we say something that does not apply to all three of them, we will say "the PC I," "the PC XT," or "the PC II," respectively.

What This Book Is For

This book assumes that your first interest is to *get results* from your PC. Thus, the goal of this book is to help you get your PC up and running with as little delay as possible. As you progress through the tutorials in Part I, you will not be slowed by technical details that are not essential for the daily operation of your PC. If you have technical questions, however, Part II and Part III provide resource assistance and guidance that can help you answer them.

What This Book Is Not For

There are several things this book will *not* do for you. It will not teach you how to write computer programs. If you are interested in programming, read the section of "Guide to Resources" that discusses programming languages to see which language is most appropriate for your needs. Then go to a computer store or bookstore to select an introductory book on that language.

This book will not make you an expert at fixing hardware or software problems. Those skills are outside the interests of most business-oriented computer users, or would take too long for them to learn.

Finally, this book will not teach you how to use specific application programs, such as word processors or accounting programs. There are far too many such programs available for a book like this one to deal adequately with even a few. For that kind of information, see the user's manuals for the programs you want to use. For many of the more popular programs, independently written "how-to" books are available as well.

How This Book Is Organized

Your IBM PC Made Easy is divided into three major parts. Part I, "Using Your PC," contains information that you are likely to need no matter what you do with your PC. It is divided into 11 chapters, and each chapter is divided into lessons. You should read Chapters 1 through 7 in order and work through the lessons' examples on your PC. If you run into a problem, you can probably solve it yourself by looking it up in the nearest "Some Things That Might Go Wrong" box. These boxes identify some of the most common problems that new users are likely to encounter, and they appear frequently in the chapters in Part I.

Chapters 8, 9, and 10 contain more specialized information that you may not need. Read only those chapters that interest you. Chapter 11 contains important information about caring for your PC. Read it before you leave Part I.

Part II, "Guide to Resources," serves as a source of information about many accessories and computer programs that may enhance your PC's ability to serve you. The six chapters in this part tell you about dealers, hardware, software, services, accessories, and supplies for your PC. They also provide specific examples of products and services. (The names and addresses of many manufacturers and distributors mentioned in these chapters are listed in Appendix B, "Index of Suppliers.")

The three chapters in Part III present detailed reference information that can help you identify and correct problems. These chapters complement the lessons in Part I. If you wish to learn more about a particular function, or if you encounter a problem that is not explained in the first part of the book, you should consult the chapters entitled "Operations and Procedures," "Problem Determination," and "Error Messages and Other Messages" in Part III.

Finally, the appendixes provide several kinds of helpful information. Appendix A discusses the different versions of PCDOS, the IBM PC's operating system. Appendix B lists some leading suppliers of the products and services discussed in Part II, "Guide to Resources." Appendix C is a glossary of technical terms used throughout the book.

IBM's PC User's Manuals

IBM publishes several manuals for the PC that contain more detailed technical information than this book provides. You will find them a useful supplement to this book's reference sections.

The *Guide to Operations* is the central manual in IBM's PC library. It is packaged with the PC and it gives you basic instructions for setting up and operating the PC and the IBM Graphic Matrix Printer. The "Problem Determination Procedures" section contains detailed procedures for diagnosing problems with your PC's hardware. The "Options" section provides space for storing the reference manuals that come with the various circuit cards that are installed in your PC or may be added to it later.

The *Disk Operating System* manual is packaged with PCDOS, the most popular operating system for the PC. It describes the commands you can enter to control PCDOS and several programs that are distributed with the system.

Other IBM manuals are listed with "Books and Periodicals" in Chapter 15 of this book.

PART I

Using Your PC

Part I familiarizes you with your IBM PC and its operating system. In the chapters that follow, you will get to know the various parts of your PC and its most commonly used accessories. You will also learn to use your PC for many day-to-day functions.

The eleven chapters that follow present a combination of tutorials (lessons that you use to learn specific operations) and informational discussions. For your easy reference, lessons are numbered by chapter, and a list of lessons and major headings appears at the opening of each chapter.

CHAPTER 1

Getting to Know Your PC

This chapter introduces you to the major parts of your Personal Computer. It provides a broad orientation rather than a hands-on tutorial, which begins in Chapter 2.

This chapter assumes that your PC is already assembled and that someone has checked it out to make sure it is in working order. But if this is not the case, do not stop reading. You can assemble the PC and check it out yourself. After reading this chapter, follow the instructions under "Assembling the PC" in Chapter 18 of this book, "Operations and Procedures." To attach and check out a printer, modem, or other external device, follow the instructions in the "Options" section of IBM's Guide to Operations *manual, or consult the user's manual for that device.*

If you do not want to do your own assembly and checkout, a technically trained person can do it for you. The retail store or sales organization that sold you your PC should be willing to do this. If you obtained your PC from some other source, you can probably find a local store or consultant who will assemble it for a fee.

The System Unit

The heart of your computer is a rectangular metal cabinet with a sloping front panel. It is called the *System Unit,* and it is shown in Figure 1-1.

There is only one control on the System Unit: the main power switch, which is the large lever on the right side near the back.

One or two rectangular panels are on the System Unit's front. Behind these panels are your PC's *disk drives,* magnetic devices that are used to store data.

The back of the System Unit has several sockets for cables that connect the System Unit to various other devices. These sockets are shown in Figure 1-2. From left to right, the sockets are used for

- A cord that supplies power to the IBM Monochrome Display, which is one of the devices that you can use to display infor-

Figure 1-1.
The System Unit

mation. (Other display devices take power from a standard electrical outlet.)

- A cord that provides the System Unit with power from an electrical outlet.
- A cable that runs to the PC's keyboard.
- A cable that connects the PC to a cassette recorder for recording and playing back computer information. (This socket is absent on the PC XT.)
- Cables that transfer data between the PC and various external devices, such as a computer display, a printer, or external disk drives. The options that are present on your PC will determine what sockets and cables are present for communication with external devices.

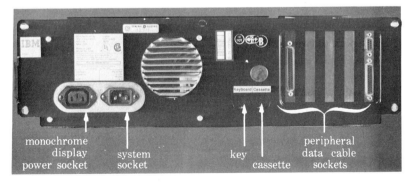

Figure 1-2.
Rear view of the System Unit

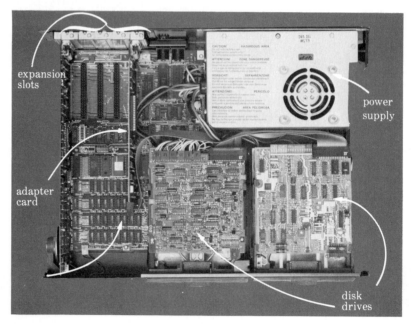

Figure 1-3.
The interior of the System Unit

Inside the System Unit

Although you probably will not spend much time puttering around inside the System Unit, you should understand what is in there, just as you should understand what is under the hood of your car even if you do not care to fix it yourself.

The inside of the System Unit is shown in Figure 1-3. Just above the bottom of the System Unit is a large printed circuit board with many electronic components mounted on it. This is the *System Board*. It contains most of the electronics that are at the heart of your PC's operations.

On the left rear corner of the System Board are several long, slot-shaped sockets. Some or all of these sockets will hold more printed circuit boards. The sockets are called *system expansion slots*. The printed circuit boards are called *option cards* or *adapter cards*, and they operate various devices such as disk drives, printers, and displays.

At the rear of most cards are one or more sockets like the ones shown in Figure 1-4. These sockets are for cabling the card to an external device like a printer. We saw these sockets when we inspected the back panel of the System Unit from the outside.

In the right rear corner of the PC is the *power supply*.

Just behind the System Unit's front panel, to the right of the

Figure 1-4.
Adapter card in PC with data cable sockets

adapter cards, are the disk drives. We saw the front of the disk drives when we examined the front panel of the System Unit.

The Display

Your PC's television-like display is its primary means of presenting information to you.

Three types of displays work with the PC. One, called a *monitor*, can display both alphanumeric data (letters and numbers) and graphics (pictures). It may display either a black-and-white or a color image.

The second type of display is called a *monochrome display*. It displays a monochrome image (most often green on black). Its *graphic* capabilities are limited, but it uses a specially developed electronic interface that produces a sharper image than a monitor does.

The third type of display is an ordinary television set connected to the PC through an *RF* (radio frequency) *modulator*. Although a television set has most of the capabilities of a monitor, it presents a poorer quality image, which makes it unsuitable for the prolonged use that your PC is likely to see in a work environment.

The Keyboard

The PC's keyboard is your primary means of communicating with the System Unit.

The keyboard can be tilted for greater typing comfort. If you want to tilt the keyboard, turn the knobs at each end of the keyboard to swing out two plastic feet that will lift the keyboard up in back. To restore it to its original position, simply press the knobs in and turn them.

The keyboard, shown in Figure 1-5, has several groups of keys in addition to the standard typing keys in the central keyboard area. We will simply point out these groups of keys now and discuss their use in later chapters.

On the far left side of the keyboard, the gray keys labeled F1 through F10 are the *program function keys*. These keys make the PC perform various functions that are defined by the computer program you are running.

The keys labeled ESC, CTRL, and ALT are directly to the left of the central portion of the keyboard. They are the *escape key*, the *control key*, and the *alternate key*, and they are used to control certain aspects of the PC's operation. We will discuss them in detail later.

Also in the left central area of the keyboard is the *tab key*, labeled ⇆. We will use the term TAB when we refer to this key later on in the book. The TAB key is similar to the tab key on a typewriter.

There are two keys labeled ⇧, one on each side of the central keyboard area. These are the *shift keys*, and we will use SHIFT to

The PC's keyboard

refer to them throughout this book.

The key to the right of the space bar, labeled CAPS LOCK, is similar to a typewriter's shift lock key, except that CAPS LOCK only affects alphabetic keys. For example, if you engage CAPS LOCK and press the A key, you will enter a capital *A;* but if you press the 3 key you will enter a 3, not a #. Pressing CAPS LOCK alternately engages and disengages (or "toggles" on and off) the caps-locking function.

The keys labeled ← and ↵ are the *backspace key* and the *enter* key. They function like the backspace and carriage return keys on a typewriter. We will use BACKSPACE and ENTER when we refer to these keys in this book.

PRTSC (print screen) and SCROLL LOCK/BREAK are used to control various aspects of the PC's operations. We will discuss the role of these keys at a later point.

The ivory keys on the right side of the keyboard make up the *numeric keypad*. These keys have two sets of functions: they can be used to enter numbers, like the keyboard of a calculator, or they can be used to control some of the PC's operations. For instance, the four cursor control keys, marked with directional arrows, are used to move the *cursor*, which is the blinking light that you will see on your display when you turn the PC on. You will be formally introduced to the cursor in Chapter 2.

The NUM LOCK key, located directly above the numeric keypad, is used to toggle the keys in the keypad back and forth between their two functions.

The gray keys labeled − and + are used to enter minus and plus signs. They are intended for use with the numeric keypad.

Your PC's Memory

Memory is the name for any part of a computer that is used to store data. Computer storage may be divided into two types, called "primary storage" and "secondary storage." You should understand these terms, since we will mention them frequently in later chapters.

Primary storage is memory that resides in your PC's circuitry and that contains data which is currently being used. When you run a program on your PC, for example, both the program and the data on which it operates are placed in primary storage.

Secondary storage consists of long-term memory devices on which the computer stores data when the data is not being used.

Magnetic disks are the PC's most common type of secondary storage.

Each kind of computer memory has a fixed capacity measured in *bytes*. A byte is the amount of memory that can hold one character of data; memory often is measured in units of 1024 bytes. (This unit is used because it is a power of 2 that is conveniently close to 1000.) If a memory device can hold 1024 bytes, it has a capacity of one *kilobyte*, or 1K. If a memory device can hold 1024K bytes, it has a capacity of one *megabyte*, or 1M.

Primary Storage: RAM and ROM

In modern computers, primary storage takes the form of *integrated circuits*, which are tiny electronic circuits encased in packages of plastic or ceramic. Many of the objects on the System Board and adapter cards are integrated circuits containing primary storage.

There are two types of primary storage. One is *random-access memory*, usually called *RAM*. A computer can store data in RAM at any time and read it back later. RAM is used to hold a computer program while it is being run and to hold the data on which the program operates.

The other kind of primary storage is *read-only memory*, or *ROM*. Data is stored in ROM when the ROM is manufactured. The computer can read the data in ROM but cannot change it. ROM is used to hold certain constant information that your PC needs in order to operate.

Two Kinds of Disks

Two kinds of disks may be used in the PC. One is a *diskette*, a 5 1/4-inch flexible disk that is coated with a magnetic recording surface and protected by a square plastic jacket. Information is recorded on a diskette and read back from it by a diskette drive. A diskette drive and a diskette are shown in Figure 1-6.

The second kind of disk, a *hard disk*, is made of metal. It requires a hard disk drive; it cannot be used in a diskette drive. Figure 1-7 shows IBM's Fixed Disk, which is an example of a hard disk in a hard disk drive.

A hard disk drive is faster than a diskette drive and can hold more data, but it is also more expensive. Diskettes are readily interchangeable, while a hard disk usually is permanently sealed into its drive.

The PC I and PC II come equipped with one or two diskette drives. An accessory called a *System Expansion Unit* can accommodate one or two Fixed Disks.

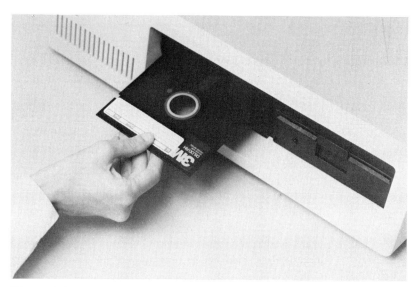

Figure 1-6.
A diskette being inserted in a diskette drive

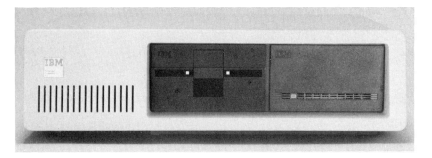

Figure 1-7.
The IBM PC XT with Fixed Disk drive on the right

The PC XT comes equipped with one diskette drive and one Fixed Disk. If you attach a System Expansion Unit to the PC XT, you can move the Fixed Disk there in order to add a second diskette drive to the System Unit. You can also add a second Fixed Disk to the System Expansion Unit.

About Software

Software is one of the most important concepts associated with computers. Once you understand what software is, you will find most of your PC's capabilities (and limitations) easy to understand.

A computer is just a machine that processes information stored in the form of numbers. You may think of it as an elaborate calculator.

When you use a calculator, you must push a button to make the calculator perform each operation. A computer pushes its own buttons. Just as it stores data, it can store a long series of instructions that tell it what operations to perform on the data. Such a series of instructions is a computer program. Computer programs are known collectively as "software."

Types of Software

There are four basic types of software: application programs, programming language processors, system utilities, and operating systems.

Application programs are programs that you run to perform a task like composing a letter, calculating your company's payroll, or keeping your appointment book. Thousands of application programs are available for the PC. Chapter 14, "Guide to Software," discusses the most important kinds of application programs. All high-quality application programs are sold with detailed instruction manuals. In addition, there are now many books on the market that teach you how to use the more popular application programs.

Programming language processors are used to develop new computer programs of all types. If you choose to learn a programming language, you can use a programming language processor to develop application programs for specialized tasks that commercially available software does not perform.

System utilities perform "housekeeping" tasks such as preparing new disks for use, setting the date and time in the PC's internal clock, and changing the way the PC displays data on a monitor. You will learn to use several PC system utilities as you read this book.

Operating systems constitute the last type of software. An operating system is a program that works behind the scenes while an application program or utility is running. The operating system takes care of such basic tasks as reading application programs from a disk, collecting keystrokes from the keyboard, and presenting an application program's output on the display.

Your PC can run any of several operating systems. The most common one, IBM's PCDOS, is described in this book. PCDOS is short for "PC disk operating system" and is generally known simply as DOS.

Options for Your PC

Many of the options available for the PC will affect the way your PC behaves in the lessons that follow. For the sake of simplicity, this book will deal only with the more common combinations of options.

We will assume that your PC has the following options:

- At least 64K of RAM.
- PCDOS 2.0 or 1.1.
- At least two diskette drives, or one diskette drive and one hard disk drive.

The options discussed in the tutorial chapters are clearly marked to enable you to identify guidelines that apply to your own PC.

CHAPTER 2

Getting Started

You learned about the components of your PC in Chapter 1; this chapter helps you begin to use it. In the lessons that follow in this chapter, you will learn how to turn on your PC, perform several kinds of simple operations, and turn off your PC.

About DOS

IBM periodically releases improved versions of PCDOS. Each version of DOS is identified by a *version number.* You can tell which version of DOS you have by looking at the printed label on the original DOS diskette that came with your PC. If you do not have that diskette, DOS will tell you what version it is when you start to run it.

This book describes DOS 2.0, which is the most current version at the time of this book's publication. DOS 2.0 can perform more functions than the two other significant versions, numbered 1.0 and 1.1. If you have an earlier version, some of the lessons in this book will not work. These lessons are marked "DOS 2.0 Only." In addition, earlier versions of DOS may display messages that are different from the messages produced by DOS 2.0. We will note these differences in the text only when they are significant enough to cause possible confusion.

We recommend that you use only version 2.0 of DOS unless you are working with a piece of hardware or software that requires an earlier version. DOS 2.0 is not expensive, and its extra features are well worth its cost.

Before You Start

To work through the lessons in this chapter, you will need a diskette containing a copy of DOS. If your PC is brand-new, you will find two diskettes in the back of IBM's *Disk Operating System* manual. Use the diskette that is labeled "DOS" (not "DOS Supplemental Programs"). If your PC is already in use, you may have a copy rather than the original DOS diskette supplied by IBM.

You will also need at least three unused diskettes. Get new diskettes if you can. Used diskettes are also fine, *as long as they contain no information that must be preserved*. This point is important, for any information on your disks will be erased when you use them in the lessons that follow.

Lesson 2-1: Starting the PC

To start the PC, you must turn it on and make it start running DOS.

Gently lift the latch on the System Unit's left-hand diskette drive. (This drive is called *drive A*.) Slip the DOS diskette out of its protective paper envelope, being careful not to touch its recording surfaces with your fingers or any other object. Hold the diskette so that its preprinted label is face up, as shown in Figure 2-1, and gently insert it into the diskette drive. Carefully lower the diskette drive latch.

If you have a monitor with its own power switch, turn it on. If you are using the IBM Monochrome Display, this step is unneces-

Figure 2-1.
The correct way to insert a diskette into a diskette drive

sary, since the display draws its power from the PC when you turn the PC on.

If you have a hard disk or System Expansion Unit with its own power switch, turn it on before you turn the PC on.

Now start the PC by lifting the red switch on the right side of the System Unit. If you do not see anything on the screen after 15 seconds or so, adjust your display's brightness control.

If you have a PC XT, you will see some numbers in the upper-left corner of the display. These numbers increment for a period of about 10 to 90 seconds as the PC XT checks itself out to be sure everything is in working order. If you have a PC I or PC II, you will see only a blinking horizontal bar while the PC checks itself out. This does not mean that anything is wrong!

When the system checkout is complete, the PC reads DOS into RAM from the DOS diskette.[1] We say that the PC *boots* DOS from the diskette—a term that may sound odd at first. The term derives from the notion of a computer "pulling itself up by its bootstraps."

When the PC boots DOS, the diskette drive makes a brief buzzing noise, and the red light on the drive flashes on. Then the PC beeps once. DOS displays something like this on the monitor's screen:

```
Current date is Tue   1-01-1980
Enter new date:
```

The flashing "_" after "Enter new date:" is the PC's *cursor*. The cursor marks the place where the next entry you type will appear on the display.

At this point, DOS is asking you to enter today's date.[2] Enter the date in the same format as DOS displayed it: month, then day, then year, with hyphens in between. Omit the day of the week; DOS computes that itself.

Thus, if today is March 23, 1983, enter the following in boldface type. (Throughout this book we will use boldface type to designate entries you make on your keyboard.)

---

[1] If you have a PC XT with DOS on its Fixed Disk, you may also boot from the Fixed Disk. Lesson 3-4 (in Chapter 3) explains how this is done.

[2] Certain PC adapter cards contain a battery powered clock that keeps track of the current date and time even when the PC is turned off. If your PC is equipped with such a card, it may set the date and time automatically when you boot. In this case you will not see the "Enter new date" and "Enter new time" prompts.

```
Current date is Tue  1-01-1980
Enter new date: 3-23-1983{ENTER}
```

If you make a mistake, you can erase it by pressing the BACK-SPACE key. When the date is complete, press ENTER to make DOS accept it.

If the date displayed by DOS is correct, you can tell DOS to use it by pressing ENTER alone.

Next, DOS displays its idea of the current time:

```
Current date is Tue  1-01-1980
Enter new date: 3-23-1983
Current time is  0:00:43.55
Enter new time:
```

Enter the correct time in the same format that DOS used. You may omit the seconds and fractions of a second. For example, if the time is 9:30 A.M., enter

```
Current time is  0:00:43.55
Enter new time: 9:30{ENTER}
```

Again, if DOS's time is correct, you can accept it simply by pressing ENTER.

Use 24-hour notation to enter times later than 12:59 P.M. For example, for 1:00 P.M. enter 13:00 and for 9:30 P.M. enter 21:30.

After you enter the time, DOS displays its version number and a copyright notice:

```
Current date is Tue  1-01-1980
Enter new date: 3-23-1983
Current time is  0:00:43.55
Enter new time: 9:30:00

The IBM Personal Computer DOS
Version 2.00 (C)Copyright IBM Corp 1981, 1982, 1983

A>
```

Now you have turned on the PC and started DOS.

Some Things That Might Go Wrong:
Booting DOS

Here are some things that might go wrong as you work through Lesson 2-1.

The PC does nothing when turned on. Remember that the PC checks itself out before booting and that the checkout can take as long as 90 seconds if the PC has a lot of RAM.

If the display does not show the PC XT's increasing numbers or the plain PC's blinking bar, the display's brightness or contrast controls may be set too low. Try adjusting them. If that does not help, make sure the monitor is turned on. If that does not help either, turn the PC off and make sure the monitor is correctly and firmly connected to its power source and to the socket that feeds it data from the PC.

If the PC does nothing when its checkout should be complete, see Chapter 19, "Problem Determination," for further suggestions.

The PC displays a message beginning "The IBM Personal Computer Basic". You probably forgot to insert the DOS diskette, or you inserted it incorrectly. Review the instructions for inserting the diskette.

If you have two diskette drives, perhaps you inserted the DOS diskette in the wrong drive. It goes into the *left* drive, drive A.

The prompt says C> instead of A>. This is what happens on a PC XT when you try to boot and the diskette drive is not ready for use, but the hard disk is present and ready. Insert the DOS diskette into drive A and reboot. Instructions for booting without turning your PC off and on again are given in the next section, "Rebooting Without Turning Off the PC."

The PC displays a message beginning "Bad or missing Command Interpreter" or "Non-System disk or disk error". Some of the things that should be on your DOS diskette are not there. Tell the person who gave you the diskette that it has no copy of COMMAND.COM; that person should know what this means and how to fix it.

If you are certain that your diskette contains a valid copy of DOS, the diskette has probably been damaged. Study the cautions on diskette handling in Chapter 3's box, "Diskette Do's and Don'ts," and then try booting with another copy of the DOS diskette.

Rebooting Without Turning Off the PC

Occasionally, a hardware or software problem makes it necessary to reboot your PC. Your PC will reboot automatically if you turn it off and then turn it on again. But turning your PC off and on frequently is unwise, because in the long run doing so will impose wear on the electronics inside. Thus, it is useful to know how to *reboot* the PC without turning it off.

Figure 2-2.
The CTRL, ALT, and DEL keys, used for rebooting

The preferred way to reboot is to hold down the CTRL and ALT keys and press the DEL key, as shown in Figure 2-2. Try rebooting your PC now by pressing this combination of keys.

In rare cases the CTRL ALT DEL combination does not work. If this happens to you, turn your PC off, wait a few seconds, and turn the PC on again.

CAUTION

Never turn off your PC unless DOS is prompting you to enter a command and the light on the disk drive is off. If you turn it off while a command is running or the light is on, the data on your disks may become scrambled.

Lesson 2-2:
Entering Two Commands—DIR and CHKDSK

This lesson starts where we left off in Lesson 2-1. If you turned your PC off after that lesson, turn it on again now and restart DOS. If you did not turn your PC off, the last line on your display should be

A>

The "A>" is a *prompt* from DOS. A prompt is simply a message inviting you to enter some information. The letter "A" appears in the prompt because you booted from disk drive A. (If you booted from the Fixed Disk, which is drive C, DOS would prompt you with "C>".)

Whenever DOS prompts you, you may respond with a line of input. Since this input instructs DOS to perform some action, it is called a *command*.[3] In this lesson, we will learn to enter two commands: the DIR command and the CHKDSK command.

The DIR Command

The DIR command lists a diskette's *directory*. The directory is a part of the diskette that tells you what information is stored on the diskette, much as a directory in an office building tells you what businesses are in the building.

Press the D key, and a "d" or a "D" will appear on the display where the cursor was. (You may enter commands in either upper- or lowercase: DOS will not care.) The cursor moves forward one column.

```
A>d
```

Press the I and R keys:

```
A>dir
```

Then press the ENTER key:

```
A>dir{ENTER}
```

When you press ENTER, the PC reads the DOS diskette for a moment and then displays something like this:

```
A>dir{ENTER}

Volume in drive A has no label
Directory of  A:\

COMMAND   COM    17664    3-08-83    12:00p
ANSI      SYS     1664    3-08-83    12:00p
FORMAT    COM     6016    3-08-83    12:00p
            .
            .
            .
MORE      COM      384    3-08-83    12:00p
BASIC     COM    16256    3-08-83    12:00p
BASICA    COM    25984    3-08-83    12:00p
        23 File(s)       31232 bytes free

A>
```

The first part of the display may disappear off the top of the screen before the last part appears. You will learn how to prevent that in a minute.

---

[3] The term "command" does not apply solely to your responses to DOS prompts. In general, your response to a prompt issued by any computer program is called a command.

Each line in DIR's output represents one *file*. A file is an area on a disk containing a collection of data. The first two columns are the two parts of the file's name; the third column shows the size of the file in bytes; and the last two columns show the date and time when the file was created or last changed (this is called the *time stamp*).

The CHKDSK Command

CHKDSK is another DOS command. As its name indicates, it checks the condition of a diskette. Try entering it now: type "chkdsk" and press ENTER. The command and the PC's resulting output should look something like this:

```
A>chkdsk{ENTER}

    179712 bytes total disk space
     22016 bytes in 2 hidden files
    126464 bytes in 23 user files
     31232 bytes available on disk

    131072 bytes total memory
    106496 bytes free

A>
```

Halting the PC in the Middle of a Command

Sometimes you may want to halt the PC in the middle of a command in order to examine what is on the display. You may have wanted to do this when you entered the DIR command and the first part of its output disappeared from the screen before the last part appeared.

To make the PC halt in the middle of a command, hold down the CTRL key and press the NUM LOCK key. To make the PC resume what it was doing, press any typing key.

Run DIR again and try this.

Lesson 2-3:
Correcting Mistakes and Discarding Commands

If you press the wrong key while entering a DOS command, it is not serious. You can erase your mistake by pressing the BACK-SPACE key. For example, enter the following:

```
A>dur
```

That is an error; you should have entered "dir". Press BACKSPACE twice to erase as far back as the incorrect character,

A>**d**

and enter the correct characters:

A>**dir**

DOS also allows you to discard an entire command line at any point before you press ENTER. To discard a command line, press the ESC key. For example, enter

A>**dir{ESC}**

DOS displays a "\", discards the command you have just entered, and moves the cursor to the next line:

A>**dir**

Now you can enter any other command you choose.

If you enter an erroneous DOS command and press ENTER, will something terrible happen? Certainly not! Try entering a misspelled command or a line of complete nonsense to see how the PC responds.

If you enter a command that you decide you should not have entered, you can abort the command in most cases by holding down CTRL and pressing BREAK. Of course, CTRL BREAK cannot undo anything the command has already done.

Many application programs have special commands for ending the program and returning to DOS. You should always use a program's "end" command, if one exists, instead of CTRL BREAK. This will ensure that the program ends in an orderly way and that the data the program was operating on is left in a usable state. Reserve CTRL BREAK for ending DOS commands and other programs that have no "end" command of their own and for emergencies when a program's "end" command does not seem to work.

Some application programs, including DOS's EDLIN, actually disable CTRL BREAK or change its function. When you run such a program, you *must* use its "end" command to return to DOS.

Lesson 2-4:
Using DISKCOPY to Back Up the DOS Diskette

Because diskettes are delicate, it is important to make a *backup copy* of every diskette you use. If the original diskette is damaged, you will be able to recover the data from the backup.

In the first part of this lesson, you will learn how to back up a diskette on a PC that has two diskette drives and no hard disk. In the second part, you will learn how to back up a diskette on a PC that has one diskette drive and a hard disk.

If you have no hard disk, work through the first part of the lesson. As an exercise, you will back up your DOS diskette. You may skip the second part.

If you have a hard disk, read the first part of the lesson but do not try to do what it says. You will back up your diskette in the second part.

Part 1:
A System With Two Diskette Drives

Make sure the DOS diskette is in the left-hand drive, and then enter the following command:

```
A>diskcopy a: b:{ENTER}
```

This command line contains something new: the "a:" and "b:" after the name of the command. These are *parameters*, and they tell the DISKCOPY command what you want it to do.

The first parameter tells DISKCOPY to copy *from* the diskette in drive A, the left-hand drive. The second parameter tells DISKCOPY to copy *to* the diskette in drive B, the right-hand drive. In DOS command lines and programs, you will almost always refer to a disk drive in this way: that is, with a letter giving the *drive name*, or *drive specifier*, followed by a colon.

DISKCOPY instructs you to insert the *source diskette* (the one to copy from) in drive A, and the *target diskette* (the one to copy to) in drive B:

```
A>diskcopy a: b:{ENTER}

Insert source diskette in drive A:

Insert target diskette in drive B:

Strike any key when ready
```

You need not act on the first instruction, since you want to copy the DOS diskette, and it is already in drive A. Insert an unused diskette in drive B and press any typing key.

DISKCOPY reads from the diskette in drive A and writes to the diskette in drive B, a process that may take several seconds. When it is done, DOS asks you if you want to copy another diskette:

```
A>diskcopy a: b:{ENTER}

Insert source diskette in drive A:

Insert target diskette in drive B:

Strike any key when ready

Copying 9 sectors per track, 1 side(s)

Formatting while copying

Copy complete

Copy another (Y/N)?
```

You are not going to copy another diskette, so press the N key to end DISKCOPY.

To copy another diskette (or make another copy of the same diskette), you would press the Y key. DISKCOPY would return to the "Insert source diskette" prompt and go through the same procedure again.

Part 2:
A System With One Diskette Drive and a Hard Disk

Enter the DISKCOPY command just as you would on a system with two diskette drives:

```
A>diskcopy a: b:{ENTER}
```

Since you have only one diskette drive, DOS uses that drive when you refer to drive A *or* drive B. DISKCOPY does not copy the DOS diskette onto itself, though. Instead, it lets you switch diskettes between operations on the source diskette and the target diskette. In this way you can process two diskettes even though you have only one diskette drive.

DISKCOPY prompts you to insert the source diskette in the drive and reads part of it. Then it prompts you to insert the target diskette in the drive and writes what it just read. Then it prompts you to insert the source diskette again, and so on, until it has copied everything. Be sure to wait for the disk drive light to go off each time you open the drive door to change diskettes.

Some Things That Might Go Wrong: Using DISKCOPY

Your PC displays the message "Not Ready Error Reading Drive A. Correct, then strike any key". DISKCOPY is trying to read the diskette in drive A, but the drive is not ready for use. Make sure the diskette is properly inserted and the drive door is closed, and then press any standard typing key.

PC displays the message "Bad program name". You may have misspelled the DISKCOPY command. If you did not misspell DISKCOPY, then DISKCOPY must be missing from your DOS diskette. Ask a more experienced DOS user for assistance.

PC takes more than a minute or so to copy a diskette, or the diskette drive makes rattling sounds. Either your target diskette is defective, or your diskette drive is out of order. Reboot the PC by holding down CTRL and ALT and pressing DEL. Try backing up the DOS diskette to a different target diskette. If your second attempt fails in the same way, and a third attempt with yet another diskette also fails, you can be virtually certain that one of the drives is out of order. Have it repaired.

PC displays a message beginning "Unrecoverable write error on target". You may be using the wrong kind of diskette for an IBM PC. Check your target diskette's part number in Table 17-1, "PC Compatible Diskettes." If you are using the right kind of diskette, the diskette is probably defective.

PC displays the message "Target disk write-protected". Your target diskette's write-protect notch (the square notch on the right edge) is covered. This prevents the PC from writing anything on the diskette. If the diskette is not one you want to protect, uncover the notch. Otherwise, use another disk.

You will also get this message if you insert the diskette upside-down.

PC displays the message "Invalid drive specification". You entered the drive name of a nonexistent drive. Try again.

Keep the Copy!

Write something like "PCDOS backup" on an adhesive diskette label, and gently press the label onto the plastic jacket of the backup diskette (see Figure 2-3.) Put the diskette in a safe place. You might need it some day.

If your original DOS diskette is the *original* original supplied by IBM, put *it* away in a safe place. Let the backup you just made be your working copy. To be especially safe, you may want to make a second copy and put that in a safe place, too.

Figure 2-3.
Attaching a label to a diskette

By the way, never write on a label that is already attached to a disk with anything but a felt-tip pen. The pressure created by the point of a ballpoint pen or a pencil can damage a disk's recording surface.

CHAPTER 3

Introducing Disks

You will be learning more about diskettes, hard disks, and drives in this chapter, and you will begin to feel comfortable with several different operations that are part of the everyday use of your PC. Before you start, it is important to understand some basic things about diskettes, for you will handle them virtually every time you operate your computer.

About Diskettes

Diskettes are sturdy enough to be used and reused many times, and if you treat them with due care, they will seldom wear out. A diskette cannot take unlimited abuse, however. Unlike a phonograph record, a diskette cannot accumulate a few scratches and still work reasonably well. Just one scratch can destroy part of the data stored on a diskette and render the whole diskette useless. Diskettes may also be damaged or ruined in many other ways that may not be obvious to new users.

It is thus important to handle your diskettes properly in order to keep your data secure. The box entitled "Diskette Do's and Don'ts" provides some guidelines for care of your diskettes. By observing them, you will greatly reduce your chances of losing computer data because of diskette failure.

The Write-Protect Notch

Something not mentioned in "Diskette Do's and Don'ts" is the *write-protect notch,* which is the square notch on the right edge of a diskette's plastic jacket. It is important to know about write-protection so that you can safeguard information on a diskette against accidental erasure.

The write-protect notch is normally uncovered, as it is on the bottom diskette in Figure 3-1. As long as it remains uncovered, the PC can both read data from and write data on the diskette. If the notch is covered by a piece of tape, however, the diskette is write-protected. (Figure 3-1 also shows a write-protected diskette.) Any

Figure 3-1.
Diskettes with uncovered write-protect notch and
with write-protect tab covering notch

attempt to copy information onto (or to *write to*) a write-protected
diskette will fail.

Every box of new diskettes comes with a sheet of write-
protection tabs that you can stick over the write-protect notch and
remove as necessary. In this way, you may write-protect any diskette that you want to protect against erasure or modification.
Many users write-protect their DOS diskettes. Your original DOS
diskette has no write-protect notch; it is permanently write-
protected.

If you try to write to a write-protected diskette, you will get a
message and a prompt like this:

```
Write protect error writing drive B
Abort, Retry, Ignore? _
```

Press the A key to abort the program you are trying to run.
Then uncover the diskette's write-protect notch, or insert a different diskette, and rerun the program.

CAUTION:

Write-protecting a diskette does not free you from the need to make
backup copies of it. Write-protection gives your diskette no immunity
against damage, wear, or loss.

Diskette Do's and Don'ts

Keep the environment clean. Diskettes are designed for use in a normal office or home. Do not use them in a place that is unusually dirty or dusty.

Protect diskettes when not in use. Keep each diskette in its paper envelope whenever it is not in the diskette drive. Store diskettes in closed boxes or other containers. Never leave them out where dust can accumulate on them.

Protect diskettes from pressure. Excessive pressure can grind particles of dirt into the recording surface. Store your diskette boxes on end and leave some loose space in each one. Never place a heavy object like a book on top of a diskette.

A pencil or ballpoint pen can exert great pressure on a small area, so *write on a diskette's label only with a felt-tip pen.*

Do not touch a diskette's recording surface with your fingers, with a cleaning tool, or with anything else. Even the softest, cleanest object may leave scratches or dirt on the diskette.

Avoid extremes of temperature and humidity. Do not leave a diskette in direct sunlight, on a radiator, or near a similar source of heat. See your diskette manufacturer's instructions for specific advice.

Protect diskettes from strong magnetic fields, which may erase the information stored on them.

Back up everything with COPY or DISKCOPY. Never, under any circumstances, assume that you are safe without a backup. Whenever you add or change information on a diskette, back up that diskette before the end of the day. Devise a routine for creating and filing backup diskettes, and stick to it!. For some suggestions on procedures for disk backup, see Chapter 18, "Operational Procedures."

Lesson 3-1:
Formatting a Diskette

Before you can store files on a new diskette, you must prepare the diskette for use by *formatting* it. Formatting a diskette consists of recording a special pattern of data over the diskette's entire surface.

The DISKCOPY command automatically formats the target diskette if that diskette is not already formatted. That was the meaning of the "Formatting while copying" message that DISKCOPY displayed when you ran it in Lesson 2-4.

If you plan to use a brand-new diskette for a purpose other than backing up another diskette with DISKCOPY, you first must format the diskette yourself. You do this with a command called FORMAT. FORMAT expects one parameter, the name of the drive on which the diskette is to be formatted.

In this lesson you are going to format one of your unused diskettes. With your DOS diskette in drive A, type

```
A>format a:{ENTER} (if your PC has one diskette drive)

A>format b:{ENTER}(if your PC has two diskette drives)
```

FORMAT prompts you to insert a diskette in drive A or B. Insert one of your unused diskettes in the appropriate drive and press any key. FORMAT proceeds to format the diskette. You can hear the drive click as its read/write head moves over the diskette's recording surface.

If you have only one diskette drive, it is OK to remove the DOS diskette from the drive to insert the new diskette, as long as the red light is not on.

When FORMAT is done, remove the formatted diskette from the drive. If you have only one diskette drive, reinsert the DOS diskette. Write some identification on an adhesive label and stick the label gently on the front of the diskette.

If you want to format more diskettes, respond to the "Format another disk?" prompt by pressing Y. FORMAT will prompt you to insert the next diskette. When you are done formatting diskettes, respond to the "Format another disk?" prompt by pressing N, and FORMAT ends.

Using the /V Option to Define a Volume Label

If you are running DOS 1.1, you will not be able to work through the examples in the rest of this lesson. Read the lesson anyway, however, because it introduces the concept of an "option," which you will need in later lessons.

DOS 2.0 allows you to record a *volume label* on a diskette when you format it. The volume label is a name that identifies the diskette. You record a volume label on a diskette by running FORMAT like this:

```
A>format a:/v{ENTER} (if your PC has one diskette drive)

A>format b:/v{ENTER}(if your PC has two diskette drives)
```

The /V after the parameter is an *option*. It gives FORMAT additional instructions on how to do its job. FORMAT interprets the /V option to mean, "After formatting each diskette, prompt the user for a volume label and record the label on the diskette."

If you are running DOS 2.0, format your new diskette again, this time using the /V option. After FORMAT formats the diskette, it prompts you to enter a volume label.

Enter a volume label and press ENTER. You may use virtually any label that you consider meaningful, although there are limitations. A volume label may be up to 11 characters long and may consist of letters, numerals, and certain punctuation characters. For a complete list of valid characters, see Lesson 4-2, "Rules for Creating a File Specification," in the next chapter.

You might choose the name "MADEEASY" for your freshly formatted disk. FORMAT records the label on the diskette and displays the diskette's data capacity. Then it asks you whether you want to format another diskette.

You need not record a volume label on a diskette, but it is always good practice to do so. By recording a unique volume label on each diskette you use, you ensure that you will always be able to tell your diskettes apart.

Note that you need not format a diskette twice to record a volume label on it, as you did in this lesson. Just use the /V option the first time you format the diskette.

More About Options

An option consists of a / followed by one other character. It may be used after a command name or after a parameter. In most commands the position of an option does not matter, but it is customarily placed after the last parameter, as in the preceding examples.

Different commands accept different sets of options and interpret them in different ways. As you progress through these lessons, you will learn about other options accepted by FORMAT and by other commands.

Using the VOL Command (DOS 2.0 Only)

Once you have formatted a disk and given it a volume label, you can display the volume label at any time with the VOL command. For example, to display the volume label of the disk in drive B, enter

```
A>vol b:{ENTER}

Volume in drive B is MADEEASY

A>_
```

A second way of displaying the volume label of a disk is to run the DIR command.

Lesson 3-2:
Using Commands With a Drive Name

In this lesson you will learn how to tell a command to act on any drive you choose.

Just as DISKCOPY accepts two parameters naming the drives you want to copy from and to, most commands accept a parameter naming the drive you want to use. For example, to run CHKDSK on a diskette in drive B, you would enter

`A>chkdsk b:{ENTER}`

CHKDSK displays information about the diskette in drive B. Again, to get a directory listing of a diskette in drive B, you would enter

`A>dir b:{ENTER}`

If you have an IBM Fixed Disk, you may check on the status of this disk by entering the following command with the DOS diskette in drive A:

`A>chkdsk c:{ENTER}`

The drive name "C" refers to the Fixed Disk. If the Fixed Disk has been properly formatted, CHKDSK displays information about the Fixed Disk.

Some Things That Might Go Wrong:
Using CHKDSK With a Drive Name

DOS displays "Disk error reading drive x
Abort, Retry, Ignore?"

The diskette in drive x has not been formatted for use with PCDOS, or it is damaged. Press the R key (for "retry"). The error may not happen again. If it does, press the A key (for "abort") to stop the operation you were trying to perform.

This message also occurs if x is a single-sided drive and you are trying to read a double-sided diskette. See the section on "Different Formats" in Chapter 5 for more information about this.

If the Fixed Disk has not yet been formatted, you will receive a message such as "Invalid drive specification." See the section "Setting Up the IBM Fixed Disk" in Chapter 18 for information about how to format the Fixed Disk.

What Drive Names Does Your PC Accept?

In many of the following lessons you will work with files that are on various disk drives. The drive names you must use in these lessons will depend on what drives your PC has and whether DOS commands and data are stored in a diskette drive or in some other drive.

Here is a summary of the rules for determining what drive names your PC accepts and which drive holds DOS:

- If your PC has two diskette drives, the left-hand drive is drive A and the right-hand drive is drive B. If you have three or four drives, the additional drives are C and D. DOS must be on a diskette in drive A.
- If your PC has one diskette drive and an IBM Fixed Disk, the diskette drive is drive A and the Fixed Disk is drive C. If you have a second Fixed Disk, it is drive D. If you have a second diskette drive, it is drive B. DOS may be on a diskette in drive A or on the Fixed Disk in drive C.
- If your PC has a non-IBM hard disk, you must experiment to find out what drive letters are assigned to each disk. Place a formatted disk in each diskette drive and run CHKDSK with different drive names (such as B, C, and D) until it displays information about the hard disk. You may find that two or more drive names address different parts of the hard disk, as though the hard disk were divided into several smaller disks. If you enter a drive name that DOS does not recognize as valid for your PC, DOS will simply display the message "Invalid drive specification." DOS is on whichever disk your hard disk's instructions tell you to boot from.

Rather than give several sets of instructions in each of the lessons that follow, we are going to proceed as if you had a PC with two diskette drives. We will use the drive name A to represent the drive holding the DOS diskette, and the drive name B to represent "any other drive." If you have a PC with a hard disk, just translate these drive names to the names appropriate for your own PC.

Lesson 3-3:
Changing the Default Drive

Most commands do not insist that you enter all the parameters they expect. If you omit a parameter, they will perform as if you had entered a *default value.*

For a command like DIR that expects a parameter giving a drive name, the parameter's default value is the name of the current *default drive.* DOS displays the current default drive name before the > in its command prompt. When DOS's command prompt is "A>", for example, the default drive is drive A. Thus, when you entered DIR with no parameter in Chapter 2, DIR assumed you wanted a listing of the disk in the default drive.

When you perform many operations on a certain disk drive, it is convenient to make that drive the default drive, so that you do not have to enter its name all the time. You make a drive the default drive by entering its drive name alone as a command. For example, this command makes drive B the default drive:

```
A>b:{ENTER}
B>_
```

DOS commands will now assume drive B whenever you omit a drive name in a parameter.

Change your PC's default drive to your second diskette drive or your hard disk, and enter DIR with no parameter. DIR displays the files on the new default drive.

You can always override the default drive by using a drive name in a parameter. For example, when drive B is the default drive, you can list files on drive A by entering

```
B>dir a:{ENTER}
```

When you are done experimenting with the default drive, reset it to drive A:

```
B>a:{ENTER}
```

You should reset the default drive because many DOS commands are fetched from disk when you run them. DOS normally gets these commands from the default disk. If you make disk B the default disk and the DOS commands are not on that disk, you will get this message when you try to run the commands:

B>**chkdsk{ENTER}**

```
Bad command or file name
```

In this case you must tell DOS that CHKDSK is on disk A (the DOS disk), not on the current default disk. Put A: before the command name:

B>**a:chkdsk{ENTER}**

Of the commands you have seen so far, all except DIR are fetched from disk when you run them. DIR is kept in RAM all the time when DOS is running, so you do not need the prefix "A:" to run it. We will return to the topic of how commands are kept on disks in Chapter 4, "Introducing Files."

Lesson 3-4:
Booting From a Fixed Disk

In Chapter 2 you learned how to boot DOS when you started your system. If you have a PC XT, you may use the method we described in that lesson. However, the normal way to start the PC XT is to boot DOS from the Fixed Disk. Now that you have read the discussion of drive names and default drives, you are ready to learn this method of starting your system.

To boot from the Fixed Disk, do not put a diskette into drive A before turning on the PC or pressing CTRL ALT DEL. The PC will try to boot from drive A, but when it finds no diskette there, it will boot from the Fixed Disk instead.

When you boot from the Fixed Disk, DOS automatically designates drive C (the Fixed Disk) as the default disk. Drive C customarily contains copies of all the standard DOS command files and data files, so you do not need a DOS diskette in drive A at all.

If you have a PC I or PC II with a non-IBM hard disk, you must boot from a diskette, but you can get most of the convenience of booting from the hard disk by making the hard disk the default disk after you boot. If you keep copies of all the DOS diskette's files on the hard disk, your PC will need the DOS diskette only for a few functions that require it to reload DOS itself.

Some Things That Might Go Wrong: Booting From a Hard Disk

The PC displays messages that indicate that it is starting some operating system other than DOS. Your hard disk is divided into several "partitions" reserved for the exclusive use of different operating systems. The "active partition" (that is, the one that starts when you boot the PC from the hard disk) is not the DOS partition. You can boot DOS from a diskette and then change the default drive to the hard disk, or you can change the active partition with the FDISK command. Refer to the hard disk manual, ask someone who is familiar with this procedure, or see Chapter 18 for more information about the FDISK command.

The PC displays a message beginning "The IBM Personal Computer Basic". The diskette drive was not ready for use when the PC tried to boot, and none of the hard disk's partitions have been made active. For more information, see the discussion of FDISK in Chapter 18.

CHAPTER 4

Introducing Files

Disks are the PC's primary media for storing information. They can store DOS and DOS commands like CHKDSK and DISK-COPY; other computer programs, such as word processors, accounting systems, and games; and data, such as business records, budget plans, and correspondence.

The basic unit of disk storage is the file. *A file is a collection of similar data, somewhat like the contents of a paper file folder. You might use a file to hold a computer program, your business's accounts receivable, or a letter you are writing to a friend.*

Lesson 4-1:
Using DIR With a File Specification

In Lesson 2-2, you used the DIR command to become familiar with the process of entering DOS commands. In this lesson, you will use it to learn how DOS uses files to store information.

Enter the DIR command as you learned to do in Lesson 2-2, and look at the information it displays. Each line in DIR's output describes one file. Look at the contents of any of the lines in DIR's output, such as this one:

```
TREE      COM      1513    3-08-83    12:00p
```

The first two words, "TREE" and "COM," are the file's *filename* and *filename extension.* The purpose of the filename is to identify the file. The purpose of the filename extension is to describe the type of data that the file contains.

When you enter a filename and extension, you must separate them with a period:

```
TREE.COM
```

The filename and the extension, taken together, make up the *file specification.* It is read "TREE dot COM."

Many DOS commands allow you to use file specifications as parameters, including DIR. Try entering DIR with "TREE.COM" as a parameter:

```
A>dir tree.com{ENTER}
```

DIR displays the same information as before, but only for the file TREE.COM rather than for every file on the default disk.

You can combine a drive name with a filename if you wish. To make DIR display information about a file named TREE.COM on the disk in drive B, you would enter

```
A>dir b:tree.com{ENTER}
```

The parameter "b:tree.com" is a complete file specification giving the file's filename and extension and the drive it is currently mounted on. You should read it "B colon TREE dot COM."

A Note on the File Specification

Since "file specification" is an awkward term, we often speak instead of "a file's name." For example, we may say, "This file is named INDEX.TXT," when we mean, "This file's file specification is INDEX.TXT."

Do not confuse "a file's name," which is really "a file's file specification," with "a filename," which is the part of a file specification that precedes the dot. When we speak of the filename, we will always write it as a single word: *filename.*

Lesson 4-2:
Rules for Creating a File Specification

List the whole contents of your DOS disk with DIR again. Notice that none of the filenames are longer than eight characters, and none of the filename extensions are longer than three characters. Those are the maximum lengths allowed for the filename and the extension.

In addition to these limitations, there are also rules governing the use of certain characters in a file's name, primarily because certain punctuation symbols have special meaning when used in or around a filename. Figure 4-1, "Legal and Illegal Characters for File Specifications," summarizes which characters or symbols are permitted and which are illegal.

If you are running DOS 1.1, you will find that you can use some of the characters that Figure 4-1 lists as "invalid" in filenames. We suggest that you stick to the characters that DOS 2.0 will accept, however, so that you will not have to rename your files when you move up to DOS 2.0.

The following characters may be used in a file specification:

! @ # $ % & ( ) ` - ` — { } ` ' ` ~
any alphabetic character
any numeral

---

*The following characters may **not** be used in a file specification:*

∧ * + = [ ] ; : " \ | , . / ? < >

Figure 4-1.
Legal and illegal characters for file specifications

It is important to choose filenames that will help you remember what is in your files. For example, you might use the filename PAYR8305 for a file containing payroll records from May 1983. In addition, you should choose filename extensions that will help you remember what *kind* of information is in your files. For example, you might use extension LTR for all your letters and RPT for all your reports.

Some Filename Extensions to Avoid

Certain filename extensions have fixed, conventional meanings. For example, BAS represents a computer program written in the programming language BASIC. You should avoid using these extensions except in their intended ways; otherwise, you are likely to confuse anyone who tries to interpret the names of your files, including yourself.

Table 4-1 lists the standard filename extensions and their accepted meanings. Notice the extensions marked with asterisks. It is particularly important to avoid using these, because they have special meanings to DOS itself.

For example, if DOS finds a file named AUTOEXEC.BAT on the DOS disk when it is booted, it will assume that the file contains a list of commands, and it will try to execute those commands before letting you type anything at the keyboard. For this reason, you should not, for example, use the name AUTOEXEC.BAT for a file that contains a letter to a company selling batteries.

Extension	Meaning
$$$	Temporary file, used within a program and then discarded. A file with this filename extension may be erased by any program at any time.
BAK	"Backup." Contains the next oldest copy of a modified file.
BAS	"BASIC." Contains a BASIC program.
BAT *	"Batch." Contains DOS commands that can be executed as though they were typed into the keyboard.
COM *	"Command." Contains a program that will be run when the filename is entered as a DOS command.
EXE *	"Executable." Similar to COM.
OBJ	"Object code." Contains a portion of a computer program.
PRN	"Print." Contains output from a program that would normally have been sent to the printer.
SYS *	"System." Contains information used by DOS to control some aspect of DOS's operation.
TMP	"Temporary." Some programs use files with this extension for temporary storage.
*This extension has a special meaning to DOS.	

Table 4-1.
Customary Meanings of Filename Extensions

Lesson 4-3:
Global Filename Characters — ? and *

Although you can type out a full file specification each time you want to make your PC operate on a file, there will be times when you want to act on a group of files all at the same time. In these cases, there is a shorthand system that lets you operate on DOS files with related names.

This shorthand system lets you use *global filename characters* to write a file specification that refers to a group of files rather than to a single file. There are two global filename characters, ? and *. They perform different functions.

The first global filename character is ?. To use it, try entering the following command with DOS in drive A:

```
A>dir disk????.com{ENTER}
```

It should list two files: DISKCOPY.COM and DISKCOMP.COM.

When you use one or more ?s at the end of a filename or extension, each ? means, "Any character or no character may be in this position." Thus the file specification DISK????.COM matches any file specification that has a filename of up to eight characters beginning with the characters DISK and a filename extension of COM.

When you use one or more ?s *within* a filename or extension, each ? must match exactly one character. Thus the file specification T???EE.COM would match TEEPEE.COM but not TREE.COM.

DOS recognizes a second global filename character, ∗, which you may use only at the end of (or in place of) a filename or extension. It means, "Any number of characters or no characters may be in this position." Thus the following command lists all files with a filename beginning with BASIC and the filename extension COM:

`A>dir basic*.com{ENTER}`

The following command lists all files with a filename beginning with F and *any* extension:

`A>dir f*.*{ENTER}`

Global filename characters can be most useful if you name your files consistently so as to create useful patterns. For example, if you have a set of files containing profit and loss statements for the 12 months of 1983, you might name them PNL8301.DAT, PNL8302.DAT, ... PNL8312.DAT. Then you could display the status of those files, and only those files, by entering DIR PNL83??.DAT. Table 4-2 provides several more examples of the use of global filename characters.

This input	would match these file specifications
PNL83??.DAT	PNL8301.DAT; PNL83QF.DAT; PNL83B.DAT; PNL83.DAT; etc.
PNL??01.DAT	PNL8301.DAT; PNL8201.DAT; PNLAB01.DAT; etc.
PNL8301.∗	Any file with the filename "PNL8301".
∗.DAT	Any file with the extension "DAT".
∗.∗	Any file (for DIR, same as no parameter at all).
PNL8∗.D∗	Any file with a filename beginning "PNL8" and an extension beginning with "D".

Table 4-2.
Examples of Global Filename Characters

When You May Use Global Filename Characters

You may use global filename characters with any DOS command that can act on a group of files. Global filename characters cannot be used with certain commands, however, because they would have no meaning.

For example, consider a command that runs a *word processing program*, a computer program with which you can create and modify text files such as contracts and letters. It would make no sense for such a program to act on a group of files all at once, so this program would not accept global filename characters.

If you try to use global filename characters with a program that does not accept them, the program will do one of three things:

- First, the program may use the first filename it finds that matches the specification and ignore any others.
- Second, the program may tell you that a file specification containing these characters is invalid.
- And third, the program may interpret ? and * as ordinary characters, creating a file that you cannot name in the parameters of most DOS commands.

A Special Filename Rule for DIR

DIR interprets its parameters somewhat differently from all other commands. DIR accepts the global filename characters we just described, but it also accepts another type of global filename notation that other commands do not accept.

DIR allows you to specify "every filename" simply by omitting the filename from the parameter and "every extension" by omitting the extension. Thus, both of the following commands produce a directory listing of all files with the filename extension COM:

```
A>dir *.com{ENTER}
```

```
A>dir .com{ENTER}
```

Both of the following commands produce a directory listing of all files with the filename EXAMPLE:

```
A>dir example.*{ENTER}
```

```
A>dir example{ENTER}
```

If you omit both the filename and the extension from DIR's parameter, DIR produces a directory listing of all the files on a disk. This is the simplest form of DIR and the first form that you learned.

The following command produces a directory listing that includes only a file named EXAMPLE:

```
A>dir example.{ENTER}
```

Because the dot is present, DIR considers the filename to have a *null* filename extension (one that is zero characters long) rather than no extension at all.

Lesson 4-4:
COM and EXE Files

Look again at the DIR listing of our DOS disk. Notice that the disk contains files like CHKDSK.COM, FORMAT.COM, and DISKCOPY.COM. (You can list them all by entering the command DIR *.COM.) These files contain programs that DOS runs when you enter commands like CHKDSK, FORMAT, and DISKCOPY. Files with the filename extension EXE also contain programs that DOS runs when you enter commands.

When you enter a command, DOS searches the default disk for a file with the command as its filename and the extension COM. If it cannot find such a file, it searches for the same filename with the extension EXE. If it cannot find that file either, it displays the error message "Bad command or file name."[1]

Files with the extensions COM and EXE contain *external commands*, which are commands that reside on a disk. When you tell DOS to run an external command, it must read the command from the disk in order to run it.

Some commands are built into DOS, so that they are in RAM all the time that DOS is running. These commands are called *internal commands*. Unlike external commands, they have no COM or EXE files. DIR is an internal command; notice that there is no DIR.COM or DIR.EXE file on your DOS disk.

DOS has several internal commands besides DIR. We will encounter some of them, including COPY, RENAME, and ERASE, later in this chapter.

As we noted in Chapter 3, you can tell DOS to run a command from a disk other than the default disk by prefixing the disk's name

---

[1]It will actually look for still a third filename extension, BAT, before displaying this error message. We will discuss the extension BAT in Chapter 9.

to the command. If you have a copy of your DOS disk in drive B, enter this command:

```
A>b:chkdsk{ENTER}
```

Notice that running a command in this way does *not* change the default drive. CHKDSK still checks on the disk in drive A unless you specify another drive in a parameter. Thus, in order to run CHKDSK from drive B and make it check the disk in drive B, you would have to enter

```
A>b:chkdsk b:{ENTER}
```

The disk from which DOS runs the command has no effect on what the command does.

You could also run CHKDSK from the disk in drive B by making drive B the default drive:

```
A>b:{ENTER}
```

```
B>chkdsk{ENTER}
```

This time CHKDSK would check the disk in drive B, since CHKDSK always operates on the default drive when no parameter is given.

Lesson 4-5:
How to Run a BASIC Program

Many PC programs are written in the programming language BASIC. A BASIC program has the filename extension BAS.

You can buy many useful BASIC programs in computer stores or from mail-order firms. You can get public-domain programs for free from other PC users, particularly if you join a user's group.

You cannot run a BASIC program by entering its filename as a command. You must run the PC's Advanced BASIC processor with the BASICA command and run the BASIC program from within BASICA.

This lesson will show you how to run a BASIC program by using some sample programs that are supplied with DOS. *If you have DOS 2.0*, the sample programs are on your DOS Supplementary Programs diskette. Put this diskette in drive B and make drive B the default drive:

```
A>b:{ENTER}
```

If you have a hard disk, copy the files on the diskette to the hard disk if they are not already on it.

If you have DOS 1.1, the sample programs are on your DOS diskette, already in drive A, or on your hard disk if you have one.

Use DIR to list the files on the diskette or hard disk that have the filename extension BAS. Each of these files contains a BASIC program, just as each file with the extension COM or EXE contains a DOS command. You are going to run the program in the file named SAMPLES.BAS.

With the DOS diskette in drive A and the diskette containing the sample programs in the default drive, you can run the file SAMPLES.BAS with BASICA like this:

```
B>a:basica samples{ENTER}
```

Note that you need not enter the filename extension BAS. Since all BASIC programs customarily have that extension, BASICA assumes it unless you enter a different one.

SAMPLES.BAS presents a title display on the display. When you press the space bar, it displays a menu of several other BASIC programs that you can run. If you have a color or black-and-white monitor, you can run any of these programs. If you have an IBM Monochrome Display, you can run any program that does not have "Color/Graphics" after its name.

Run a program by pressing the letter key opposite the program's name. SAMPLES reads the program you selected from the default drive.

Follow the instructions shown on the display by the program you selected. When you have had enough, return to the menu and select another program or press ESC to end SAMPLES.

When you leave SAMPLES, the display goes blank and you see the word "Ok" in the upper-left corner. This is BASIC's command prompt, just as "A>" is DOS's command prompt. Respond like this:

```
Ok
system{ENTER}


A>_
```

SYSTEM is a BASIC command that means "return to the operating system" (that is, return to DOS).

About BASICA and BASIC

Look at a DIR listing of your DOS disk. Notice that there is a file named BASIC.COM, as well as BASICA.COM. BASIC.COM is Disk BASIC, another BASIC processor.

BASICA.COM is the preferred BASIC processor because it has several useful features that BASIC.COM lacks. Because the file BASIC.COM consumes somewhat less RAM than BASICA.COM, however, BASIC.COM allows you to run a larger program. If your PC has only 64K of RAM, you will occasionally find programs that must be run with BASIC.COM so that they will have enough RAM to run on your PC. If you have 96K of RAM or more, this should never happen to you, and you should never need BASIC.COM.

More Information About BASIC

As in DOS, you can halt a BASIC program temporarily by entering CTRL NUM LOCK. Press any standard typing key to make the PC resume running.

In most cases you can halt a BASIC program permanently by entering CTRL BREAK. This returns you to the "Ok" prompt. Most BASIC programs accept some sort of "stop" command, however. If such a command exists, it is a better way to stop a program than CTRL BREAK. It allows the program to finish any processing it is doing and stop in an orderly way.

After you halt a program with CTRL BREAK, you can restart it at the beginning with the following command:

```
Ok
run{ENTER}
```

You can restart a program at the point where you interrupted it with the following command:

```
Ok
cont{ENTER}
```

For more information about Disk BASIC and Advanced BASIC, see the IBM BASIC user's manual provided with your PC.

Lesson 4-6:
Using the COPY Command

We saw in Lesson 4-4 that DOS contains several internal commands that are not listed in its disk directory. This lesson teaches you to use one of these commands, COPY, and in the following lessons we will use other internal commands.

The COPY command is used to make a copy of a file. COPY expects two parameters. The first parameter describes the file to copy *from*; the second describes the file to copy *to*.

Make drive A the default drive. With the DOS diskette in drive A, put one of your formatted diskettes into drive B and enter the following command:

```
A>copy chkdsk.com b:xyzq.com{ENTER}
```

This command says, "Copy file CHKDSK.COM to B:XYZQ.COM."

Now display disk B with DIR. Notice that there is now an XYZQ.COM file there.

Try running XYZQ.COM:

```
A>b:xyzq{ENTER}
```

XYZQ does the same thing as CHKDSK since it is a copy of CHKDSK. It even has the same time stamp. DOS does not consider a copy of a file to be "created or modified," so a copy has the same time stamp as the original had when the copy was made.

Now let's try something else. Enter

```
A>copy chkdsk.com b:{ENTER}
```

There are two parameters here, but the second one is not a complete file specification; rather, it is just a drive name. In this case, COPY makes the "to" file's name the same as the "from" file's name. If you run DIR on the disk in drive B, you should now find that CHKDSK.COM is listed on it.

What happens if you omit the second parameter completely, like this?

```
A>copy b:xyzq.com{ENTER}
```

COPY makes the "to" file's name the same as the "from" file's name and puts the "to" file on the disk in the default drive. If you check the directory of drive A, you will see that XYZQ.COM is now listed on it.

CAUTION

If you tell COPY to write a file on a certain disk, and there is already a file with the same name on that disk, the copy completely replaces the original file. Be careful of this—it is easy to wipe out important data by copying other data over it, particularly when you use COPY with global filename characters.

If you have backed up your disks conscientiously, of course, you can always recover the lost data when you discover your mistake.

Using COPY With Global Filename Characters

Just as you use COPY to copy a single file, you can also use COPY with global filename characters to copy more than one file at a time. For example, the following command

```
A>copy *.com b:{ENTER}
```

would copy every file on the disk in drive A with the extension COM to the disk in drive B.

By using global characters with the COPY command, you may copy a whole group of files to a new group of files with different names. For instance, the command

```
A>copy b:july.* b:august.*{ENTER}
```

would make a copy on the disk in drive B of every file on that disk that has the filename JULY, giving the copy the filename AUGUST. (The file extension would remain the same on each new file.)

COPY can do many more things that we will not discuss here. After you have become comfortable with DOS, you may wish to learn more about COPY from IBM's *Disk Operating System* manual.

Some Things That Might Go Wrong: Using COPY

COPY displays the message "Write-protect error writing drive x; **Abort, Retry, Ignore?"** You are trying to copy a file to a diskette whose write-protect notch is covered. Press the A key to abort the command. If you are certain that the material on the disk does not need to be protected, uncover the write-protect notch and enter the command again.

If the write-protect notch is not covered, this message may indicate that the diskette is improperly seated in the drive, or that the drive's write-protection sensor is stuck. To seat the diskette properly or unstick the write-protection sensor, open the drive's door and gently jiggle the diskette. If this does not work, have the drive repaired.

COPY displays the message "File cannot be copied onto itself". You tried to copy a file to an identically named file on the same disk. This is a meaningless operation, and COPY therefore refuses to do it.

This situation can arise if the second parameter of COPY has the same drive name as the first parameter and no filename. It can also arise if the first parameter refers to a file on the default drive and the second is omitted.

Lesson 4-7:
Using the RENAME Command

RENAME is another internal command. It changes the name of a file on a disk.

Like COPY, RENAME takes two parameters. The first is the "from" name and the second is the "to" name. For example, the following command would change the name of CHKDSK.COM to CHEKDISK.COM (provided the DOS diskette is not write-protected):

```
A>rename chkdsk.com chekdisk.com{ENTER}
```

If you change the name of a command such as CHKDSK, you should use RENAME again to restore its original name:

```
A>rename chekdisk.com chkdsk.com{ENTER}
```

When you rename a file on a disk other than the default disk, enter the drive name with the first parameter *only*. Since it makes no sense to rename a file to a different drive, DOS does not expect a drive name with the second parameter:

```
A>rename b:xyzq.com abcd.com{ENTER}
```

You may use global filename characters to rename a group of files:

```
A>rename *.com *.moc{ENTER}
```

This command would change every COM file on the default drive to a MOC file. (If you make this change, undo it immediately, or you will not be able to execute any of those commands.)

```
A>rename *.moc *.com{ENTER}
```

Lesson 4-8:
Using the ERASE Command

ERASE is still another internal command. You use ERASE to remove a file from a disk, freeing the space it occupied for use by other files.

ERASE expects one parameter, the name of the file to be erased:

```
A>erase b:abcd.com{ENTER}
```

ERASE, like COPY and RENAME, allows you to use global filename characters. When you use the global file specification "*.*" to erase all the files on a disk, DOS will ask you if you are sure before proceeding.

CAUTION

Once you have erased a file, it is *gone*. The only sure way to get an erased file back is to restore it from a backup disk.

Practice the use of ERASE by erasing all of the strangely named files you created with COPY and RENAME. Be careful to include the correct disk drive parameter, as you do not want to erase important files on your DOS diskette.

CHAPTER 5

More About Disks

In Chapter 3 you learned about disks and disk drives. You learned how to format a diskette, to use commands with a drive name, and to boot from a Fixed Disk. There is more to learn, however, and this chapter gives you some more information about formatting, data storage, and disk capacity; about creating bootable diskettes; and about backing up disks.

Different Diskette Formats

You have already learned how to use FORMAT to prepare a new diskette for use. The formatting procedure you learned in Chapter 3 can be used with any IBM PC and any version of DOS. FORMAT will format a disk in different ways, however, depending on what version of DOS you use and what options your PC has.

These differences are important to you for two reasons. First, they affect a diskette's capacity (the amount of data that you can store on it). Second, they affect your ability to format disks on one PC and use them on another. For example, if you want to format a disk under DOS 2.0 and use it under DOS 1.1, you must run FORMAT with a special command option that tells it to use a disk format that DOS 1.1 can read.

Variations in DOS disk formats are of two types. First, FORMAT may format one or both sides of a diskette. Second, FORMAT may create eight or nine *sectors* of data per *track* of a diskette. Sectors and tracks are illustrated in Figure 5-1 and explained in the box called "How Data Is Stored on a Disk."

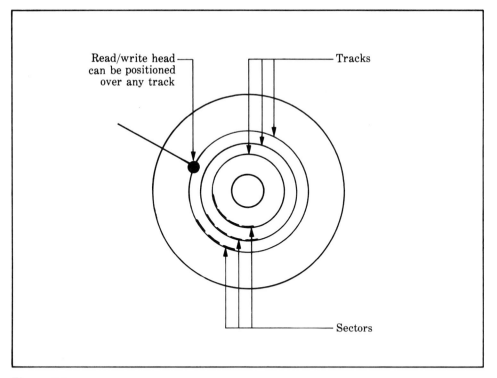

Figure 5-1.
How data is stored on a disk

How Data Is Stored on a Disk

Diskettes and hard disks store data in essentially the same way. Data may be recorded on either one or both sides of a disk. Some hard disk drives contain two or more disks, which rotate together on a common spindle. Such a drive must have one read/write head per recording surface, since it must be able to reach any of the surfaces at any time.

Data is recorded on each recording surface of a disk in *tracks*, which are like rings around the center of the disk. Each track is divided into *sectors*, which are segments of data of equal length. A sector is the smallest amount of data that can be read or written on a disk. Tracks and sectors are illustrated in Figure 5-1.

To read or write a particular piece of data, the PC must move the disk drive's read/write head over the proper track, wait until the beginning of the proper sector is under the head, and then perform the read or write operation.

Whether FORMAT makes a diskette single- or double-sided depends on the version of DOS you are running and the type of disk drives your PC has. DOS 1.0 can only make (and use) single-sided diskettes. Later versions of DOS make only single-sided diskettes on single-sided diskette drives (that is, on drives with only one read/write head), but they normally make double-sided diskettes on double-sided drives.

The number of sectors that FORMAT creates per disk track depends only on the version of DOS you use. DOS 2.0 creates either eight or nine sectors per track, nine being the default. Earlier versions of DOS can create only eight sectors per track. These variations combine to create four possible diskette formats, which are shown in Table 5-1.

Reading and Writing to Diskettes With Different Formats

If your version of DOS can handle a diskette's format at all, it automatically adjusts itself to use the proper format when you insert the diskette in the drive. Thus, you need not be concerned with how to make DOS use a diskette that has a certain format, but only with whether it can use the diskette at all.

The DISKCOPY command is a special case. Since it copies a diskette rather than the files on a diskette, it always leaves the target diskette with the same format as the source diskette. It automatically reformats the target diskette if that is necessary.

DOS version	Can read/write	Approx. capacity	Files per diskette	Normally reads/writes
Version 1.0	1 side 8 sector	160K	64	1 side 8 sector
Version 1.1	1 side 8 sector 2 sides 8 sector**	160K 320K	64 112	1 side 8 sector* 2 sides 8 sector**
Version 2.0	1 side 8 sector 2 sides 8 sector** 1 side 9 sector 2 sides 9 sector**	160K 320K 180K 360K	64 112 64 112	1 side 9 sector* 2 sides 9 sector**

*On single-sided drives.
**On double-sided drives only.

Table 5-1.
Diskette Format Compatibility

Lesson 5-1:
Formatting Diskettes With Different Formats

The FORMAT command normally formats a diskette of the type listed in the "Normally reads/writes" column of Table 5-1. You can get a different type of diskette—if the diskette drive and DOS version permit it—by running the FORMAT program with an option specifying the format you want. Table 5-2 shows the options that FORMAT accepts.

You can make FORMAT create a single-sided diskette by running it with the /1 option:

```
A>format b:/1{ENTER}
```

Notice that there is approximately half as much storage space available on the diskette when you format only one side. To reformat the diskette to use both sides, simply repeat the FORMAT command with no options:

```
A>format b:{ENTER}
```

You can make FORMAT create an eight-sector diskette under

Option	Valid in			Not compatible with	Effect on format
	DOS 1.0	DOS 1.1	DOS 2.0		
/1	no	yes	yes	Fixed Disk	Formats single-sided disk even on double-sided drive
/8	no	no	yes	/V; Fixed Disk	Formats eight sectors/track
/B	yes	yes	yes	/S /V	Formats eight sectors/track; reserves space for DOS on diskette but does not copy DOS to diskette
/S	yes	yes	yes	/B	Copies DOS to diskette
/V	no	no	yes	/8 /B	Stores volume label on disk

Table 5-2.
Options for FORMAT

DOS 2.0 by running it with the /8 option:

A>**format b:/8{ENTER}**

To convert a diskette from one format to another, format a new diskette with the desired format. Then copy all the files from the old diskette to the new one, using the COPY procedure described in Lesson 4-6.

The Disk Directory And the Capacity of a Disk

There is a limit to the number of files that you can store on a diskette: 64 files for a single-sided diskette and 112 files for a double-sided diskette, as shown in Table 5-1. These limits are imposed by the size of a diskette's *directory*.[1]

If you try to store more data on a diskette than will fit, the program you are running displays the following message:

`Insufficient disk space`

If you try to store more files on a diskette than will fit in the directory, the program you are running displays the following message:

`File creation error`
`Disk directory full`

If you see either of these messages, run CHKDSK to determine whether the disk or directory is really full. If the disk or directory is full, erase some unnecessary files or copy some files to another disk and then erase them from the first disk.

Lesson 5-2: Creating a DOS Diskette

When you ran FORMAT in Lesson 5-1, you created a diskette that did not have a copy of DOS on it. You cannot boot from such a

---

[1]Hard disks have capacities ranging from about 5 million bytes to 30 million bytes or more, and they can generally hold several hundred files.

diskette; you can only use it to store files.

If you have no hard disk and you use more application programs than will fit on one diskette, you may find it inconvenient to have only one bootable DOS diskette. After you boot, you must replace the DOS diskette with a program diskette to run an application program. To format a diskette you must change back to the DOS diskette, and so on. The way out of this difficulty is to keep all of your programs on DOS diskettes.

One way to make a bootable diskette is to copy your original DOS diskette with DISKCOPY. This method is inconvenient, however, because many of the files on the standard DOS diskette would be superfluous on a diskette that is going to hold programs. After making the copy, you would have to erase most of the files from it.

A better way to make a bootable diskette is to run FORMAT with the /S option:

```
A>format b:/s{ENTER}
```

This means, "Format the diskette in drive B *and* put a copy of DOS on it." The option letter "S" comes from the word "system." FORMAT runs just as before, except that it copies DOS from your current DOS diskette to the target diskette. When it has done this, it displays the message "System transferred".

After you have formatted a bootable diskette, you may copy some of your standard DOS diskette's files to it if you wish.

What Is on a Bootable Diskette?

A bootable diskette is different from other diskettes because it holds three files that contain all the parts of DOS that your PC keeps in RAM. The three files occupy a total of about 20K to 40K, depending on what version of DOS you run.

Two of the three files are *hidden*; that is, they do not appear in your DIR listing, and you cannot erase or rename them. Run CHKDSK, however, and it will tell you how many hidden files are on the diskette and how much space they take up.

The third file on a bootable diskette is COMMAND.COM, and it is not hidden. COMMAND.COM contains the part of DOS that reads and executes the commands you type in. Never delete this file from a diskette that you must boot from!

Changing Diskettes

Once you have booted DOS, you may remove the bootable diskette from drive A and insert a diskette containing only programs and data. You generally will not need to reinsert a bootable diskette until you want to boot again. A few commands require that a bootable diskette be mounted in drive A and will prompt you to insert one if necessary.

In general, you should *never change a diskette in either drive when a command is running*—change a diskette only when DOS is prompting you for a command. If you change a diskette while a command is running, the command may write data onto the new diskette that it should have written to the old one. This can destroy some or all of the data stored on the new diskette.

There are exceptions to this rule. Some commands, like FORMAT, explicitly prompt you to change diskettes while they are running. Others permit it at certain times. But unless you are quite sure when diskette changing is allowed, play it safe by ending the command, changing the diskette, and running the command again.

Lesson 5-3:
Backing Up a Fixed Disk (DOS 2.0 Only)

A Fixed Disk is more reliable than a diskette, since it runs in a sealed, dust-proof case. Even Fixed Disks fail occasionally, though, and their data is no safer against accidental change or erasure than is data on diskettes. You should back up your Fixed Disk regularly, just as you would back up diskettes.

You cannot use DISKCOPY to back up a Fixed Disk, since it will only copy the contents of one disk to another identical disk. DOS 2.0 provides another command, BACKUP, for backing up a Fixed Disk on a diskette. Most makers of non-IBM hard disks provide backup programs of their own. BACKUP also works with many of these disks. Check your disk's instruction manual to see whether BACKUP will work with it.

In the lesson segments that follow, you will learn how to back up either all or some of the files on a Fixed Disk.

Running BACKUP

BACKUP expects two parameters: the drive name of the disk to back up and the name of the diskette drive on which to make the backup.

Before you run BACKUP, you must format enough diskettes to hold all the files on the hard disk. BACKUP, unlike DISKCOPY, cannot format a diskette automatically. Run DIR against your hard disk and add up the approximate amount of space used by all the files listed. Divide the sum by the capacity of a diskette to find out how many diskettes you will need.

Run BACKUP like this:

```
A>backup c: a:{ENTER}
```

For "C:", substitute the drive name of your hard disk. For "A:", substitute the drive name of your diskette drive.

BACKUP prompts you to insert a diskette in the diskette drive. Insert a formatted diskette and press any typing key. BACKUP erases any files already on the diskette, and then begins backing up the files that are on the hard disk.

If the first diskette cannot hold all the files, BACKUP prompts you to insert another diskette when the first one is full. This process continues until all the files on the hard disk are backed up.

Label the backup diskettes with their contents, date, and the order of use as you remove them from the drive. As you will see in the section "Restoring Files Saved with BACKUP," this information will be important when the time comes to use your backup files.

A Partial Backup by Filename

The backup you just made was a *full backup*—that is, a backup of all the files on the hard disk. BACKUP also can make a *partial backup* that includes only files you have created or modified. When you have modified only a few files on the hard disk, you can quickly make a partial backup to protect yourself against losing data.

One way to make a partial backup is to back up the individual files you have changed. To do this, specify a filename in BACKUP's first parameter. Global filename characters are allowed. For instance, if you wanted to back up all files whose filenames began with "ar83", you would type

```
A>backup c:ar83??.* a:{ENTER}
```

A Partial Backup With the /D Option

Another way to make a partial backup is to back up only files created or modified since the last full backup. To do this, run BACKUP with the /D (for "date") option. This option means, "Back up files with a time stamp on or after this date." Here is an example of BACKUP with /D, which backs up files created or changed on or after July 4, 1983:

```
A>backup c: a:/d:7-4-1983{ENTER}
```

There is one catch to /D: namely, certain DOS commands create and modify files without setting their time stamps. The most important such command is COPY, which gives a new file the same time stamp as the file it is copied from. You can force COPY to give a new file a current time stamp by putting "+,," after the source file name:

A>**copy a:example.txt+,, c:{ENTER}**

This COPY procedure will provide BACKUP with a new time stamp as an accurate reference point.

A Partial Backup With the /M Option

Another way to make a partial backup is to back up files created or modified since the last backup of any sort. To do this, run BACKUP with the /M (for "modified") option.

A>**backup c: a:/m{ENTER}**

This option means, "Back up all files modified since the last full or partial backup." BACKUP can tell if a file must be backed up because it marks a file's directory entry when it backs up the file, and DOS erases the mark if the file is later modified.

Restoring Backup Files With the RESTORE Command

The files on a diskette created by BACKUP cannot be used directly, since they are in a special format that enables BACKUP to back up a file larger than a diskette can hold. Before you can use such files, you must restore them to a hard disk. You can do this with another DOS command, RESTORE.

There are two reasons why you might run RESTORE: to recover a specific file that was lost or damaged, or to reconstruct the contents of your hard disk when you must run it on another PC or when your hard disk has failed and been repaired.

RESTORE expects two parameters: the diskette drive name from which it should read the backup and the drive name of the hard disk to which it should restore the file.

Like BACKUP, the RESTORE command can be used to restore all the files on a disk or only selected files. To restore all the files from drive A to drive C, you would enter

A>**restore a: c:{ENTER}**

RESTORE prompts you to insert the first backup diskette in the diskette drive. Insert the diskette and press any typing key. The RESTORE command begins restoring files from the backup diskette to the hard disk.

If your backup spans several diskettes, RESTORE prompts you to insert each one in turn. *Be sure to insert the backup disks in the order in which they were created.*

To restore specific files rather than all the backup files on a diskette, put the file name in the second parameter. Global file-name characters are allowed. For instance, the following command would restore to drive C all the files with the filename extension DAT:

A>**restore a: c:*.dat{ENTER}**

Unlike BACKUP, RESTORE does not erase files from the target disk; it adds the restored files to the files that are already there. (Of course, RESTORE will write over any file with the same name, since it makes no sense to have two identically named files on the same disk.)

If you have made a partial backup with /D, you can restore the entire contents of the Fixed Disk by restoring the full backup and then restoring the most recent partial backup. If you have made partial backups with /M, you can restore the entire contents of the Fixed Disk by restoring the full backup and then restoring *all* the partial backups, starting with the oldest. In either case, the Fixed Disk will end up containing any files that you deleted after the full backup, since BACKUP has no way of noting the fact that a file has been deleted.

If your Fixed Disk fails and the data on it has become unusable, you must reinitialize the disk before you can restore the files. See the discussion of Fixed Disks in Chapter 18 for more information.

Fragmented Disk Space
And How to Cure It

As you create and erase files on a disk, the storage space on the disk tends to become *fragmented:* bits of files and free space appear all over the disk. To see why this happens, consider the following example.

Suppose you have created two files named F1 and F2 on a newly formatted disk. We might represent the use of space on the disk like this:

DOS	F1	F2	Free space

Now you run a program that reads F1, creates an updated copy of it, and then deletes the original. Now the disk's space looks like this:

DOS		F2	F1	Free space

Next you run a program that updates F2 in the same way. The updated version of F2 is a little larger than the space left by the original version of F1. DOS reuses the freed disk space by putting the new F2 in the hole left by the old F1. But since all of F2 will not fit, the file becomes fragmented:

DOS	F2		F1	F2	Free space

When a program reads F2, DOS fetches the blocks of the file in the proper order to make this fragmentation invisible. But the PC's performance is reduced because DOS must move the disk drive's read/write head across the disk to fetch the blocks of the fragmented file. If a disk becomes very fragmented, this can slow down the PC substantially.

You can estimate how fragmented a disk is by running CHKDSK against the disk. Enter a parameter naming the file that you want to check for fragmentation. You may use global filename characters. To check every file on the disk, you may enter "*.*":

A>chkdsk b:*.*{ENTER}

After the summary of disk status, CHKDSK displays a message like this for any file that is fragmented:

B:\EXAMPLE.TXT

    Contains 2 non-contiguous blocks.

When a diskette becomes very fragmented, copy all the files from the diskette to an empty diskette. As COPY copies each file, it writes the file to the target disk in a single block.

You can use virtually the same procedure when a hard disk becomes too fragmented, although you cannot use the COPY command. Instead, copy all the files to diskettes with BACKUP (or a non-IBM hard disk's own backup utility), and then copy them back with RESTORE.

CHAPTER 6

Editing Files With EDLIN

DOS files can contain many types of data: commands, numeric data, letters, and so forth. This data can be in various forms. For example, command files contain sequences of computer instructions in a form that is meaningful to the hardware inside your PC but meaningless if displayed on the screen.

One of the most important types of data you can store in a file is character data, often called ASCII *data.[1] A file containing character data is called an ASCII file or a* text *file. You can use text files to store letters, research papers, customer lists, tax records, and so forth.*

What EDLIN Is

EDLIN is a *text editor*—that is, a program you can use to create and modify files containing character data. If you do not have a word processing program, you may find EDLIN useful for certain functions. For instance, you can use it to prepare data files for input to application programs and to create batch files (files containing DOS commands), which are explained in Chapter 9.

However, EDLIN cannot perform some other functions that you might expect from a word processor. For instance, EDLIN will not permit you to type text in continuous paragraphs. Instead, it allows you to create one numbered line of text at a time, limiting the length of each line to 253 characters (about 3 1/3 screen lines). What is more, EDLIN makes you display and edit the contents of a file one line at a time. This makes it much less convenient than most word processors, which display a screenful of text and let you edit it by moving the cursor around the screen and typing directly over the text displayed there.

---

[1]"ASCII" stands for "American Standard Code for Information Interchange." It is the method that most computers use for representing displayable information in their memories.

Thus, if you have a word processing program for your PC, by all means skip this chapter and learn to use your word processing program instead.

Lesson 6-1:
Editing a File With EDLIN

To create an EDLIN file, enter the EDLIN command with a parameter giving the name of the file:

```
A>edlin b:example.txt{ENTER}
New file
*_
```

If EDLIN finds no file with the given name, it creates an empty file and displays the message "New file". If EDLIN does find a file with the given name, it reads in that file and displays the message "End of input file". The "*" is EDLIN's prompt, just as "A>" is DOS's prompt.

Once you have created the file, you insert and modify text by entering various EDLIN commands. EDLIN's commands are described in the following sections and are summarized in Table 6-1.

Since the newly created file contains no text, inserting text is the only operation that makes sense. EDLIN's insert command is I. You may enter it in upper- or lowercase:

```
*i{ENTER}
     1:*_
```

The "1" that appears on the screen is the *line number* of the line you are about to insert. You insert the line simply by typing it and pressing ENTER. Then EDLIN prompts you for the next line, and so forth:

```
*i{ENTER}
     1:*This is the first line inserted in the file.{ENTER}
     2:*This is the second line;{ENTER}
     3:*this is the third.{ENTER}
     4:*_
```

If you make a mistake, you may erase it with BACKSPACE as long as you are still on the same line. (You will soon learn how to correct an error on a preceding line.)

Editing command	Function	Leaves current line
A *n* A	Append data to RAM from old disk file. Append *n* lines to RAM from old disk file.	—
m,n,t C *m,n,t,c* C	Copy lines from *m* through *n* before line *t*. If *m* and/or *n* is omitted, it defaults to the current line. *c* is the number of consecutive copies to make; if omitted, it defaults to 1.	Line after copy of last line copied (originally *t*)
D *m* D *m,n* D	Delete current line. Delete line *m*. Delete lines *m* through *n*.	Line after [last] deleted line
E	Save file, rename old file to *.BAK, and return to DOS.	—
I *n* I	Insert lines before current line. Insert lines before line *n*.	Line after [last] inserted line
L *n* L *m,n* L	List 23 lines centered on current line. List *n* lines starting at current line. List lines *m* through *n*.	Unchanged
m,n,t M	Same as C (copy), but deletes lines *m* through *n* from their original location as it copies them to their new one. C's *c* parameter is not allowed.	Line after last line moved (originally *t*)
P *n* P *m,n* P	Same as L, but makes last displayed line the current line, allowing you to "page" through the file.	Last line displayed
Q	Return to DOS but do not save modified file.	—
R*fr*{F6}*to* *n* R*fr*{F6}*to* *m,n* R*fr*{F6}*to*	Replace each *fr* with *to*. Replace each *fr* with *to*, line *n* to end. Replace each *fr* with *to*, line *m* though *n*	Last line changed, if any
?	As a prefix to R, makes EDLIN prompt "O.K.?" before doing each replacement.	—
S*str* *n* S*str* *m,n* S*str*	Search file for first *str*. Search line *n* to end for first *str*. Search lines *m* through *n* for first *str*.	Line containing first occurrence of *str*, if any
?	As a prefix to S, makes EDLIN prompt "O.K.?" and continue searching until you reply Y.	—
T *filespec* *n* T *filespec*	Insert a copy of the file named by *filespec* before line *n* of the file being edited. If *n* is omitted, it defaults to the current line.	Line after insertion (originally *n*)
W	Write 3/4 of RAM data to new disk file.	—
n W	Write first *n* lines of RAM data to new disk file.	
n	Edit or replace line *n* with editing keys.	Unchanged

Table 6-1.
EDLIN Commands

After entering the last line, press ENTER to end the line. Then press CTRL BREAK to break out of insert mode:

```
3:*this is the third.{ENTER}
4:*{CTRL}{BREAK}
```

*_

If you subsequently want to add more lines, enter I again. You will be able to resume entering text on the same line number at which you left off.

Adding and Listing Lines With I and L

The I command allows you not only to enter text, but also to insert new lines among the lines you have already written. For instance, you can insert a line directly before line 3 by entering the line number 3 followed by the I command. (If you are still in the insert mode, you will need to press CTRL BREAK first.)

```
*3i{ENTER}
```

EDLIN's response will be the following prompt:

```
3:*_
```

Any material you add at this point will be inserted before the original line 3. For instance, you may add

```
3:*This is a new line number three.
```

Do not be surprised that you cannot see the effects of your editing. EDLIN will not show you that your new line now follows line 2 and that the original line 3 is now line 4, unless you command it to list your text. To do this, press ENTER to end the line you are inserting, and press CTRL BREAK to leave insert mode. Then enter EDLIN's list command L.

```
3:*This is a new line number three.{ENTER}
4:*{CTRL}{BREAK}
```

```
*L{ENTER}
```

Now EDLIN will display all the lines of text you have entered so that you can see the changes you made.

To list only one line of text, you may simply use the L command preceded by that line's number:

```
*4L{ENTER}
    4: This is the third.
```

*_

To display a group of lines, precede the L command with the first and last line numbers in that group, separated by a comma:

```
*2,4L{ENTER}
    2: This is the second line.
    3: This is a new line number three.
    4: This is the third.

*_
```

You have now learned to insert new lines and to display the editing you have done.

Deleting Lines With D

EDLIN also permits you to delete lines with the D (delete) command. If you enter the D command with one line number, like this,

```
*2d{ENTER}
```

EDLIN deletes the specified line. If you enter it with two line numbers, like this,

```
*1,2d{ENTER}
```

EDLIN deletes the two specified lines and all lines between them.

When you add or delete lines in a file, the remaining lines are immediately renumbered. For example, if you add two lines before line 3, they become lines 3 and 4; the former line 3 becomes line 5. If you delete lines 1 and 2, the former line 3 becomes line 1.

The Current Line

You may have noticed as you have been using EDLIN that the line on which you are working is usually marked by an asterisk just to the right of the line number. This asterisk marks the *current line*. At any time, one of the file's lines is the current line, and most EDLIN commands operate on that line if entered with no parameter. For example, if you enter D with no parameter, EDLIN deletes the current line.

Many EDLIN commands change the current line. For example, I makes the line after the last inserted line the current line, while D makes the line after the last deleted line the current line.

You can also change the location of the current line yourself. To do this, leave insert mode. Then enter the number of the line you wish to make the current line:

```
*l{ENTER}
    1:*This is the first line inserted in the file.
    1:*{ENTER}

*_
```

Notice that you must press ENTER *twice* when you change the line number: once after you enter the number and a second time after EDLIN displays the line. This is because EDLIN has gone into its Edit Line command, a powerful feature that lets you change the contents of a line without typing the whole line in again. When you press ENTER the second time, you tell Edit Line that you do not want to edit the line, and it returns to command mode.

If you neglect to press ENTER twice, Edit Line will use the next line you enter to modify the contents of the current line. This will introduce errors into your file.

You will learn to use the Edit Line feature in a later lesson in this chapter.

Other Ways of Referring to Lines: . and

In any EDLIN command, you may use a dot (.) in place of a line number to indicate the current line. For example, to delete the current line, you could enter

```
*.d{ENTER}
```

Just as you can refer to the current line by using a dot instead of a line number, you can refer to the end of the file by using a pound sign (#). This symbol means "the line after the last actual line in the file."

For example, you can insert text after the last line in the file by entering

```
*#i{ENTER}
```

Since the actual line number of the end of the file may not be obvious unless you break from editing to display lines with L, the pound sign is very useful. It is a more reliable and convenient technique than entering a line number that you *hope* is greater than the last line number in the file.

Relative Line Numbers (DOS 2.0 Only)

The dot and pound signs are two quick ways of accessing lines of text; DOS 2.0 provides yet a third way. Wherever you may use an ordinary line number, you may also use a *relative line number*— that is, a number that gives the position of a line relative to the current line.

A relative line number is preceded by a plus sign (+) for a line that is after the current line or a minus sign (−) for a line that is before the current line. For example, to delete the line after the current line, you would enter

*+1d{ENTER}

To delete the line three lines before the current line, you would enter

*-3d{ENTER}

To delete the last line in the file, you would enter

*#-1d{ENTER}

Ending EDLIN With E or Q

When you are ready to stop editing with EDLIN, there are two ways to return to DOS. The first one saves the file you have been editing; the second abandons the edited version of the file.

To return to DOS and save the file you have been editing, enter the E (end) command. If you have been editing an existing file, E preserves the original copy of the file by changing its filename extension to BAK. For example, if you edit an existing file named EXAMPLE.TXT, E changes the name of the original version to EXAMPLE.BAK before saving the new, edited version under the name EXAMPLE.TXT.

If you wish to reedit your file later, simply enter the EDLIN command with the name of the file. EDLIN will respond with the message "End of input file" and prompt you.

If you wish to return to DOS *without* saving the edited file, enter the Q (quit) command. EDLIN first asks you if you are sure you want to do this:

```
*q{ENTER}
Abort edit (Y/N)?_
```

If you press the Y key, EDLIN discards the new version of the file and does not rename the old version.

Lesson 6-2:
Searching for and Replacing Text

You now know everything you need to know about EDLIN to edit files, but EDLIN has several more commands that can make your work easier. Some of these commands allow you to search for information in a file and replace lines or parts of lines in a single operation.

For this lesson we will use a new text file. Use EDLIN to create this file now. Enter the file just as it is shown, errors and all, since you will be correcting the errors in the course of the lesson. You may give the file any name you want, but we will refer to it as GIRAFFES.TXT:

```
A>edlin b:giraffes.txt{ENTER}
New file
*i{ENTER}
    1:*Everyone knows giraffes have long necks.{ENTER}
    2:*Animals with long necks need wide neckties.{ENTER}
    3:*In my dreamn I sawa agiraffe.{ENTER}
    4:*It was eatinkg hay from the trunk of a car.{ENTER}
    5:*Giraffes alon among yngr ungulates, are voiceless.{ENTER}
    6:*{CTRL}{BREAK}
*e{ENTER}

A>_
```

Save GIRAFFES.TXT, if you have not already done so, and reload it. It is important to save it first, because we will abandon and reedit modified versions of the file in the coming lessons.

Replacing a Line

You can replace a line by typing its line number. EDLIN will display the line:

```
*3{ENTER}
    3:*In my dreamn I sawa agiraffe.
    3:*_
```

Then type the replacement and press ENTER:

```
*e{ENTER}
    3:*In my dreamn I sawa agiraffe.
    3:*In my dream, I saw a giraffe.{ENTER}

*_
```

If you decide not to change the line after you have begun typing its replacement, press CTRL BREAK to make EDLIN discard your edited line.

Searching for a String With the s Command

A *string* is a sequence of consecutive characters within a line. For example, "Everyone", "yon", and "e know" are all strings that may be found in the first line of GIRAFFES.TXT.

You can search your file for a string with the s (search) command. Enter the s command like this:

*1sgiraffe{ENTER}

This means, "Search the file for the first occurrence of the *search string* 'giraffe', beginning at line 1 and ending at the end of the file." (You can also enter s with two line numbers to make it search the file from the first line to the second.)

EDLIN lists the first line containing "giraffe" and makes it the current line. In this case, the first line containing "giraffe" is already the current line, so the current line is not changed.

Notice two important things about the s command. First, it searches for a string—a sequence of characters—not a word. It happened to find "giraffe" in the word "giraffes". If you had told it to search for the string "ffes ha", it would have found that string in the same place.

Second, notice that there is no space between the "s" and the first character of the search string. If you put a space there, EDLIN will look for a string that begins with a space, which may or may not suit your needs.

Now enter s again, with no line number and no search string:

*s{ENTER}
        3:*In my dream, I saw a giraffe.

EDLIN displays line 3. Why?

Here is what happened. First, when you enter s with no line number, EDLIN searches *from the line after the current line* to the end of the file. Second, when you enter s with no search string, it searches for the same search string as the most recently entered s command.[2] This means you can search for consecutive occurrences of a string by entering s commands with no line number and no search string.

Enter s again with no line number and no search string. This

---

[2]Actually, EDLIN searches for the most recently entered s or R (replace) command. You will learn about R later in this lesson.

time EDLIN displays the message "Not found" and the current line is not changed.

Why did EDLIN not find "Giraffe" in line 5? The reason is that EDLIN considers upper- and lowercase significant when it searches for a search string. The search string "giraffe" with a lowercase "g" does not match "Giraffe" with a capital "G." "G" and "g" are entirely different letters as far as EDLIN is concerned.

If a file contains several occurrences of a string and you are not sure which one you are looking for, put a ? before the S, like this:

*1?sgiraffe{ENTER}

After finding the first occurrence of the search string, EDLIN asks you if it is the one you want:

```
*1?sgiraffe{ENTER}
    1:*Everyone knows giraffes have long necks.
O.K.? _
```

If you press the Y key, EDLIN ends the search and makes this line the current line. If you press any other key, EDLIN searches for the next occurrence of the string and prompts "O.K.?" again.

Searching for a String and Replacing It

You can search for a string of characters and replace it with another string with the R (replace) command. R is similar to S, except that you have to specify a *replacement string* as well as a search string.

Quit EDLIN without saving GIRAFFES.TXT (using the Q command) and reedit the file. Then enter the R command like this:

```
*1rdreamn{F6}dream{ENTER}
    3:*In my dream, I sawa agiraffe.
```

EDLIN searches for all occurrences of the search string, not just the first one, between line 1 (the line you designated) and the end of the file. It replaces each one with the replacement string. It lists each changed line after each change. The last changed line is made the current line.[3]

Now with line 3 as the current line, try to change "sawa a" to "saw a", like this:

```
*rsawa a{F6}saw a{ENTER}
Not found
```

---

[3]This is true in DOS 1.1's version of EDLIN. If you are running DOS 2.0, however, you may find that the line before the last line changed will become the current line, due to a bug in DOS 2.0's EDLIN. This will affect the operation of the following step in this lesson.

The reason this doesn't work is that R uses exactly the same line number rules as S. In particular, if you enter no line number, R searches from the line *after* the current line to the end of the file. In the example above, this made R miss the error we wanted to correct.

The solution to this problem is that if you want to replace something in the current line, enter the current line as a line number. It is wise to specify the current line as both the beginning *and* ending line numbers, so that R will not search to the end of the file and possibly make some replacements you did not foresee:

```
*.,.rsawa a{F6}saw a{ENTER}
     3*In my dream, I saw a giraffe
```

Now let's correct "eatinkg" in line 4:

```
*4,4rnk{F6}n{ENTER}
     4:*It was eating hay from the trunk of a car.{ENTER}
     4:*It was eating hay from the trun of a car.{ENTER}
```

As you can see, R replaces every occurrence of the search string in the range of lines it searches, producing an unintended result. The moral is that it is safer to enter a long search string that is likely to be unique. If we had searched for "eatinkg" and replaced it with "eating", this problem would not have occurred.

R, like S, can be used with a ? before the command letter to get an "O.K.?" query before each replacement is performed. That is another good way to prevent R from making unforeseen changes, since ? makes R ask permission to make each change before making it.

If you enter R with nothing after the command name, like this,

```
*r{ENTER}
```

it uses the same search string as the most recently entered S or R command and the same replacement string as the most recently entered R command.

If you enter R with a search string but no replacement string, like this,

```
*rgiraffe{ENTER}
```

R replaces each occurrence of the word "giraffe" with the most recently entered replacement string.

If you enter R with a search string and then press F6 and ENTER without designating a new replacement string, like this,

```
*rgiraffe{F6}{ENTER}
```

each occurrence of the search string is replaced with the *null string* (a string zero characters long). Thus, in effect, R deletes each occurrence of the search string.

Lesson 6-3:
Editing a Line

Earlier in this chapter you learned that you can replace a line by entering the number of the line to be replaced and then typing the replacement. That was just a simple case of something much more powerful: EDLIN's Edit Line feature.

Edit Line lets you edit a line in much the same way that EDLIN itself lets you edit a file. You can enter line editing commands to find, insert, and delete characters within a line. The line editing commands are described below and are summarized in Table 6-2.

Edit Line is actually a feature of DOS that is used by EDLIN and by many other programs that deal with lines of data. Once you understand how Edit Line works in EDLIN, you can use it the same way when you enter DOS commands, and in other places, too.

Editing key	Function
Typing keys	Insert characters in the edited line and skip over characters in the template, in effect replacing old characters with new ones.
{F1} or →	Copy the next character from the template to the edited line.
{F2}x	Copy all characters up to (but not including) the next x from the template to the edited line.
{F3}	Copy all remaining characters from the template to the edited line.
{F4}x	Skip all characters up to (but not including) the next x in the template.
{F5}	Copy the edited line back to the template and restart line editing.
{DEL}	Skip the next character in the template, *in template*, in effect deleting it from the edited line.
{INS}	Enter insert mode. Following typing keys insert characters in the edited line without skipping characters in the template. The next editing key (INSERT or any other) ends insert mode.
{BS} or ←	Backspace edited line and template.

Table 6-2.
Editing Keys for EDLIN's Line Editing Feature

Use EDLIN to edit GIRAFFES.TXT again. Press the 3 key, and then press ENTER as if you were going to replace line 3:

```
*3{ENTER}
     3:*In my dreamn I sawa agiraffe.
     3:*_
```

Instead of replacing the line, press F1 a few times. This key "copies" one character from the original line into the edited line. Press F1 11 times, and you will see this:

```
3:*In my dreamn I sawa agiraffe.
3:*In my dream_
```

To replace the "n" with a comma, just type the comma:

```
3:*In my dreamn I sawa agiraffe.
3:*In my dream,_
```

Now type a few characters of nonsense:

```
3:*In my dreamn I sawa agiraffe.
3:*In my dream,x6yxtr_
```

Backspace over the nonsense and start pressing F1 again. You will get the contents of the original line, not the nonsense:

```
3:*In my dreamn I sawa agiraffe.
3:*In my dream, I saw_
```

This happens because F1 copies characters to the edited line from an area called the *template*. Each time EDLIN displays a complete line of text, it stores that line in the template. Typing characters into the edited line does not affect the template.

To delete the extra "a" after "saw," press the DEL key. DEL advances one character in the template without copying that character to the edited line:

```
3:*In my dreamn I sawa agiraffe.
3:*In my dream, I saw{DEL}_
```

After deleting the "a", press F1 twice more:

```
3:*In my dreamn I sawa agiraffe.
3:*In my dream, I saw a_
```

Now you must insert a blank. Press the INS key. This puts EDLIN in insert mode, which lets you type characters into the edited line without skipping over characters in the template. Insert the blank:

```
3:*In my dreamn I sawa agiraffe.
3:*In my dream, I saw a _
```

Press F1 several more times to copy the rest of the template to the edited line. (Pressing any editing key ends insert mode automatically. You could also end insert mode without affecting the line by pressing INS a second time.)

```
3:*In my dreamn I sawa agiraffe.
3:*In my dream, I saw a giraffe._
```

To store the edited line in the file (and the template), press ENTER.

Using the Cursor Control Keys

You can use the CURSOR LEFT and CURSOR RIGHT keys at the right side of the keyboard to control the cursor while you are editing a line. CURSOR LEFT has the same effect as BACKSPACE. CURSOR RIGHT has the same effect as F1.

These keys double as the numeric keypad's 4 and 6 keys. When you boot, they function as cursor control keys, but pressing the NUM LOCK key makes them function as numeric keys instead. To restore their cursor control function, press NUM LOCK again.

Advanced Line Editing

We are not quite done with the Edit Line feature. Let's see how some additional functions can enable us to edit the line more easily. We will do this by applying Edit Line to line 5 of GIRAFFES.TXT:

```
*5{ENTER}
    5:*Giraffes alon among yngr ungulates, are voiceless.
    5:*_
```

The F2 key copies characters from the template to the edited line, *up to* a specified character. Press F2 and then the N key to copy up to the first "n" in the line:

```
5:*Giraffes alon among yngr ungulates, are voiceless.
5:*Giraffes alo_
```

We have gone too far. We should insert a comma after "Giraffes". Let's correct this error by starting over. Press ESC. EDLIN displays a backslash (\) and discards the edited line:

```
5:*Giraffes alon among yngr ungulates, are voiceless.
5:*Giraffes alo\
5:*_
```

Press F2 and the space bar to copy up to the space. Then press INS and type in the missing comma:

```
5:*Giraffes alon among yngr ungulates, are voiceless.
5:*Giraffes alo\
5:*Giraffes _
```

Now press F2 and N to copy up to the "n", F1 to copy the "n", and INS, then E, to insert the missing "e":

```
5:*Giraffes alon among yngr ungulates, are voiceless.
5:*Giraffes alo\
5:*Giraffes, alone_
```

Now press F2, then Y, to copy up to the "y":

```
5:*Giraffes alon among yngr ungulates, are voiceless.
5:*Giraffes alo\
5:*Giraffes, alone among _
```

Since "yngr" was a mistake, you can delete it. Press F4 then U, to skip up to the next "u". (You will not see any immediate results, since you have deleted material.) If you press F3 to copy to the end of the template, however, you will see that "yngr" is no longer included in your line.

```
5:*Giraffes alon among yngr ungulates, are voiceless.
5:*Giraffes alo\
5:*Giraffes, alone among ungulates, are voiceless._
```

At this point, there is one error left: we should insert "the" after "among". The F5 command allows us to do this.

Press F5. EDLIN displays an @ at the end of the edited line, *copies the edited line to the template,* and resumes editing:

```
5:*Giraffes alon among yngr ungulates, are voiceless.
5:*Giraffes alo\
5:*Giraffes, alone among ungulates, are voiceless.@
5:* _
```

Since the template is now correct except for the missing comma, we can finish editing this line with seven more keystrokes. Which seven? You figure it out.

Lesson 6-4:
Rearranging Blocks of Lines (DOS 2.0 Only)

In addition to the operations we have described so far, EDLIN has commands that you can use to manipulate blocks, or groups, of lines. The C (copy), M (move), and T (transfer) commands each let you rearrange blocks in different ways.

Copying Lines With the c Command

You can copy a block of lines from one part of a file to another with the C (copy) command. You enter the command like this:

*m,n,tc{ENTER}

Here *m* represents the number of the first line you want to copy; *n* is the number of the last line; and *t* is the number of the line you want to copy to. The block of lines is inserted before line *t*, just as if you had used the I command with a line number of *t*.

If you omit the first or second parameter, the C command defaults to the current line. For example, this command copies three lines beginning with the current line to the end of the file:

*,+3,‡c{ENTER}

The first comma indicates that the first parameter is omitted; "+3" is the second parameter.

This command copies the current line alone to the end of the file:

*,,‡c{ENTER}

An optional fourth parameter tells EDLIN to copy the specified block of lines more than once. For example, this command makes eight copies of line 5 before line 23:

*5,5,23,8c{ENTER}

Moving Lines With the M Command

A second command, M (move), lets you move a block of lines from one part of a file to another. The M command works just like the C command, except that it deletes the specified lines from their original location as it moves them to their new one. The fourth parameter (number of copies to make) may not be used.

*m,n,tm{ENTER}

Lines *m* through *n* will be deleted from their original position and inserted before line *t*.

Transferring Blocks With the T Command

While the C and M commands let you manipulate blocks of lines within a file, the T (transfer) command lets you copy an entire ASCII file from disk into the file you are editing.

You enter the T command like this:

*ntfilespec{ENTER}

The contents of the file named by the file specification *filespec* are inserted before line *n* in the file you are editing. If *n* is omitted, the contents of the file will be inserted before the current line.

Editing a Very Large File

If you use EDLIN to edit a file that is too big to fit in RAM, you cannot edit the whole file at one time. EDLIN reads in as much of the file as it can but does not display the message "End of input file". The absence of that message warns you that the whole file is not in RAM.

To edit the rest of the file, you must first enter the W (write) command, which makes EDLIN write the first part of the file, with changes, to disk. If you enter W without a parameter, EDLIN writes out three-fourths of the data it is holding in RAM. If you enter W preceded by a parameter *n*, EDLIN writes out the first *n* lines.

After you write the first part of the edited file to disk, you can read in the next part of the unedited file with the A (append) command. If you enter A with no parameter, EDLIN again reads as much data as it can, or reads to the end of the file if it can. If you enter A preceded by a parameter *n*, EDLIN reads the next *n* lines. EDLIN displays the message "End of input file" when it has read the whole file.

You can edit a file of any length by repeatedly writing edited lines out and reading unedited lines in.

CHAPTER 7

Using a Printer

A printer is a device that your PC can use to print information on paper. For most PC users, a printer is an indispensable tool. This chapter tells you how to load the IBM Graphic Matrix Printer with paper and a ribbon and how to operate its controls. It also tells you how to operate any sort of printer from the keyboard of the PC.

The IBM Graphic Matrix Printer

IBM sells a printer for the PC called the 80 CPS Graphic Matrix Printer. (CPS stands for "characters per second," and 80 cps is the printer's nominal printing speed.) This device is typical of a kind of printer called a *dot matrix printer,* so named because each character is formed by a matrix of dots. Dot matrix printers are moderately priced devices that produce moderate quality printing at moderate to high speeds. The Graphic Matrix Printer is shown in Figure 7-1.

If you have an IBM Graphic Matrix Printer or a similar printer, lift your printer's hinged plastic top and look inside. Notice that the printer does not hold the paper with a rubber platen as a typewriter does. Instead, it holds and moves the paper with a *tractor,* which has a pair of wheels with pins on their rims. The printer uses *continuous form* paper, also known as *pin-feed* or *fan-fold* paper. This type of paper has a row of perforations along each edge that fit over the tractor pins. After printing is completed, these perforated edges often can be torn off, leaving a straight edge.

The printer's print head contains a matrix of movable pins that point toward the paper. The print head prints characters by driving various combinations of pins against the paper through an inked ribbon.

On the right side of the printer is a knob for advancing the paper by hand. Below the knob and toward the rear of the printer is a rocker switch that controls the printer's power.

On top of the printer are three square buttons. The *Online* button controls whether the printer will accept data from the PC and

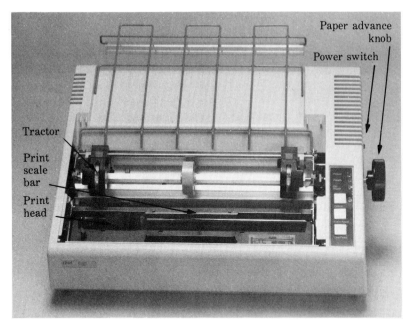

Figure 7-1.
The IBM Graphic Matrix Printer

print it. The *Form Feed* button advances the printer to the top of the next sheet of paper. The *Line Feed* button advances the printer one line.

Next to the three buttons are four indicator lights. *Power* indicates that the power switch is on. *Ready* indicates that the printer is ready to print. *Paper Out* gives you a warning when the printer has reached the end of a stack of paper. *Online* (unlabeled, but next to the Online button) indicates that the printer is prepared to receive data from the computer.

The *forms thickness control* is a lever just inside the printer's left side, near the print head's leftmost position. You may adjust this control for the most pleasing print density. Move the control toward the back of the printer to print on single-sheet paper and toward the front for multi-part paper.

Lesson 7-1:
Installing a Ribbon

The Graphic Matrix Printer's ribbon comes in a large plastic cartridge. You install the ribbon under the printer's hinged cover.

To install a ribbon, lift the printer's cover. Hold the ribbon cartridge by the fin on its top and press it into place, as shown in Figure 7-2. Notice the two tabs on the left side of the cartridge; they must fit into slots on the printer's frame for the cartridge to slip into place.

Once the cartridge is in place, slip the ribbon between the print head and ribbon shield as shown in Figure 7-3. You can use a pencil to handle the ribbon without getting ink on your fingers.

Take up any slack in the ribbon by turning the knob near the left end of the ribbon cartridge counterclockwise. Then lower the plastic cover.

Lesson 7-2:
Loading Paper

The printer should be placed on a printer stand or on a table with its back near the table edge.

Lift the printer's cover and raise the hinged shield mounted over each wheel of the tractor. Pull the print scale bar forward.

Figure 7-2.
Installing the ribbon cartridge

Figure 7-3.
Slipping the ribbon into place

Put a stack of paper behind and below the printer. Feed the paper into the printer by inserting it between the forms rack and the plastic roller, as shown in Figure 7-4. Push it under the print scale bar, behind the tractor mechanism, and up between the tractor and the print head.

Figure 7-4.
Feeding the paper into the printer

Pull the paper a couple of inches past the print head. Then slip the edge holes over the pins on each tractor wheel. If you need to adjust the spacing of the tractor wheels, push forward on the lever next to each wheel to unlock the wheel. Push back on the levers to lock them again when you are done. Set the wheels so that the paper's left edge perforation is just left of the print head's leftmost position and so that there is just a little slack in the paper when the tractor wheels engage the edge holes.

Lower the shields over the wheels. Finally, push the print scale bar back against the paper and lower the printer cover.

Lesson 7-3:
Checking Out the Printer

Before you turn the printer on, roll the paper forward so that the top of a sheet is just above the print head. This will enable the printer to position the paper at the top of a new sheet when you press the Form Feed button. Never turn the knob while the power is on or you may damage the nylon gear mechanism.

Turn on the PC, and then turn on the printer. Check the printer's indicator lights. The Power, Ready, and Online lights should be on. The Paper Out light should be off.

Notice that if you tap the Line Feed and Form Feed buttons, nothing happens. This is because these buttons have no effect when the printer is on-line. Press the Online button. The Online and Ready lights should go off. Now the printer is *off-line.*

Tap the Line Feed button again. The paper should advance one line. Try it a few times, and then hold the button down for a few seconds. The paper should advance continuously until you release the button.

Tap the Form Feed button. The paper should advance to the top of the next sheet (11 inches below the top of the first sheet).

Press the Online button again. The Online and Ready lights should go back on; the printer is back on-line.

Before you begin using the printer in the lessons that follow, you can conduct a short self-test to make sure that the print is the right darkness and that it is centered correctly.

To make sure that the printer is operating as you want it to, first turn off the printer. Then press and hold the Line Feed button while you turn the printer on. The printer will print line after line of characters until you turn it off.

Some Things That Might Go Wrong: Turning On the Printer

Power light does not go on when power is turned on. The printer is not plugged in.

Ready light is not on; Paper Out light is on. The paper is not properly loaded. The printer has a "paper out" detector under the bar behind the tractor mechanism. If the paper is not fed under the bar, the printer thinks no paper is loaded.

Form Feed and Line Feed do not work. The paper is not properly loaded.

Paper does not feed evenly. Either you inserted the paper unevenly, or the tractor wheels are not properly spaced; they are probably too close together. See the instructions for adjusting the tractor wheels in Lesson 7-2.

Paper pin-feed holes tear. If the holes tear on the sides near the edges of the paper, the tractor wheels are too far apart. Lesson 7-2 tells you how to adjust them.

If the holes tear at the tops, something is pulling back on the paper as it feeds into the printer. Find the obstruction and remove it.

About Form Feeds

There are two ways to make your printer do a *form feed* (that is, skip to the top of the next sheet of paper). One is to set the printer off-line and tap the Form Feed button. The other is to send the printer a special nonprinting character, called a *form feed character*, in the stream of printed data. Many computer programs use the form feed character to start a new page of output.

Your printer has no way of knowing where the top of a page actually is. Instead, the printer simply assumes that it is set at the top of a page when you turn it on. It keeps track of lines printed so that it always knows how far to advance to get to the top of the next page. If you roll the paper forward by hand, the printer loses its place, so that a form feed operation will advance it to the wrong place on a page.

When you are printing pages of output that should be aligned with the actual page breaks on the paper, you can keep the paper properly aligned in either of two ways:

- Use the Form Feed or Line Feed buttons. Never roll the paper forward by hand.
- After you roll the paper forward, or after you insert a new stack of paper while the printer is on, press the Form Feed

button if the printer is not already aligned at the top of a page. Then roll the paper forward until it is actually positioned at the top of a page.

If You Have a Non-IBM Printer

Most non-IBM printers have indicators and controls similar to those on the IBM Graphic Matrix Printer. Some common differences are as follows:

- *Letter quality printers* print characters as a typewriter does, by striking a raised type element against the paper through a ribbon. Such printers are slower and more expensive than dot matrix printers, but they produce higher quality printing. They are often used for word processing.
- Some printers lack an on-line control. Such a printer is always on-line when paper is properly loaded. The manual controls, if present, work at all times.
- Some printers have a rubber roller instead of a tractor and use cut sheets or rolls of paper. Some printers have both a roller and a tractor and can use cut sheets, rolls, or continuous forms.
- Some printers have an interlock mechanism that makes the printer go off-line when the cover is raised. To make the printer start again, you must lower the cover and sometimes press a "reset" button.

Consult your printer's instruction manual for detailed information.

Serial and Parallel Interfaces

The electrical connection between your PC and your printer may be either of two types. One type is called a *parallel interface* or *Centronics interface*. The other type is called a *serial interface* or *RS-232C interface*.

The IBM Graphic Matrix Printer has a parallel interface. That is the kind of interface the PC can "talk to" most easily. For a printer with a serial interface, you must do some extra preparation before you can begin printing.

You can tell which kind of interface your printer uses by looking at the cable between the printer and the PC. If the plug that fits into the PC is male, the printer has a parallel interface; if it is female, the printer has a serial interface.

Device Names for Serial and Parallel Interfaces

Just as you can refer to your disk drives with drive names like A and B, you can refer to other devices by device names.

Several of DOS's device names refer to the PC's interface adapters. The name LPT1 (for "line printer #1") refers to a parallel interface; the name COM1 (for "communications device #1") refers to a serial interface. These are the device names normally associated with a parallel or serial interface printer. A complete table of DOS device names and their uses is given in Chapter 18, "Operations and Procedures."

Preparing to Use a Serial Interface Printer

If your printer has a serial interface, you must execute two commands each time you boot before you can use the printer.

There are two ways you can execute these commands. First, you can enter them from the keyboard after you boot. Second, you can store the commands in an *AUTOEXEC file*, which the PC will read and execute automatically when you boot.

You will learn how to set up an AUTOEXEC file in Chapter 9. If your PC has been set up or used by another person, however, it may already have an AUTOEXEC file that prepares it to use a serial printer.

To find out if your PC has an AUTOEXEC file, enter this command, with the default drive set to the diskette or hard disk from which you normally boot:

```
A>type autoexec.bat{ENTER}
```

If there is an AUTOEXEC file, this command displays it on the screen. If not, it produces the message "File not found".

If there is an AUTOEXEC file, examine its contents (the TYPE command displays the file) to see if it contains the two commands we are about to describe. If it does, DOS will execute the necessary commands automatically when you boot, and you may skip the rest of this section.

The first preparation command tells DOS how data sent to the PC's serial interface should look. You enter it like this:

```
A>mode com1:baud,n,8,1,p{ENTER}
```

For *baud*, substitute your printer's *baud rate* — a number giving the rate at which the printer expects the PC to send data.[1] If you do not know what number to use, ask a technically informed person or study the printer's instruction manual. The most likely values for *baud* are 300 and 1200.

The second command instructs DOS to send printed data to the PC's serial interface rather than to its parallel interface. You enter the command like this:

A>**mode Lpt1:=com1{ENTER}**

After you have entered this command, your PC is ready for use with the serial interface printer.

Lesson 7-4:
Printing the Contents of the Screen

You can print the current contents of the screen at any time by holding down the SHIFT key and pressing the PRTSC (print screen) key. After you have started DOS and gotten your printer ready, try printing the contents of the screen.

Printing Graphics From the Screen (DOS 2.0 Only)

If your PC has an IBM Color/Graphics Monitor Adapter, it can display graphics (pictures) on the screen as well as text. This adapter card allows a program to display graphics, text, or both on the screen at once.

SHIFT PRTSC normally can print only character data, not graphics. However, if you have an IBM Graphic Matrix Printer and version 2.0 of DOS, you can enable SHIFT PRTSC to print a screen of graphics by running the GRAPHICS command:

A>**graphics{ENTER}**

You need run this command only once after booting DOS. It may be run automatically by an AUTOEXEC file.

If your printer is not an IBM Graphic Matrix Printer but is capable of printing graphics, a program equivalent to the GRAPHICS command may be available for it. Consult your dealer for more information.

---

[1]*Baud* is a shortened form of "Baudot," a method used by early teletype printers to encode characters as digital information. To translate a baud rate into an approximate number of characters per second, divide by 10.

Some Things That Might Go Wrong: Printing the Screen's Contents

The printer ignores SHIFT PRTSC. The printer is not ready to print. Find and correct the problem, and try again.

The PC freezes when you press SHIFT PRTSC. The printer is not connected or is not turned on. If you have a serial printer, it may be connected and turned on but not ready to print. If you have a serial printer, you may have neglected to enter the MODE commands needed to make DOS use the serial interface.

The printer prints nonsense. You are using a serial printer, and your PC's serial interface is not configured the same way as the interface on the printer. Either you used the wrong baud rate in the first MODE command, or you have an unusual printer for which the other MODE parameters ("n,8,1,p") are not appropriate.

Study your printer's instruction manual to determine how your printer is configured. Look for information on "baud rate," "character length," "stop bits," and "parity."

To learn how to set the PC's serial interface, study the description of the MODE command in the "DOS Commands" chapter of IBM's *Disk Operating System* manual. If you cannot figure out how to enter the MODE command, experiment. The worst thing you can do is print some more nonsense.

You do not have to reenter the second form of the MODE command after reentering the first form.

Lesson 7-5:
Slaving the Printer to the Screen

Slaving the printer to the screen means telling DOS to begin printing whatever it displays on the screen. Slaving is meaningful only for text displays, not for graphics displays. You slave the printer to the screen by holding down the CTRL key and pressing the PRTSC key.

Press CTRL PRTSC now and enter some command such as DIR. DOS should print the DIR command, DIR's output, and the DOS prompt that follows the command, at the same time as all of this appears on the screen. To make DOS stop printing what it displays, enter CTRL PRTSC again.

Using TYPE to Display a Text File

This method of slaving the printer to the screen can be put to use in many ways. For instance, it may be used to print a text file.

The simplest way to print a text file is to enter CTRL PRTSC and then to run the TYPE command:

`A>{CTRL}{PRTSC}type b:giraffes.txt{ENTER}`

Be sure to toggle this function off by pressing CTRL PRTSC when you are finished experimenting with it.

Some Things That Might Go Wrong: Using TYPE

TYPE displays strange characters (such as Greek letters) in a file. The printed copy of the file may be formatted strangely. A part of each byte that is not normally used to store a character contains other information in this file. The PC interprets the whole byte as a character value and displays unusual characters.

This often happens when you use TYPE to display a file that was created with a word processing program. It has no effect on the way the word processor itself will display or print the file.

Lesson 7-6:
Controlling Print Spacing With MODE

You can control the horizontal and vertical spacing of the IBM Graphic Matrix Printer's output with the MODE command. The format of MODE for this purpose is

`A>mode Lptl:h,v{ENTER}`

For h, substitute the number of characters you want to print per 8 1/2-inch line. This value may be either 80 or 132. When you turn the printer on, its default setting is 80 characters per line.

For v, substitute the number of lines you want to print per vertical inch. This value may be either 6 or 8. When you turn the printer on, it prints six lines per inch.

Once you set the printer's spacing with MODE, it does not change until you set it again with MODE, until a program sets it, or until you turn the printer off.

CAUTION

This form of the MODE command makes DOS send printed data to the PC's parallel interface, undoing the effect of a previous command like MODE LPT1:=COM1. Thus, you should enter this form of MODE *only if you are using a parallel interface printer attached to LPT1.*

In addition, since this command writes data that is meaningful only to the IBM Graphic Matrix Printer, you should not use it unless you have that printer or an equivalent printer, since MODE is likely to produce unexpected results or nothing.

Lesson 7-7:
Queuing Files for Printing (DOS 2.0 Only)

In version 2.0 of DOS, you can order DOS to print a file, and then you can run other programs while DOS prints the file. You can even *queue* several files for printing and run other programs while DOS automatically prints each one. This is an important time-saving technique, since most PC programs generate printed output faster than your printer can print it.

Later on, in Chapter 8, you will learn how to redirect the printed output of any program to a file so that you can queue the output for printing instead of printing it as it is produced.

Queuing Files: The PRINT Command

Before you queue a file for printing, be sure that your printer is on-line and ready for use. If you have a serial interface printer, you must run the MODE commands needed to make the PC send printed output to its serial interface.

You queue a file for printing by entering the PRINT command with the print file's name as a parameter. Use the PRINT command to print a text file such as GIRAFFES.TXT, which you created in Chapter 6:

`A>`**`print b:giraffes.txt`**`{ENTER}`

PRINT displays the following prompt:

`Name of list device [PRN] : _`

PRINT is asking you what device name you want queued files to be printed on. You may respond PRN ENTER or just ENTER. After you respond to the "Name of list device" prompt, PRINT queues the file for printing. Since no files are ahead of it in the queue, DOS begins printing the file immediately.

GIRAFFES.TXT may be so short that it will be done printing before you can enter another command, but if you queue a longer file, you can run any other command while the file is printing.

Once you have queued a file for printing, you may not remove the disk containing the file or erase or modify the file until it has been completely printed.

You cannot use CTRL PRTSC or SHIFT PRTSC while DOS is printing a queued file. After DOS has emptied the print queue, however, you may use those commands again.

When DOS finishes printing a queued file, it advances the printer to the top of a new page. This keeps the printout of each file separate from the next.

Some Things That Might Go Wrong: Using PRINT

You see the message "Not ready error on device PRN. Abort, Retry, Ignore?" You have tried to slave the printer to the display while DOS is printing a file that was queued with PRINT, or you have tried to queue a file with PRINT while the printer is slaved to the display.

Press CTRL PRTSC to unslave the printer. Then press A (for "abort") or R (for "retry") to make DOS resume running.

You must stop the printer while printing queued files to adjust the paper or replace the paper or ribbon. Enter CTRL NUM LOCK. This halts all of the PC's activity, including printing of queued files. Press any typing key to make the PC resume running.

If your printer has an "off-line" control, you may try stopping the printer by switching it off-line. With some printers, this stops the printer while allowing the PC to continue running a program. With other printers, it makes you lose part of your printed output because the printer does not notify the PC that it is off-line, and DOS therefore continues trying to print queued files.

The PC prints nonsense, prints nothing, or freezes when the first PRINT command is entered. See the list of things that might go wrong when a file is printed with SHIFT PRTSC.

These symptoms may also be caused by responding to the "List device?" prompt with the name of a device that is not attached to your PC.

The printer stops printing before the end of the print queue, and the PC freezes. The printer has run out of paper or otherwise entered a nonready state. Correct the problem and bring the printer back on-line.

Queuing More Files

You can queue more files with PRINT at any time. PRINT will not reprompt you for the name of a list device after the first time you use it.

You can queue several files at once by using global filename characters in a PRINT parameter or by entering PRINT with several parameters. For example, this command line queues the names of three files:

```
A>print a.txt b.txt c.txt{ENTER}
```

The DOS print queue can hold up to ten filenames at a time.

Listing and Controlling the Print Queue

You can display the names of the files currently in the print queue by entering PRINT with no parameters:

```
A>print{ENTER}
```

You can remove any file from the print queue (including the file currently being printed) by entering PRINT with that file's name followed by the /C (cancel) option:

```
A>print b.txt/c{ENTER}
```

If you use /C in a command line with more than one parameter, /C affects the *immediately preceding* file and *all following* files. For example, the following command line queues D.TXT and removes B.TXT and C.TXT from the queue:

```
A>print d.txt b.txt/c c.txt{ENTER}
```

You can remove all files from the print queue by entering PRINT with the /T (terminate) option:

```
A>print/t{ENTER}
```

On to Application Programs

You have now learned enough about your PC and about DOS to begin applying your PC to useful tasks.

We suggest that you take a break from this book and learn to use one or more application programs on your PC. Then you will be able to start using your PC in your work. The experience you acquire will help you consolidate your understanding of the PC and DOS.

If you do not have strong ideas about what sort of application to learn, we suggest you try a word processing program or a spreadsheet program. These types of programs (and many others) are discussed in Chapter 14, "Guide to Software."

Return to Chapter 8 of this book after you have become comfortable with the basic use of DOS and with one or two application programs.

CHAPTER 8

Advanced File Features Of DOS 2.0

This chapter introduces several powerful techniques for manipulating and organizing files. You will learn how to redirect a program's displayed output or keyboard input to a file and how to "pipe" one program's displayed output directly to another program's keyboard input. You will also learn how to create sub-directories, which group together a number of related files as though they were on a separate disk.

Lesson 8-1:
Redirecting Input and Output

Version 2.0 of DOS allows you to make almost any program write its output to a file instead of to the display. Similarly, it lets you make a program read its keyboard input from a file instead of from the keyboard. This facility is called *I/O redirection.*[1] I/O redirection makes it easy for you to do things that would otherwise be impossible, such as

- Printing a program's display output.
- Queuing the display output file with PRINT so that the PC will print it while you run other programs.
- Modifying the display output file with a text editor before you print it.
- Printing more than one copy of the file or saving it to be displayed or printed again at a later time.
- Making one program read its keyboard input from another program's display output file, instead of from the PC's keyboard.

---

[1] Devices that are attached to the PC are often called "I/O devices." *I/O* is short for "input/output," and thus an I/O device is simply a device for getting data into and out of your PC. Some common I/O devices include printers, modems (for transferring data by telephone), and disk drives.

Redirecting Output

To redirect a program's display output to a file, enter the command line followed by the name you want to give the file. To distinguish the file's name from a parameter, you must prefix it with a greater-than sign (>). You may think of > as an arrow pointing from the command to the output filename.

For example, to use DIR to write the directory of a disk in drive B to a file named DISKB.DIR, you would enter

A>dir b: >diskb.dir{ENTER}

Enter this command now. DIR's listing of the directory of disk B will be stored in the file DISKB.DIR. To display the contents of the output file, enter the following command:

A>type diskb.dir{ENTER}

What if you decide that you would like DISKB.DIR to contain the display output of a second command? You can add the output of a second command to the material that is already in a file by using two greater-than signs (>>) instead of one. For instance, to add disk B's CHKDSK listing to the file DISKB.DIR, enter

A>chkdsk b: >>diskb.dir{ENTER}

Be sure to use >> instead of > as the prefix to the output file's name in this command. The prefix > would cause CHKDSK's output to *replace* the existing contents of the file rather than being added to the file.

Use the TYPE command again now to display the contents of DISKB.DIR. CHKDSK's output is displayed along with DIR's output.

Redirecting Input

To redirect a command's keyboard input to a file, enter the command line followed by the name of the file you want the command to read. Prefix the file's name with a less-than sign (<). You may think of < as an arrow pointing from the input file's name to the command.

For example, to edit a file named ABC.TXT with EDLIN and make EDLIN read its keyboard input from a file named EDITCMDS.IPT on disk B instead of from the keyboard, you would enter

A>edlin abc.txt <b:editcmds.ipt{ENTER}

In the next lesson you will learn some new commands that suggest much more practical uses for redirection of input.

You can use input and output redirection in the same command line if you wish. It does not matter which file name is first. See the discussion of the SORT filter in Lesson 8-2 for an example of this.

Redirection does not work with some programs because they do not do their keyboard input or display output through standard programming facilities that DOS provides. Many word processors, spreadsheet programs, and other application programs that "paint" text on the screen fall in this category.

Lesson 8-2:
Filters

A *filter* is a program that copies text data from one place to another, making some type of systematic change in the data as it copies. A simple example of a filter is a program that copies only those lines that contain a certain sequence of characters, ignoring the rest.

Filters are useful for processing the display output of a DOS command such as DIR after it has been redirected to a file. They can be applied to the output of any other program if it is in an appropriate form.

The SORT Filter

For an example of how to use a filter, consider the following problem. You want a directory listing of your DOS disk that is sorted in alphabetical order by filename.

This problem can be solved in two steps. The first step is to run DIR and write the directory listing to a file. We will call this file NOORDER.DIR, and we will put it in drive B:

```
A>dir a: >b:noorder.dir{ENTER}
```

The second step is to run a filter called SORT. SORT reads input from the keyboard, sorts it in alphabetical order, and writes it to the display. We can see a sorted directory listing by running SORT and redirecting its keyboard input to NOORDER.DIR:

```
A>sort <b:noorder.dir{ENTER}
```

If we want to store the sorted directory in a file, we redirect the output of SORT as well. Then we can print the file with the PRINT command:

```
A>sort <b:noorder.dir >b:inorder.dir{ENTER}
A>print b:inorder.dir{ENTER}
```

Try running these commands on one or more of your disks to become familiar with the use of the SORT filter.

Variations on SORT

You can make SORT sort a file in reverse order by running it with the /R option. Notice that the option goes *before* the names of the redirection files:

A>**sort/r <b:noorder.dir >b:revorder.dir{ENTER}**

You can make SORT begin sorting at some point after the beginning of each input line by running it with the $/+n$ option, where n is the number of the column at which sorting should begin.

For example, the filename extension begins in column 10 on each line of a DIR listing. To sort a DIR listing by filename extension, you would enter

A>**sort/+10 <b:noorder.dir >b:extorder.dir{ENTER}**

Again, you may wish to sort the DIR listing by file size. If you examine a directory listing, you can see that the file size begins in column 14 of each line. Thus, you would enter

A>**sort/+14 <b:noorder.dir >b:sizorder.dir{ENTER}**

The SORT filter cannot process a file larger than 63K bytes. This is not a serious limitation, however, since filters are intended mainly for processing short files, like the redirected output of DIR.

The FIND Filter

FIND is another useful filter. You can use FIND to display or count all lines containing a string (a specified sequence of characters) in the keyboard input.

For instance, to display all the lines containing the string "EXE" in NOORDER.DIR, you would enter this:

A>**find "EXE" <b:noorder.dir{ENTER}**

Note that uppercase and lowercase must be replicated exactly any time you use a string. If you had entered "exe" in your command line rather than "EXE", FIND would have ignored all lines where "EXE" appeared only in uppercase.

Here is a problem FIND can solve: you want a directory listing of all the files on a disk whose filenames end with the characters DISK. All the filenames are not the same length, so global filename notation will not help.

You can redirect DIR's output to a file and then run FIND to display only those lines which contain "DISK∅" (where the symbol "∅" represents a blank):

```
A>dir a: >b:noorder.dir{ENTER}
A>find "DISK " <b:noorder.dir{ENTER}
```

The blank after "DISK" guarantees that FIND will display only lines in which the filename *ends* with "DISK" and not filenames in which "DISK" is embedded.

If you enter FIND with two parameters, the second naming a file, FIND searches the file instead of its keyboard input. Thus the following commands

```
A>find "DISK " b:noorder.dir{ENTER}
A>find "DISK " <b:noorder.dir{ENTER}
```

would produce the same results.

Variations on FIND

The FIND filter accepts several options. You may specify its options *only* after the command name, not after the search string or file name.

The /V option makes FIND display all lines in a file that do *not* contain a specified string. Thus, the following command line would display all lines in INORDER.DIR that do not contain the word "COM", delimited by blanks:

```
A>find/v " COM " b:inorder.dir{ENTER}
```

Another option you can use with the FIND command is /C (count). The /C option makes FIND display only the number of lines that contain a designated string, not the lines themselves. To find out how many "COM" files are contained in the file named INORDER.DIR on disk B, for instance, enter

```
A>find/c " COM " b:inorder.dir{ENTER}
```

Since strings are always designated by quotation marks, you may have wondered how to type a command in which the string itself contains quotation marks. For instance, how would you enter a command that would make FIND display all the instances of the string 'A "sticky wicket"'?

You would represent each quotation mark in the string by a pair of quotation marks, as in the following example:

```
A>find "A ""sticky wicket""" abc.txt{ENTER}
```

This command would cause FIND to list all the lines in the file ABC.TXT that contain this string.

The MORE Filter

The MORE filter can be used to display a file one screen (24 lines) at a time. At the end of each screen, MORE displays the message

```
--More--
```

and waits for you to press any typing key. Then it displays the next screen. This will continue until MORE has displayed the entire input file.

MORE reads its input from the keyboard. Thus you must use input redirection to apply it to a file. For example, to display INORDER.DIR one screen at a time, you would enter

```
A>more <b:inorder.dir{ENTER}
```

A Final Note on Filters

Filters are among the most powerful tools in DOS. The three filters provided with DOS only begin to address the potential uses for filters.

There is nothing magical about a filter; it is just a computer program that reads input from the keyboard or a file and writes output to the display, performing some alteration in between. If you choose to learn how to write computer programs, you can develop your own filters.

Lesson 8-3:
Pipes

A *pipe* is a direct connection between the display output of one program and the keyboard input to another. You use a pipe like this:

```
A>program1 | program2{ENTER}
```

When you enter a command line like the preceding one, DOS runs PROGRAM1 and then PROGRAM2. It redirects the display output of PROGRAM1 to the keyboard input of PROGRAM2.

For example, you could display a sorted directory listing of a disk with one command line, like this:

```
A>dir | sort{ENTER}
```

This command line runs DIR, then runs SORT. DIR's display output becomes SORT's keyboard input. Thus the command line is exactly equivalent to the following three command lines:

```
A>dir >%pipel.$$${ENTER}
A>sort <%pipel.$$${ENTER}
A>erase %pipel.$$${ENTER}
```

In fact, a pipe works by creating a temporary file with a name like %PIPE1.$$$ on the default drive and then erasing the file when it is no longer needed.

You can connect three or more commands with pipes if you wish. The following command line produces a sorted DIR listing that includes only those lines containing a word that ends with the numerals "83":

```
A>dir ¦ find "83 " ¦ sort{ENTER}
```

Pipes do not enable you to do anything that you could not do with plain redirection, but they are a great convenience when you want to use one program's display output file only as the next program's keyboard input file. You can get the effect of creating the file, using it, and deleting it by entering a single command line.

About Sub-Directories

Up until now, each of your disks has had one directory that contains pointers to all the files on the disk. This arrangement is perfectly adequate so long as a disk contains only a few files.

As you learned in Chapter 5, however, there is a limit to the number of files that a diskette will hold in its main directory. In addition, directories are difficult to read when they become too long.

Version 2.0 of DOS lets you deal with these problems by defining several directories on a disk. One directory—the one you have been using up to now—is the *root directory*. The root directory may hold both data files and *sub-directories*, which are files that contain more directory information. Each sub-directory may hold both data files and other sub-directories, and so forth. There is no limit to the number of files you can store in a sub-directory, nor to the number of sub-directories you can define on a disk.

Figure 8-1 illustrates how the contents of a disk might be organized using sub-directories. The figure shows a disk whose directory contains two data files and three sub-directories. Some of the sub-directories contain their data files and more sub-directories. We will discuss Figure 8-1 in the next several paragraphs; in Lesson 8-4, you will learn to duplicate Figure 8-1's sub-directories and files on your own disk.

The branching structure shown in the figure is often called a *tree*. If you turn the figure upside down, you will see that "tree" is an apt term. The root directory is at the root of the tree. The sub-directories are the branches, and the files are the leaves.

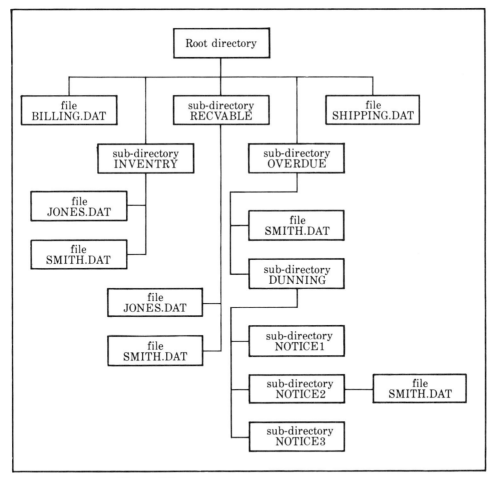

Figure 8-1.
Structure of a disk with sub-directories

Whenever you are using a disk, one of that disk's directories is its *current directory*. For most purposes, the files in the current directory are the only ones on the disk that you can see.

You can change the current directory with the CHDIR command, described in a later lesson. Once you change the directory, it remains as you set it until you change it again, reboot, or put a new disk in the disk drive. (When DOS detects the new disk, it makes the disk's root directory the current directory.)

Notice that several of the sub-directories contain files with the same names. This does not create a conflict, any more than having files with the same name on several different disks would create a conflict. In fact, giving two files in different sub-directories the same name can be a very useful way of emphasizing a connection between them.

Using Paths to Refer to Sub-Directories and Files

Every sub-directory has a name, just as every file has a name. A sub-directory's name follows the same rules as a file's name: it may be one to eight characters long, followed by an optional dot and an extension of one to three characters.

There are two ways you can refer to a sub-directory or a file in a sub-directory. First, you can identify each sub-directory between the root directory and the sub-directory or file you want. Second, you can name each sub-directory between the current directory and the sub-directory or file you want. The second way is shorter, as long as the file you want is part of the same "branch" as the current directory. However, the first way lets you refer to any sub-directory or file on a disk, no matter what directory is current.

For example, if the current directory is OVERDUE in Figure 8-1, you can refer to NOTICE2 either as "sub-directory NOTICE2 in sub-directory DUNNING in the current directory," or as "sub-directory NOTICE2 in sub-directory DUNNING in sub-directory OVERDUE in the root directory." Either kind of reference is called a *path*.

Table 8-1 shows how to express a path in a command line. In each case the backslash (\) is used to separate sub-directory names from each other and from the file's name, if any. Notice that in the first two lines of the table, the first name is preceded by a backslash. This signifies that the first directory in the path is found in the root directory. If the first name is *not* preceded by a backslash, it is found in the current directory.

There is no limit on the number of directories in a path. There is a limit on the length the path's name may have, however. A path name, from the \ representing the root directory to the last directory name, may be no longer than 63 characters.

Notation	Example	Expresses
\dir\...\dir	\OVERDUE\DUNNING\NOTICE2	Sub-directory name relative to root directory
\dir\...\dir\fn	\OVERDUE\DUNNING\NOTICE2\SMITH.DAT	Filename relative to root directory
dir\...\dir	OVERDUE\DUNNING\NOTICE2	Sub-directory name relative to current directory
dir\...\dir\fn	OVERDUE\DUNNING\NOTICE2\SMITH.DAT	Filename relative to current directory

Table 8-1.
Expressing Paths in Command Lines

Some Examples of Paths

Here are some examples of how paths may be used in command lines.

The following command refers to sub-directory NOTICE2, relative to the root directory of the disk in the default drive. (This command's function is to make that sub-directory the current directory.)

A>**chdir \overdue\dunning\notice2**{**ENTER**}

The following command types file SMITH.DAT in sub-directory NOTICE2:

A>**type \overdue\dunning\notice2\smith.dat**{**ENTER**}

The following command is the same, but refers to disk B:

A>**type b:\overdue\dunning\notice2\smith.dat**{**ENTER**}

The following command is the same, but refers to the file relative to the current sub-directory (which presumably is DUNNING):

A>**type b:notice2\smith.dat**{**ENTER**}

The following command is the same, but refers to the file relative to the current sub-directory, when the current sub-directory is NOTICE2:

A>**type b:smith.dat**{**ENTER**}

Observe how the path name reduces to only the filename when the file is in the current directory.

Lesson 8-4:
Creating Sub-Directories and Sub-Directory Files

Just as you must create a file before you can tell a program to read the file, you must create a sub-directory before you can tell DOS to put a file in the sub-directory. You create sub-directories, one at a time, with the MKDIR (make directory) command.

As a learning exercise, you will create the directory structure shown in Figure 8-1 on a diskette. Then you will create the data files that belong in the directories.

Of course, this is not the only order in which you could create Figure 8-1's directory structure. If it suited your purposes, you could create some files, then some sub-directories, then some more files, and so forth. The only restriction is that you may only create a file or a sub-directory in a directory that already exists.

Using MKDIR to Create Sub-Directories

Start with an empty, formatted diskette. Insert the diskette in your drive B, or whatever diskette drive is free on your PC.

First, use the MKDIR command to create the three sub-directories that reside in the root directory. MKDIR expects one parameter, the path to the sub-directory being made.

To make the sub-directories INVENTRY, RECVABLE, and OVERDUE in the root directory, enter these commands:

```
A>mkdir b:inventry{ENTER}
A>mkdir b:recvable{ENTER}
A>mkdir b:overdue{ENTER}
```

Now you must make the sub-directory DUNNING in the sub-directory OVERDUE. You can do it like this:

```
A>mkdir b:overdue\dunning{ENTER}
```

Notice that you typed this path with no leading \. That was just to save yourself the trouble of pressing the extra key. As long as the root directory is the current directory, it does not matter whether you enter the leading \ or not. Do you see why?

Next, you must make three more sub-directories in DUNNING. You could do it by entering three MKDIR commands with parameters like "OVERDUE\DUNNING\NOTICE1", but if you make DUNNING the current directory you can save yourself most of that typing.

Use the CHDIR (change directory) command to make the sub-directory DUNNING the current directory:

```
A>chdir b:overdue\dunning{ENTER}
```

Now you can define the three sub-directories NOTICE1 through NOTICE3 like this:

```
A>mkdir b:notice1{ENTER}
A>mkdir b:notice2{ENTER}
A>mkdir b:notice3{ENTER}
```

At this point you could *not* get the same result if you entered a \ at the beginning of the path. "MKDIR B:\NOTICE1" would make a sub-directory in the root directory, not in DUNNING.

Creating Files in Sub-Directories

Now you must create the files shown in each sub-directory in Figure 8-1. We are only concerned with the diskette's directory structure, so you may create these files in any convenient manner — for example, by making copies of files on the DOS disk.

Now that the directory structure is complete, it does not matter in what order you define the files. To keep things orderly, however, we will return to the root directory and go through each of the sub-directories one level at a time.

To make the root directory the current directory, enter the CHDIR command like this:

```
A>chdir b:\{ENTER}
```

This is the first type of reference to a directory reduced to its simplest form: a leading \, meaning "start at the root directory," followed by no sub-directory name.

Create the files BILLING.DAT and SHIPPING.DAT by any convenient means. For example:

```
A>copy chkdsk.com b:billing.dat{ENTER}
A>copy chkdsk.com b:shipping.dat{ENTER}
```

Now you must create the files JONES.DAT and SMITH.DAT in the sub-directory INVENTRY. You can do it like this:

```
A>copy chkdsk.com b:inventry\jones.dat{ENTER}
A>copy chkdsk.com b:inventry\smith.dat{ENTER}
```

Now copy JONES.DAT and SMITH.DAT to the sub-directory RECVABLE. Instead of copying the files the way you copied them into INVENTRY, you can save some keystrokes by making RECVABLE the current directory:

```
A>chdir b:\recvable{ENTER}
A>copy chkdsk.com b:jones.dat{ENTER}
A>copy chkdsk.com b:smith.dat{ENTER}
```

Notice that you entered CHKDSK.COM, not \CHKDSK.COM, even though the current directory is RECVABLE and you were copying from the root directory. That is because you were copying from the root directory of disk A and on disk A the root directory is still current. Every disk on your system has its own current directory, independent of every other disk.

Next, make OVERDUE the current directory and then copy SMITH.DAT to it from sub-directory INVENTRY:

```
A>chdir b:overdue{ENTER}
A>copy b:\inventry\smith.dat b:smith.dat{ENTER}
```

Here you have used a path in COPY's first parameter to refer to a file that is neither in the current directory nor in the root directory. You need no path in the second parameter because you are copying to the current directory.

The exercises you have just performed should have familiarized you enough with paths that you can finish up on your own. Do this by making NOTICE2 the current directory and then creating a SMITH.DAT file in it.

Displaying Sub-Directory Data With CHDIR, DIR, and TREE

Now that you can create sub-directories and create files in them, you need to know how to display information about sub-directories. You can do this with the CHDIR and DIR commands.

Using CHDIR and DIR

You can display the path to a disk's current directory by entering CHDIR with no parameter or with only a drive name in the parameter:

```
A>chdir b:{ENTER}
```

When you enter DIR with no parameter or with no path in the parameter, it displays information about the current directory.

On a disk with sub-directories, DIR's output contains some things that you have not encountered yet. Enter the following commands to see an example:

```
A>chdir b:\overdue{ENTER}
A>dir b:{ENTER}

 Volume in drive B is JASONS
 Directory of B:\OVERDUE

.              <DIR>     9-08-83     3:17p
..             <DIR>     9-08-83     3:44p
```

```
SMITH     DAT      6016    3-08-83   12:00p
DUNNING           <DIR>    9-08-83    3:50p
        4 File(s)     343005 bytes free
```

A>_

The second line of DIR's display shows the current directory's path. Looking back at earlier DIR displays, you now can see the reason for the puzzling "Directory of B:\" entry: it displayed the path of the root directory.

In the directory listing, each sub-directory is listed with the notation "<DIR>" after its name. It has no size value.

Each sub-directory contains two special directory entries. The entry with the "name" of "." contains information about the sub-directory itself. The ".." entry contains a pointer to the sub-directory's *parent directory*. In Figure 8-1, the parent directory of OVERDUE is the root directory. The parent directory of the sub-directory DUNNING is OVERDUE.

You can use DIR to display a directory other than the current directory by including a path in the parameter. For example, to display the contents of sub-directory NOTICE2 in sub-directory DUNNING in the current directory, you would enter

A>**dir b:dunning\notice2{ENTER}**

You can also use global filename characters with paths, if you want to display only a certain type of file in a sub-directory. For instance, you could use the following command to display files with the filename extension DAT in sub-directory INVENTRY in the root directory:

A>**dir b:\inventry*.dat{ENTER}**

Using the TREE Command

While the DIR command will list the contents of one directory at a time, you may want to scan all the directories and sub-directories on a disk. The TREE command lets you do this by displaying a complete picture of the directory structure of a disk. The TREE command expects one parameter identifying the disk you want to display:

A>**tree b:{ENTER}**

TREE displays the path to each sub-directory on the disk and the names of any sub-directories defined in the sub-directory. If you use the /F (files) option, it also displays the names of any files in each sub-directory.

Removing a Sub-Directory With RMDIR

You learned how to create sub-directories earlier in this chapter. You may also want to remove a sub-directory from a disk. Use the RMDIR (remove directory) command to do this. RMDIR expects one parameter, the path to the directory, to be removed. For example, to remove the sub-directory NOTICE3 from the disk described by Figure 8-1, you could enter

A>**rmdir b:\overdue\dunning\notice3**{ENTER}

If DUNNING were the current directory on this disk, you could also remove NOTICE3 like this:

A>**rmdir b:notice3**{ENTER}

You cannot remove a sub-directory from a disk while it contains any files or any lower-level sub-directories. If you want to remove such a sub-directory, you must first erase all the files and remove all the sub-directories that are in it. Also, you cannot remove a sub-directory while it is the current directory.

CAUTION

Do not try to remove a sub-directory with ERASE. If you do, DOS will delete every file in the sub-directory. In addition, do not try to rename a sub-directory with RENAME. If you try, DOS will rename the first file in the sub-directory. To do the equivalent of renaming a sub-directory, you must create a new sub-directory, copy all the files in the old sub-directory to the new one, delete all the files in the old sub-directory, and remove the old sub-directory.

Referring to a Parent Directory

You can use a double dot (..) in a path to represent the parent directory of a sub-directory. For example, if DUNNING in Figure 8-1 were the current directory, you could make OVERDUE the current directory like this:

A>**chdir b:..**{ENTER}

If NOTICE2 were the current directory, you could make NOTICE1 the current directory like this:

A>**chdir b:..\noticel**{ENTER}

And if NOTICE2 were the current directory, you could type the file SMITH.DAT in OVERDUE like this:

```
A>type b:..\..\smith.dat{ENTER}
```

If you created SMITH.DAT by copying CHKDSK.COM, of course, displaying it would be pointless. TYPE is used for displaying text files, and a COM file is not a text file.

Double-dot notation is useful mainly with a disk whose directory structure is rather complex and very regular.

Backing Up Disks With Sub-Directories

Backing up a diskette with a sub-directory is simple. The DISKCOPY command, presented in Lesson 2-4, copies the entire disk, sub-directories and all.

Backing up a hard disk is a little more complex. You must take account of the fact that a hard disk has sub-directories if you want to back up the disk properly.

BACKUP normally backs up only one directory—the current directory, if you specify no path in BACKUP's first parameter. Use the /S (sub-directory) option to make BACKUP back up all the files in the specified directory *and* in sub-directories below it in the directory tree. For example, to back up sub-directory OVERDUE and all sub-directories whose paths go through OVERDUE, you could enter

```
A>backup c:\overdue a:/s{ENTER}
```

To back up an entire hard disk, back up the root directory and its sub-directories:

```
A>backup c:\ a:/s{ENTER}
```

Ordinarily, the RESTORE command restores files that were backed up from the directory that you specify in the second parameter (or from the current directory, if no directory is specified). In every case, RESTORE will only restore a file to the directory that held it when it was backed up.

For example, let's suppose the disk structure in Figure 8-1 is defined on a hard disk. If you back up the entire hard disk by running BACKUP on the root directory with the /S option, and then restore to OVERDUE, like this,

```
A>backup c:\ a:/s{ENTER}
A>restore a: c:\overdue{ENTER}
```

only the files and sub-directories in OVERDUE will be restored. That is because you named OVERDUE in RESTORE's second parameter, and the RESTORE command restores files only to the directory from which they were originally saved.

Again, if you back up the files in INVENTRY and try to restore them to OVERDUE, like this,

```
A>backup c:\inventry a:{ENTER}
A>restore a: c:\overdue{ENTER}
```

no files will be restored, because none of the files on the backup diskette came from OVERDUE.

You can make RESTORE restore files to a directory and all its sub-directories by running RESTORE with the /S option. Thus, if you ran this RESTORE command on a backup of the whole hard disk,

```
A>restore a: c:\overdue/s{ENTER}
```

it would restore everything in and below OVERDUE in the directory tree: that is, a total of two files and four sub-directories.

To restore all the files on the backup diskette, restore to the root directory with /S:

```
A>restore a: c:\/s{ENTER}
```

When you run RESTORE with /S, it still restores each file to the directory it was backed up from. If the necessary directory does not exist, RESTORE creates it and any other sub-directories on the path to it.

When you run RESTORE without /S, it does not create sub-directories. If you want to restore files to a particular sub-directory, you must first create that sub-directory with MKDIR, if it does not already exist.

Lesson 8-5:
Searching for Command Files With PATH

Sub-directories are helpful for running internal commands like COPY and TYPE, but what if you want to run external commands and application programs? Suppose, for example, you are using a word processing program on text files stored in many different sub-directories. Must you keep a copy of the program in every sub-directory?

One way to avoid that would be to make the directory containing all your programs the current directory and refer to your data files with their path names. This is a nuisance, however, especially if you build a directory structure in which many sub-directories are nested within other sub-directories. And many application programs can't operate on files that aren't in the current directory.

Another way to solve the problem is to keep all of your programs on one disk and all of your data on another. If your PC has two diskette drives, for example, you can keep programs and command files in the root directory on disk A and data files in various directories on disk B. No matter what directory is current on disk B, DOS will fetch programs and command files from disk A.

If you have one hard disk, however, that solution is unsatisfactory. You want to keep both the programs and the data on the hard disk because of its speed and capacity, but you cannot have two different current directories on the same disk at the same time.

The PATH command solves this problem by letting you define a *search path:* that is, a path to a directory that DOS uses to search for programs and command files that it cannot find in the current directory.

For example, suppose your PC has a hard disk as drive C. The drive's root directory contains DOS commands and other programs, including a word processing program called WP. The root directory also contains a sub-directory named CLIENTS, which in turn contains a sub-directory named LETTERS, which contains correspondence with your business's clients.

Using the PATH Command

To make \CLIENTS\LETTERS the current directory and tell DOS to search the root directory for any programs not found in \CLIENTS\LETTERS, you would enter

```
C>chdir \clients\letters{ENTER}
C>path \{ENTER}
```

Now you can enter a command such as:

```
C>wp{ENTER}
```

or

```
C>chkdsk{ENTER}
```

without concern for the fact that the necessary program files are in the root directory rather than the current directory. When DOS fails to find a program in the current directory, it automatically searches the directory defined by PATH.

PATH itself is an internal command, so you need not enter it with a path or keep a copy of it in each of your directories.

To replace the current search path with a new one, simply run PATH again.

To cancel the current search path without defining a new one, run PATH with a null parameter:

```
C>path ,{ENTER}
```

(The solitary comma—as opposed to no comma at all—tells DOS that there is a null parameter.)

To display the current search path, execute PATH with no parameters:

```
C>path{ENTER}
```

Multiple Search Paths

You can define two or more search paths by running PATH with two or more path names separated by semicolons. DOS will search the paths in the order that you entered them.

Some Things That Might Go Wrong: Using Search Paths

DOS displays the message "Bad command or filename". DOS did not find the command filename in the command line in the current directory or in any of the currently defined search paths.

You may have misspelled a path's name when you ran PATH. PATH does not check the validity of a path name, and if a path does not exist when DOS tries to search it, DOS just ignores the missing path and tries the next path in the list, if any exists.

An application program displays an error message like "Overlay files cannot be found". An *overlay* is a part of a program that is kept in a file other than the COM or EXE file and that is loaded into RAM by the program itself when it is needed. Large programs often reduce the amount of RAM they need by loading several overlays into the same part of RAM, one at a time.

The program is telling you that it cannot find an overlay file that it needs. This is probably because the overlay file is in the same sub-directory as the COM or EXE file, and the program, unlike DOS, does not know how to find a file through the search path.

Consult your dealer. He may be able to show you how to make this program find its overlay files through the search path.

If there is no way to make a program use the search path, you must copy the overlay files into the current directory before you can run the program. Batch files offer a useful tool for doing this; they are introduced in Chapter 9. The discussion of sub-directories in Chapter 18, "Operations and Procedures," shows a sub-directory that will automatically copy the overlay files to the current directory, run the program, and delete the overlay files.

For example, suppose you want to keep your word processor program in a separate sub-directory named WP. You might wish to do this in order to separate the files associated with several different application programs. You want to define a search path leading to WP, but you also want to define a search path leading to the root directory so that you can execute DOS commands. To define these two search paths, enter PATH with these two path names:

```
C>path \wp;\{ENTER}
```

Now if DOS fails to find a program in the current directory, it will search WP, and if it fails to find the program in WP, it will search the root directory.

Each time you run PATH, it replaces all the existing search paths with a new set.

CHAPTER 9

Batch Files

A batch file *is a file that contains DOS commands. You can make DOS run the commands in a batch file by entering a single command through the keyboard. Batch files have many uses, some of which are*

- *Entering a sequence of many commands that must be run the same way many times.*
- *Entering one or more commands with long, complex parameters.*
- *Entering a sequence of long-running commands while you attend to other tasks.*
- *"Packaging" a sequence of commands so that an inexperienced person can run them by typing one command line.*

Lesson 9-1:
Creating and Using a Batch File

A batch file must have the filename extension BAT. You run the batch file by entering its filename through the keyboard, just as if it were a command.

A batch file may have any filename that is not the same as the name of a command in the same directory. If a batch file and a command have the same filename, entering the filename makes DOS run the command. You cannot run the batch file until you change its name.

Use EDLIN or a word processor to create a file named EXAMPLE.BAT on your DOS disk. Put the following three lines in it:

```
dir *.com
chkdsk
dir *.bas
```

After you have created this batch file, enter its filename as a command:

A>**example{ENTER}**

DOS displays and runs each command in the batch file, just as if you had entered the commands from the keyboard.

Batch Files on Other Disk Drives or Directories

If a batch file is not on the default disk, you can run it by entering its filename with a drive name:

A>**b:example{ENTER}**

Lesson 9-2:
Using a Dummy Parameter in a Batch File

In the preceding lesson you learned how to create a batch file that runs the same sequence of commands each time it is used. You can also write a batch file that takes parameters and does different things depending on what parameter values it is run with. For example, you can write a batch file, like the preceding lesson's EXAMPLE.BAT, that takes a drive name as a parameter and runs its commands for that drive.

You accomplish this by using *dummy parameters* in the lines in the batch file. Each time you run the batch file, DOS substitutes a parameter value from the command line you entered for each dummy parameter in the file. By entering different parameter values in the command line, you can make DOS behave as though the lines in the batch file itself contained different parameter values.

The following example will help make this concept clear. Edit your batch file so that it looks like this:

```
dir %1*.com
chkdsk %1
dir %1*.bas
```

"%1" is a dummy parameter. Every dummy parameter consists of the percent sign (%) followed by a numeral.

Now put a formatted diskette in drive B and enter

A>**example b:{ENTER}**

As DOS processes the batch file, it substitutes the parameter value "b:" for the dummy parameter "%1" wherever "%1" occurs. The effect is just as if you had entered

```
dir b:*.com
chkdsk b:
dir b:*.bas
```

Now run the batch file with no parameter:

A>**example{ENTER}**

The file produces exactly the same result as before you modified it. Since you entered no parameter in your command, the dummy parameter assumed the null value (a value that is zero characters long). In effect, the dummy parameter disappeared from the file. The result was as if you had entered the commands you put in EXAMPLE.BAT in the preceding lesson.

A Batch File With Multiple Parameters

A batch file may have up to nine dummy parameters, "%1" through "%9". When you run the batch file, DOS replaces each "%1" with the first parameter value, each "%2" with the second parameter value, and so forth.

For example, suppose you create the following batch file under the name COPYDIR.BAT:

```
copy %1 %2
dir %2
```

If you run the batch file like this,

A>**copydir *.com b:{ENTER}**

DOS will process the batch file like this:

```
copy *.com b:
dir b:
```

All the command files will be copied from disk A to disk B, and then DOS will display the directory of disk B.

Parameter substitution simply replaces a symbol with a string of characters; it need not produce a whole parameter or even a valid result. For example, given the preceding definition of EXAMPLE.BAT, this command line

A>**example disk{ENTER}**

would be processed like this:

```
dir disk*.com
chkdsk disk
dir disk*.bas
```

The two DIR commands are meaningful and would produce the expected results, but "disk" is not a valid parameter for CHKDSK, and it would produce an error message.

Since a parameter value is not necessarily a file name, its length is not limited in the way that the length of a file name is. In fact, a parameter value may be any length that allows it to fit on a command line.

Batch File Parameter Rules

Here are DOS's rules for the use of dummy parameters in batch files:

1. There are nine dummy parameters, "%1" through "%9".

2. The nth parameter value in a command that executes a batch file corresponds to the dummy parameter "%n".

3. As DOS executes a batch file, it replaces each dummy parameter with the corresponding parameter value *for this execution only*. The contents of the batch file are not changed.

4. If you want to use % as a character in a command in a batch file, you must type two %'s. This is because a single % in a batch file signals the beginning of a dummy parameter.

5. If there are more dummy parameters in the batch file definition than there are parameters in the command line that executes it, null parameters (zero characters long) are substituted for the excess dummy parameters.

You may use the dummy parameter "%0" in a batch file, too. DOS replaces this dummy parameter with the drive name and filename of the batch file being executed.

Aborting the Execution
Of a Batch File

CTRL BREAK has its normal effect on the execution of a command in a batch file: it either aborts or does not abort the command, depending on whether or not the command has disabled it.

If CTRL BREAK does abort the command, DOS displays the following prompt:

```
Terminate batch job (Y/N)?
```

If you press the Y key, DOS abandons the batch file and gives you its next prompt. If you press the N key, DOS executes the next command in the batch file.

Commands That May Be Used With Batch Files

DOS supports several commands that may only be used in batch files, or that may be entered from the keyboard but are useful mainly in batch files. The next few sections describe these commands.

The PAUSE Command

The PAUSE command halts your PC's operation and displays a message of your choice followed by the prompt "Strike a key when ready". Nothing else happens until you press a typing key. The format of the PAUSE command is

A>**pause <u>message</u>{ENTER}**

You may use PAUSE in a batch file to prompt yourself (or another user) to take some action. For example, you might put the following PAUSE command in a batch file:

`pause Insert the data diskette in drive B;`

When DOS gets to the PAUSE command in the course of executing the batch file, you will see this on your display:

```
A>pause Insert the data diskette in drive B;
Strike a key when ready . . . _
```

After taking the action suggested by the message, you signal DOS to proceed to the next command in the batch file by pressing any typing key.

The REM Command

The REM (remark) command presents a message like PAUSE, but it does not halt the PC. You may use it to present a message that does not require the PC to wait while you take action. For example:

`REM Each program should run for about 12 minutes.`

DOS also interprets a command line beginning with a dot as a comment. Thus,

`.Each program should run for about 12 minutes.`

means the same thing as the preceding REM command.

The ECHO Command (DOS 2.0 Only)

The ECHO command has two functions. First, it can control whether DOS displays the command lines from a batch file as it executes them. Second, it can display a message on the PC's screen.

DOS normally displays each command line in a batch file as it runs the command. If you think the command lines would be distracting or you do not want the user of a batch file to see what is in it, you can make DOS stop displaying command lines by running the following command:

```
A>echo off{ENTER}
```

ECHO OFF also makes DOS stop displaying its command line prompt, "A>". ECHO OFF does not affect information displayed by commands, such as error messages or directory listings; it only stops the listing of the command line prompts and the command lines themselves.

To make DOS start displaying command lines and prompts again, run the following command:

```
A>echo on{ENTER}
```

To display a message, use ECHO followed by the message

```
A>echo Disk directories follow{ENTER}
Disk directories follow
A>_
```

This form of ECHO is useful for displaying a message from a batch file while ECHO OFF is in effect. REM cannot be used for this purpose because REM's message is displayed as a part of the command line itself, and so is not visible with ECHO OFF.

The CLS Command

The CLS (clear screen) command erases the PC's screen and moves the cursor to the upper left corner. You may use it at the beginning of a batch file to erase possibly distracting things that were displayed before the batch file began.

The DATE and TIME Commands

Two additional commands, DATE and TIME, may be entered from the keyboard but are often used in batch files. You can use the DATE command to change the DOS date. Enter the date as a parameter:

```
A>date 3-15-1983{ENTER}
```

Alternatively, you may enter DATE with no parameter to display the current DOS date and then enter a new date if you wish, just as you do when you boot:

```
A>date{ENTER}
Current date is Tue   3-15-1983
Enter new date: _
```

If you want to see the DOS date but not change it, press ENTER and the DOS command line prompt will appear.

You can use the TIME command to change the DOS time. It works the same way as DATE. To simply change the current time, enter the time as a parameter:

```
A>time 9:33{ENTER}
```

You may enter TIME with no parameter to display the current DOS time and then enter a new time if you wish:

```
A>time{ENTER}
Current time is 9:24:17.17
Enter new time: _
```

A Sample Batch File

The following batch file illustrates three of the commands you have just learned: PAUSE, REM, and ECHO. It supposes that disk A contains a program named DSCAN, which subjects diskettes to some unspecified operation called "scanning."

```
rem     Each time "NEXT" is displayed, insert another
rem     diskette and press any typing key.
rem
pause   Insert first diskette to be scanned;
echo off
dscan b:
echo            Next
pause
dscan b:
echo            Next
pause
dscan b:
echo on
rem     End of DSCAN procedure.
```

This batch file would display the following output on the screen (assuming DSCAN did not display anything while running):

```
A>rem     Each time "NEXT" is displayed, insert another
A>rem     diskette and press any typing key.
A>rem
A>pause   Insert first diskette to be scanned;
Strike a key when ready. . .
```

```
A>echo off
            Next
Strike a key when ready. . .

            Next
Strike a key when ready. . .

A>rem    End of DSCAN procedure.
A>
```

The initial REM commands are displayed normally. So is the PAUSE command. Then PAUSE displays the message "Strike a key when ready".

After the user presses a key, DOS runs ECHO, which turns off echoing. Now command line prompts and command lines cease to be displayed. Thus the DSCAN command is invisible, and so is each following ECHO command, although ECHO still displays its message, "Next". PAUSE is invisible, but displays "Strike a key when ready" and waits for the user to press a key.

Notice that a PAUSE command with the message parameter "Next" would not display the message "Next" because echoing is turned off. That is why we need an ECHO command with a message, followed by a PAUSE command with no message.

After a second "DSCAN ... ECHO ... PAUSE" sequence and a third DSCAN command, we turn echoing back on and display a remark that says the procedure is ended.

Lesson 9-3:
Decision Making in Batch Files (DOS 2.0 Only)

DOS has a group of commands with which you can write batch files that automatically make decisions like "Run this command only if that file exists" or "Run this command once for each batch file parameter." These commands enable you to write batch files so powerful that they can take the place of computer programs in many cases.

The FOR Command

The FOR command lets you execute another command once for each of a list of file names. FOR may be used only in batch files; if you try to enter it directly through the keyboard, DOS displays the error message "Syntax error".

Here is an example of FOR:

```
for %%f in (b:.jan b:.feb b:.mar) do dir %%f
```

When this command is run, it makes DOS run the following four commands:

```
A>dir b:.jan{ENTER}
A>dir b:.feb{ENTER}
A>dir b:.mar{ENTER}
```

Here are explanations of the parts of this command:

1. "for" is the command name.
2. "%%f" is a symbol that represents a variable file name, much as a parameter symbol does. It must consist of two percent signs (%%) followed by a letter.
3. "in (...)" defines a *set* of filenames. In this case, the filenames refer to files on drive B with the filename extensions JAN, FEB, and MAR. (Remember the special rule for DIR parameters: that omitting the filename entirely is the same as entering *.)
4. "do dir %%f" causes DOS to run "dir %%f" once for each file name in "in (...)". Each time "dir %%f" is run, one of the file names in the set is substituted for "%%f".

If you use a global filename character in one of the file names in the set, DOS expands the file name into as many file names as it finds on the disk. For example, if you run the following command,

```
for %%f in (b:*.jan . . .) do dir %%f
```

DOS runs DIR once, with a specific file name, for every JAN file on the disk. This makes FOR useful for simulating global filename notation in commands that do not otherwise accept it (such as TYPE). This is also the reason why we used the unusual form "b.jan" in our first example of FOR. If we had used a *, we would have gotten many separate DIR listings, each containing one file.

If you use a global file specification that does not match any file names, DOS "runs" a command line with nothing on it, as though you had pressed ENTER at the keyboard.

You can use FOR's set to enter parameters other than file names if you wish. Note that if your parameter values include the characters * and ?, DOS will interpret them as global file name characters whether you intend the parameters to be file names or not.

The IF Command

The IF command lets you execute another command if a certain condition is true and skip the command if the condition is false. A *condition* is an assertion like "%1 (dummy parameter 1) has the value 'b:index.txt'," or "There exists a file named C:DOG.RCD."

Here is an example of an IF command:

```
if %1 == b:index.txt dir b:index.*
```

In this example, the condition is "dummy parameter 1 is equal to 'b:index.txt'." (The double equal sign (==) represents "is equal to.") The expression, "dir b:index.*" is a *conditional command* which is run if and only if the condition is true.

DOS considers upper- and lowercase characters to be unequal in an IF condition. Thus, an example of a false condition would be "b:index.txt == B:INDEX.TXT".

The EXIST Condition for IF

Another form of condition for the IF command looks like this:

```
if exist b:noorder.dir type b:noorder.dir
```

The condition "exist b:noorder.dir" is true if there exists a file named B:NOORDER.DIR and false if not.

EXIST is useful for doing something to a file that may or may not exist when a batch file is run. By putting a command into an IF command, you can run it if and only if the file it works on is there.

You may use global filename characters in a file specification with EXIST. The EXIST condition is true if and only if there exists at least one file that fits the file specification. For example, the following command runs DIR only if there exists at least one file on disk B with the filename extension DIR:

```
if exist b:*.dir dir b:*.dir
```

The ERRORLEVEL Condition for IF

Another form of condition for the IF command can test the DOS *error level*, a number that a program can set to indicate whether it ran successfully. Here is an example of ERRORLEVEL:

```
if errorlevel 1 dir b:
```

The condition "errorlevel 1" is true if the error level is 1 or more and false if it is less than 1. Thus, this IF command runs DIR if and only if the error level has been set to a value equal to or greater than 1.

You can use this form of IF to make a batch file run other commands if a certain command ran successfully (or did not run successfully). For example, you could use it to display a prominent warning message after running BACKUP if BACKUP failed to run successfully.

It is customary for a program to set the error level to 0 for successful completion and to various positive values for various kinds of errors, with larger values indicating more serious errors.

At present the only DOS commands that set the error level to useful values are BACKUP and RESTORE, which set the values shown in Table 9-1. All other external commands set the error level to 0. Internal commands leave it unchanged.

Application programs also set the error level to meaningful values, and their values may differ from those shown in the table. Consult each program's user's manual to see if that program sets a value that you can usefully test with ERRORLEVEL.

The NOT Condition for IF

NOT is a condition that reverses the effect of any other condition. For example, the condition "errorlevel 1" is true if the error level is equal to or greater than 1 and false if not; the condition "not errorlevel 1" is true if the error level is 0 and false if not.

Here is an example of one use of the NOT condition:

```
if not errorlevel 1 echo Backup successful.
```

Using Command Labels With the GOTO Command

A *label* is a line that gives a name to a certain point in a batch file. You may use the GOTO command in a batch file to make DOS "go to" a label and begin reading command lines at the first line after the label.

A label always begins with a colon. It may be any length, but only the first eight characters after the colon are meaningful. For example, you could define a label named ":DOCUMENTS" and go to it with "GOTO DOCUMENTATION", since the first eight characters of DOCUMENTS and DOCUMENTATION are the same. This is more likely to be a source of confusion than a useful technique, so you will be wise to avoid using labels that are more than eight characters long.

Error level	Meaning
0	Successful completion
1	No files found to back up or restore
3	Run terminated by user entering CTRL BREAK
4	Run terminated due to I/O error or hardware error

Table 9-1.
Meaning of Error Level Values for BACKUP and RESTORE

The following batch file illustrates the use of both a label and the GOTO command:

```
echo off
backup b:/m
if not errorlevel 1 goto ok
echo *****************************
echo *Error in backup of disk b!!!!*
echo *****************************
goto end
:ok
echo Backup complete.
:end
echo on
```

After setting ECHO OFF and running BACKUP, this batch file tests the error level. If the error level is 0, DOS goes to the label OK, echoes "Backup complete." and sets ECHO ON. If the error level is greater than 0, DOS does not go to the label OK; rather it displays a prominent warning message, goes to the label END, and sets ECHO ON.

DOS considers uppercase and lowercase characters to be the same in labels. For example ":loop", ":LOOP", and ":Loop" are all the same label. You could go to any version of this label with "goto loop", "goto LOOP", or "goto Loop:".

The SHIFT Command

The SHIFT command shifts each parameter symbol in a batch file one parameter to the right. That is, the first time SHIFT is executed in a batch file, it makes "%1" refer to the second parameter, "%2" refer to the third, and so forth. The second time it is executed it makes "%1" refer to the third parameter, "%2" refer to the fourth, and so on.

The SHIFT command has no parameters:

```
shift
```

Here is a very simple example of a batch file that uses SHIFT:

```
type %1
shift
type %1
shift
type %1
```

Suppose this batch file were run by the following command line:

A>**type3 x.txt y.txt z.txt{ENTER}**

The first TYPE command would type file X.TXT. The first SHIFT command would make "%1" refer to the second parameter. Thus the second TYPE command would type file Y.TXT. The second SHIFT command would have the same effect again; thus the third TYPE command would type file Z.TXT.

Here is a more realistic example of a batch file using SHIFT. This batch file can erase any number of files with a single command:

```
:loop
  if %1. == . goto end
  erase %1
  shift
  goto loop
:end
```

If this batch file were named ERASES.BAT, you might run it as follows to erase three files named A.TXT, B.TXT, and C.TXT:

A>**erases a.txt b.txt c.txt{ENTER}**

The IF tests the value of the first parameter. If the parameter is not null, ERASE is run on it. Then SHIFT makes "%1" refer to the second parameter, and GOTO LOOP makes the process repeat. After the last parameter has been processed, SHIFT makes "%1" refer to a parameter that does not exist. The next time through the loop, IF goes to END.

Notice the trick that this IF uses to express the idea "If %1 is absent, go to END." It compares "%1" with a dot added to the end to a dot alone. If the value of "%1" were "A.TXT", for example, IF would compare "A.TXT." to ".". If the two were equal, "%1" would have to be empty (that is, absent). Note that there is nothing magical about the dot; any other ordinary character would work as well.

Lesson 9-4:
The AUTOEXEC File

Many users have a series of commands that they run each time they boot. If you have a serial interface printer, for example, you must run two MODE commands each time you boot before you can print anything, as we saw in Chapter 7. If you have a battery-powered clock card in your PC, you may run a program provided with the card that sets the DOS date and time from the card.

If you use such a series of commands, you have probably realized that you can run them more conveniently by putting them in a batch file. In fact, you can do even better: you can make DOS run the batch file automatically whenever you boot.

All you need to do to accomplish this is to store the batch file in the root directory of your DOS disk and name it AUTOEXEC.BAT. When DOS is booted, it checks the root directory of the DOS disk for an AUTOEXEC.BAT file. If it finds such a file, it runs it.

When DOS finds an AUTOEXEC.BAT file, it does not prompt you for the date and time as it otherwise would. This is so that you will not be bothered by DOS's date and time prompts if one of the commands in AUTOEXEC.BAT sets the date and time from a clock card. If you want to get the usual date and time prompts with an AUTOEXEC.BAT file, you must include the DATE and TIME commands in the file.

CHAPTER 10

Some Useful Techniques

This chapter discusses a number of valuable techniques that have not yet been presented. You will learn more about the numeric keypad and the function of the NUM LOCK key as well as about three commands: SYS, BREAK, and SET. You will also learn about the CONFIG.SYS file.

Lesson 10-1:
The Numeric Keypad and the NUM LOCK Key

In an earlier chapter you learned to use both CTRL and NUM LOCK to halt a running program temporarily. NUM LOCK has another function when used by itself: it changes the function of your keyboard's numeric keypad.

When you first boot DOS, the keys on the numeric keypad perform control functions that vary from program to program. In EDLIN and DOS, for example, you can use the CURSOR LEFT and CURSOR RIGHT keys to duplicate the functions of the BACKSPACE and F1 keys, respectively. Pressing NUM LOCK makes the numeric keypad enter numerals instead. Pressing it again makes the keypad perform control functions again.

Boot DOS, if necessary, and run a command such as DIR. Try pressing the CURSOR RIGHT key on the numeric keypad. Observe how it moves the cursor to the right and copies characters from the preceding command line, just as F1 would. CURSOR LEFT backspaces the cursor, just as BACKSPACE would.

Press NUM LOCK once. Now if you try pressing the number keys, they will enter numbers, just like the top row of typing keys on the main part of the keyboard. Press NUM LOCK again to return the numeric keypad to its control-function mode. Use the CURSOR LEFT and CURSOR RIGHT keys to erase the numbers you entered, and complete the command.

The SYS Command

When you purchase a new application program, you may have to use the SYS command to transfer a copy of DOS to the *distribution diskette* that the program comes on. The instructions accompanying the new program should tell you whether to do this or not.

To use SYS, you must have a bootable diskette in drive A. Put the distribution diskette in drive B, and run SYS like this:

```
A>sys b:{ENTER}
```

SYS requires a bootable disk in the default drive so that SYS has a source from which to copy DOS. If the disk in the default drive is not bootable, SYS prompts you to change it.

Why Is SYS Necessary?

The safest way to deal with a distribution diskette is to copy its files to another diskette (which is bootable if you have formatted it with the /S option) and put the original away in a safe place. If you use a distribution diskette this way, you have no need for SYS.

However, this is not always possible. Most software vendors license their products for use on a single PC, and many of them *copy-protect* the distribution diskette to prevent purchasers from giving away or selling unauthorized copies. If a diskette is copy-protected, you can run a program from it, but you cannot copy it to another disk. Thus the only way you can run the program from a bootable disk is to make the distribution disk bootable by using SYS to put a copy of DOS on it.

You cannot use SYS to make one of your own nonbootable diskettes bootable. The copy of DOS on a bootable diskette must go at the very beginning of the diskette's file space, and on a nonbootable diskette other files already occupy that space. On a software distribution diskette, the necessary space is reserved for SYS to use.

Note that after you run SYS, you may need to copy the file COMMAND.COM from the boot disk as well.

The BREAK Command

In an earlier lesson you learned that CTRL BREAK generally interrupts a running program and returns control to DOS.

There are two reasons why CTRL BREAK might not have this effect. First, certain programs change the function of CTRL BREAK because they use it for another purpose, or because they must not allow themselves to be interrupted at certain times. EDLIN is one such program. As Chapter 6 shows, it uses CTRL BREAK to halt one of its commands. To return to DOS, you must enter either the E (end) or Q (quit) command.

The other reason why CTRL BREAK might not have its usual effect is that DOS detects and acts on a pending CTRL BREAK only when the program that is running tries to do an I/O operation on the screen, keyboard, printer, or serial interface. If a program malfunctions, it might never try to do such an I/O operation, preventing you from ever interrupting the program. What is more, some programs frequently run a long time without trying to do such operations.

With the BREAK command, you can make DOS check for CTRL BREAK whenever a program asks DOS for *any* service, such as a disk I/O operation or the time of day. You enter the command like this:

```
A>break on{ENTER}
```

When BREAK ON is in effect, no correctly functioning program is likely to run very long after you enter CTRL BREAK, and the chances that CTRL BREAK will be unable to interrupt a malfunctioning program are significantly decreased. The cost of setting BREAK ON is that it will make DOS and all your application programs run a little slower.

You can reverse the effect of BREAK ON by entering

```
A>break off{ENTER}
```

You can check the current status of BREAK by entering the BREAK command with no parameter:

```
A>break{ENTER}
```

The VERIFY Command

The VERIFY command makes DOS verify all data it writes to disk by reading back the results of each write operation. This is a way of ensuring that critical data is written correctly. However, VERIFY slows down all programs that do substantial amounts of disk writing.

To set verification on, enter the following command:

`A>verify on{ENTER}`

To set verification off again, enter the following command:

`A>verify off{ENTER}`

To display the current verification setting, enter VERIFY with no parameters:

`A>verify{ENTER}`

The /V Option for COPY

You can use write verification for a single file copying operation by running COPY with the /V (verify) option. For example, to copy a file named CRITICAL.DAT from disk A to disk B with write verification, you would enter

`A>copy critical.dat b:/v{ENTER}`

The /V option provides a way of write-verifying critical data without going to the trouble of turning verification on and off with separate commands.

Lesson 10-2:
Program Parameters
And the SET Command (DOS 2.0 Only)

DOS reserves an area in RAM for lines of data that may be used by either DOS or application programs. Among programs that use this data, most use it to decide how they should function: that is, to decide what path to use for a group of application files;

whether the user wants long, informative messages or brief, terse ones; and so on. This area in RAM is called the *environment*, and lines of data in the environment are called *environment strings*.

The environment typically looks something like this:

```
PATH=
COMSPEC=A:\COMMAND.COM
PROMPT=$N$G
CACPATH=C:\CAC\DB
TEXDRIVERS=C:\TEX\DRX
```

Each environment string consists of a word, an equal sign (=), and some additional text. The word before the = identifies the purpose of the environment string; the text after the = is the environment string's value.

You can use the SET command to display DOS's environment. Enter SET now to display the environment:

A>set{ENTER}

Your environment will not look exactly like the one shown here. You will understand the meaning of each string in the environment after you have read the next section.

How Environment Strings Are Set

You can set or change the value of any environment string by entering the SET command with a parameter. For example, to set the environment string TEXDRIVERS to the value "c:\tex\drx", you would enter this command:

A>set texdrivers=c:\tex\drx{ENTER}

Enter this command now. Then run SET with no parameters to display the environment. Notice that TEXDRIVERS is now in it.

SET forces the name of the string (TEXDRIVERS in this case) to uppercase, but leaves the value (c:\tex\drx) in lowercase if you enter it that way.

You can remove an environment string from the environment by "setting" it to a null value:

A>set texdrivers={ENTER}

Enter this command and then display the environment. The string TEXDRIVERS should be gone.

If you want to set the value of an environment string whenever you boot, you can do it by including an appropriate SET command in your AUTOEXEC.BAT file.

Some environment strings can be set in other ways: by entering a special command or by putting the appropriate data in the

CONFIG.SYS file. Special commands for setting environment strings are discussed in the next section. CONFIG.SYS is described in a later section.

You can increase the size of the environment by adding strings or lengthening the values of strings until you run a command that loads a new part of DOS into RAM, such as PRINT, GRAPHICS, or certain forms of MODE. When you run such a program, it puts the new part of DOS immediately after the environment. After this, you may increase the size of the environment only within the following limitations:

- DOS sets aside 127 bytes for the environment when you boot, so you can always expand the environment to that size.
- You can add or lengthen a string after deleting or shortening a string, so long as the total size of the environment does not increase beyond what it was when you first ran PRINT, GRAPHICS, and so on.
- Rebooting wipes the slate clean. You can expand the environment freely until you enter PRINT, GRAPHICS, and so on again.

What Environment Strings Do

Many environment strings have meanings to particular application programs. Since DOS does not know what strings your application programs recognize, it cannot tell whether a given string is "valid" or "invalid." It just recognizes certain strings as its own and ignores the others.

In the preceding sample environment listings, CACPATH and TEXDRIVERS represent environment strings for hypothetical applications. Their meanings would depend entirely on how they were interpreted by the applications that recognized them. The environment strings PATH, COMSPEC, and PROMPT are used by DOS. We will look at each of these environment strings in turn.

PATH describes the current search path. Its default value is null, indicating a search path that includes only the root directory on the default drive. The PATH string is changed when you enter the PATH command. PATH, not SET, is customarily used to change the value of this string.

COMSPEC gives the drive, sub-directory, and file name of the *command processor*, the program that prompts you for DOS commands and interprets the command lines you enter. Its default value is x:\COMMAND.COM (where x is the name of the default disk when you boot), unless some other value is set by the file named CONFIG.SYS, as we will see later.

You can change the appearance of DOS by changing the value of COMSPEC to refer to a different command processor. Writing a command processor is a job for an experienced programmer, however.

PROMPT describes DOS's command line prompt. By changing the value of this string you can change DOS's command line prompt. For example, you can make the prompt contain the current time of day followed by a colon.

The PROMPT string's default value is null (that is, it is absent from the environment), indicating that DOS uses a command line prompt like "A>"—the kind you have seen all along. You can change the PROMPT string with the PROMPT command as well as with SET.

Since changing the command line prompt is an unusual operation, this book does not discuss how to set the value of the PROMPT string to get a particular prompt. If you are interested in doing this, see the discussion of the PROMPT command in Chapter 10 of IBM's *Disk Operating System* manual, "Advanced DOS Commands."

The CONFIG.SYS File

You can set certain characteristics of DOS each time you boot by storing *configuration commands* in a file named CONFIG.SYS. You must store CONFIG.SYS in the root directory of your boot disk.

When you boot, DOS looks for CONFIG.SYS in the root directory of the boot disk. If DOS finds the file there, DOS sets its characteristics from the information in the file. If DOS finds no file, it sets all of DOS's characteristics to their default values.

If you define CONFIG.SYS, you must make it a text file with one configuration command per line. The configuration commands that you can use without a detailed technical understanding of DOS will be discussed in a moment.

CAUTION

Do not confuse configuration commands with DOS commands. Configuration commands go in CONFIG.SYS. DOS commands go in batch files or are entered through the keyboard. The two cannot be interchanged.

The configuration command BREAK determines whether DOS's initial state will be "break on" or "break off." "Break on" and "break off" were explained earlier in the section on the DOS command BREAK.

The configuration command BREAK looks like this:

`BREAK=ON`

or

`BREAK=OFF`

The configuration command SHELL sets the initial value of the environment string COMSPEC, which names the DOS command interpreter. SHELL is so named because in UNIX, the operating system that originated the idea of a replaceable command interpreter, the command interpreter is called "the shell."

The configuration command SHELL looks like this:

`SHELL=A:\COMMAND.COM`

For "A:\COMMAND.COM", substitute the drive, path, and file name of the command interpreter you want to use.

It is better to set COMSPEC with the configuration command SHELL than with the DOS command SET. If you use SET, you must keep COMMAND.COM on a DOS disk to interpret the SET command. If you use SHELL, this is unnecessary; you need only keep the command processor that COMSPEC is to refer to.

CHAPTER 11

Caring
For Your PC

The PC is a very reliable computer. Like any other device, how-ever, it does sometimes malfunction. This chapter shows you how to take the best possible care of your PC, and it also prepares you to deal with a breakdown if and when this occurs.

Routine Care

Your PC needs very little routine maintenance. Most of your care will be a matter of common sense: protecting it from physical abuse, coffee spills, and so forth.

You may clean your PC with a cloth moistened with water or a mild household cleaner. Do not wet the cloth so much that liquid may drip into the PC's parts. Do not use abrasive cleaners, strong chemicals, or alcohol, which may damage your PC's plastic surfaces.

If you want to protect your PC and peripherals from dust, you can buy specially fitted dust covers from many computer stores and computer supply firms.

Cleaning the Diskette Drives

The read/write heads of diskette drives tend to get dirty with use, and this can cause errors in reading from and writing to diskettes. You can avoid such problems by cleaning the heads on a regular basis.

You can clean the diskette drives with a kit that contains a diskette made of special cleaning material. Such kits are made by several manufacturers. See Chapter 17, "Guide to Supplies," for names.

Carefully follow the instructions of the disk cleaning kit's manufacturer when you use the kit. The instructions will involve inserting the cleaning diskette in the diskette drive and operating the drive. You can operate the drive by attempting to execute DIR enough times to give the read/write head on each drive the recommended amount of cleaning.

Do not feel obligated to clean your drives as often as the cleaning kit recommends, since that recommendation was written by people who would like to sell more cleaning kits. Unless your PC resides in a dirty environment, three or four cleanings a year will be quite sufficient.

Cleaning a hard disk's mechanism is both impossible and unnecessary, since the disk is permanently sealed in a dust-proof plastic case.

Cleaning Your Printer

The interior of a printer tends to accumulate bits of paper fiber, which wear out the moving parts of the printer and shorten its life. You can minimize this problem by periodically cleaning the inside of your printer with a vacuum cleaner and nozzle attachment. Be careful not to damage the printer's moving parts or knock them out of alignment. You may want to use a miniature vacuum cleaner, which has a smaller nozzle than a full-size one. These are available at many computer supply firms and department stores.

If you use a letter-quality printer, you can preserve the quality of your printed output by cleaning the printing element periodically. This is more important with fabric ribbons than with multistrike (film) ribbons, since fabric ribbons tend to deposit sludge in the hollow parts of letters like *a* and *e*. Typewriter cleaning kits are appropriate for this task.

About Electrical Power

Avoid turning your PC on and off frequently. Its circuits suffer more stress from being turned on and off than from being left on for long periods. Many computer users prefer to turn their systems on and off no more than once a day.

Any computer contains delicate circuits that are easily damaged. Your PC is designed to protect itself from most problems caused by changes in line voltage, but you should still use common sense in operating it. Try not to use your PC during electrical storms or at times when power failures are likely.

If the commercial power in your area is "dirty" (that is, subject to peaks and dips that last a fraction of a second), you may want more protection than is built into your PC and the other parts of your system. Power regulators and power supplies can help you deal with dirty power. They are discussed in Chapter 16, "Guide to Accessories." Consult your computer dealer or service person if you are not sure whether or not you should get such a device.

About Static Electricity

Some of the components in your computer are quite sensitive to static electricity. A static spark can disrupt the operation of your computer, destroy data, and sometimes damage the electronics.

Several types of floor coverings and sprays are available to help control static electricity. These are described in Chapter 16.

You can help protect your PC against damage from static electricity, with or without the aid of antistatic products, by observing these rules:

- Connect your PC and all other computer devices to a properly grounded source of power. This is the single most important thing you can do to protect your computer equipment.
- If your floor surface tends to produce static electricity when you walk on it, you should touch a grounded object like a water pipe before touching the PC. If no grounded object is available, press your hand against a wall.
- In cold weather, do not let the air become too dry. Moist air reduces buildups of static electricity.
- Do not use an ion generator in your computer room. The ions may make you feel good, but they tend to affect computers the same way that static electricity does.

Dealing With Disk I/O Errors

If you use diskettes, sooner or later you are going to have difficulty reading from or writing to one. Although hard disks tend to be much more reliable than diskettes, they are not entirely immune to problems either.

When you get I/O errors on a disk, you must respond by doing three things:

1. You must respond to the immediate symptom of the error. This usually means halting the program that is running.
2. You must identify and correct the probable cause of the error. This usually means replacing a faulty diskette. More rarely, it means having your PC repaired.
3. You must recover any lost data. The simplest and most reliable way to recover lost data is to restore it from a recent backup. There are several ways to recover data from the

problem disk itself, although they require more work and are not always successful.

The most frequent symptom of a disk problem is one of the following messages:

```
Disk error reading drive x
Abort, Retry, Ignore? _

Disk error writing drive x
Abort, Retry, Ignore? _

File allocation table bad, drive x
Abort, Retry, Ignore? _
```

The meaning of the first two messages is self-evident. The last one means that something has happened to the part of the disk that is used to keep track of the location of each file on the disk.

When you get one of these messages, *do not remove the disk from the drive where the error occurred* until you have responded to the prompt that accompanies the message. You can respond in any of these ways:

- Press R to retry the read or write operation that produced the error.
- If the error is a read error, press I to ignore it. The system will simply try to read the next part of the file.
- Press A to halt (abort) the program that is running. DOS returns you to the command line prompt; you may then remove the disk that caused the error.

I/O errors may also be revealed by data that is *corrupted* for no apparent reason. You may find "garbage" (unexplainable characters) in a text file, or you may find that one copy of a program ceases to work.

Chapter 18, "Operations and Procedures," discusses the causes of disk I/O errors and what you can do about them. When you have problems, you should consult it for more detailed information.

When Something Goes Wrong

When you have a problem with your PC, it is important to be able to make an informed judgment about what kind of thing is wrong. That judgment will govern how you correct the problem:

call a repair person, report an error in software, or fix things yourself.

You can divide apparent computer problems into three classes:

1. *Operational problems.* In these cases, you are doing something wrong. When you find your error and correct it, the problem goes away.
2. *Software problems.* Here the computer program is not doing what it should.
3. *Hardware problems.* Some part of your computer system is not doing what it should.

Classifying the Problem

Unless you are absolutely certain that you are using your PC correctly, *check the instructions* before you assume something is broken. If you call a repair person to correct an operational problem it will cause an unnecessary delay in your work, and it may cost you money. Ask a more experienced user for assistance if you think you may have an operational problem but you cannot identify it.

If you are dealing with an operational problem on your own, it is important to *look up error messages or other symptoms* in order to get as much information as possible about the problem you are having. Do not assume that a message means what it says and no more. When you look an error message up, you may find useful information about the message's implications.

Chapter 19, "Problem Determination," discusses the causes of many puzzling problem symptoms on the PC. Chapter 20, "Error Messages," lists all the error messages that you can get from DOS and the DOS commands described in this book. IBM's *Disk Operating System* manual also lists DOS error messages. Although it is slightly less thorough than this book, the *Disk Operating System* manual does list messages for a few DOS commands that this book does not discuss.

If you have a hardware or software problem, record as much information about the problem as you can. Write down every error message so that you can describe it in a useful way. Note whether the problem is a hard failure (that is, something does not work at all) or a malfunction (something does not work the way it should). If you have this sort of information, a repair person may be able to resolve the problem by phone, or at least know what spare parts your system will need.

It is also useful to determine whether the problem is consistent or intermittent. If it seems intermittent, consider whether you are doing something differently that makes the problem occur some times but not others. You may discover an operational problem this way. If you have a real hardware or software problem, being able to demonstrate it consistently will make the problem easier for a qualified person to diagnose and fix.

Useful Techniques for Identifying Problems

Substitution often helps identify problems. For example, if you have two parallel-interface printers and one does not work, try substituting the second printer for the first. If it works, you can be pretty sure the problem is in the first printer. If *neither* printer works, it is more likely that something is wrong with your PC.

Substitution is equally useful for distinguishing among hardware, software, and operational problems. For example, if your printer does not work with a particular program but works when you use it the same way with other programs, you have an operational problem or a software problem. If your printer does not work with any program, software is a less likely cause, and you should suspect an operational problem or a hardware problem.

If you have a System Expansion Unit and suspect a hardware problem in the System Unit, try running the PC with the System Expansion Unit and System Unit disconnected. (*Turn everything off* before disconnecting them.) If the error goes away, the System Expansion Unit or one of the adapter cards in it is probably at fault.

If you are not sure where a problem originates, ask yourself what has changed lately. Any change in your computer system or your use of the system is a possible trouble spot. You may be making an error in an unfamiliar procedure, or you may have found a malfunction in a new or previously unused piece of software or hardware. New and recently repaired pieces of hardware are more likely to break than those that have been running without trouble for a long time.

The cause of a computer problem is always logical, but this is often clear only *after* the problem has been located. Locating a problem can be very tricky, so you should test every assumption you make. For example, if you have two parallel-interface printers and neither one works, does that mean the problem has *got* to be in the PC? No! If you used the same data cable with both printers, the problem might be in the cable. You can test this by substituting a different cable. If both printers then work, you have identified not only an incorrect assumption about the problem but also the problem itself.

Techniques for Solving Hardware Problems

Look at the obvious things first. Are your system's components cabled together correctly? Are all the plugs fully connected? (*Turn everything off* before checking or tightening cables.) Is everything plugged into a source of power, and is the power on?

IBM provides a number of diagnostic procedures that can help you isolate problems in a particular component of your PC. If you think you have a hardware problem in your System Unit or in some other component of your PC that is made by IBM, these diagnostics can help you identify the problem.

IBM's diagnostics are of two types: power-on diagnostics and diagnostic programs. *Power-on diagnostics* are tests that the PC runs automatically when you turn it on. It runs these diagnostics during the delay that occurs after you turn the PC on and before the PC boots the operating system. *Diagnostic programs* are on a special diskette that comes with the PC. You run them by booting from the diagnostic diskette and making choices from the menus that the programs on the diskette present to you.

Detailed instructions for using both types of diagnostics are given in the "Problem Determination Procedures" section of the IBM PC *Guide to Operations*. Consult that manual if you want to use the diagnostics.

Planning Ahead

The best rule for dealing with hardware failure is to be prepared. When you need to make arrangements for service, you should know where to call, who to ask for, and what to say.

Be sure to find out how long it will take to get your PC repaired. If the repair time estimate seems like more time than you can afford, you may want to get a different kind of service, arrange to rent or borrow a PC if yours breaks, or even buy a second PC for backup.

Moving the PC

If you must move your PC, consult the instructions for disassembling and packing it that are provided in Chapter 18, "Operations and Procedures."

Before you begin to take apart your PC, you should also review Chapter 18's instructions for *reassembling* it. If your PC has any unusual adapter cards or peripherals not covered by the instructions, note how they are connected so that you can reconnect them properly.

PART II

Guide to Resources

In the short time that the IBM PC has existed, a significant industry has grown up around it. Hundreds of companies offer add-on hardware, software, or services especially for the PC. Others have products and services that are useful with the PC although not specifically intended for it. The competing claims of all these vendors could well bewilder a new PC user. This "Guide to Resources" will help you make sense of it all.

The "Guide to Resources" could not possibly mention every kind of product available for the PC. Instead, the Guide discusses only products that are likely to interest people who use the PC primarily in their work and that can be readily used by people who do not have a lot of technical knowledge.

Each section mentions some specific products that, in the author's opinion, are widely accepted or have unusual and useful features. The author and publisher do not endorse these products, nor do they mean to imply that products not mentioned are inferior to those that are.

For names and addresses of the manufacturers and suppliers mentioned here, see the "Index of Manufacturers" in Appendix B. For a more complete and up-to-the-minute list of PC-compatible products, see the product directories discussed in the "Publications" section of Chapter 15, "Guide to Services."

CHAPTER 12

Guide to Dealers

Most products and services sold for the IBM PC are not available directly from the manufacturer, but rather must be purchased through a dealer. This is a generally advantageous situation for you as a computer user since it means that many of your computer needs can be met by a single source.

The selection of a dealer you can work with and who will work with you is a vitally important task. It is your responsibility to check out dealers to make sure that they are willing and able to provide you with the services you require. A little bit of homework done before you buy can save you a great deal of grief if things later go wrong.

Types of Computer Equipment Dealers

There are several common types of dealers, whose differences consist mainly in the level of *customer support* they provide. Customer support includes all the services that you get before and after your purchase: advice on what to buy, expert help in installing a product and adapting it to your needs, training, and repair.

Some kinds of dealers charge a premium for their products and in return provide a high level of customer support. Others emphasize low prices and do not have the kind of professional staff needed to give support. No matter who you buy from, you will have to pay for the support you get, whether you do so directly or by paying top dollar for the products you buy. The more support you want, the more you should expect to pay.

An *independent sales organization* (ISO) generally offers you the most support at the highest price. An ISO operates out of an office rather than a store. It expects you to purchase a complete computer system. It may do computer programming or other customizing work to deliver a system exactly fitted to your needs. After the sale, it supports you by selling accessories and supplies, providing repair service, and helping to adapt your PC to your changing requirements.

A *full-service computer store* charges list prices and provides the same kind of support as an ISO. The full-service store carries a broader range of products than most ISOs do but may not be equipped to do as much customizing work on a system as an ISO would.

A *discount computer store* offers lower prices but less support than other computer stores. It caters mainly to technically oriented computer users who know exactly what they want and how to use it.

A *mail-order firm* tends to offer the lowest prices and the least support. Ethical mail-order firms ship orders promptly and honor manufacturers' warranties, but few provide any other services.

Evaluating Dealers

Before choosing a dealer, decide what type of dealer you want. Decide if you are likely to need support for the product you are buying. Be conservative: paying for support you do not need is not nearly so bad as needing support you did not pay for and so cannot get.

If you do not know exactly what you want, go to a computer store or an ISO. They have sales people who are competent at giving advice and willing to take the time to do so.

If you purchased your PC from an ISO, you probably should make all your purchases there. The ISO should ensure that any product you buy will work with the ones you already have. The ISO will also continue to think of you as a client and will be more inclined to help you if you have a problem. In addition, if you value having an individual relationship with a sales person, you will find it easier to maintain one at an ISO than in a store. A sales person in a store must talk to anyone who walks in the door and so is less likely to remember or care who bought a PC from him a year ago.

When you evaluate a particular dealer, check out the following points:

- Is this organization an authorized IBM PC dealer? If it is, you know that it meets fairly rigorous business and technical qualifications. For example, an authorized dealer will have an in-house service staff and at least one person on that staff who has been trained in PC repair by IBM. If the organization is not an authorized PC dealer, it may be equally qualified, but you should check its credentials further.

- How long has this organization been in business? Does it seem stable? Can you be sure it will continue to provide support?
- If you are buying hardware, can this organization fix the hardware if it breaks, or will they have to ship it back to the manufacturer? Will they loan you a working replacement while your equipment is being fixed?
- Do the sales people seem technically informed enough to know what products are suitable for you? Can they demonstrate the products and explain them clearly? Be wary of sales people who use a lot of technical jargon. They may be hiding the fact that they do not know much, or they may be computer whizzes who cannot communicate effectively with laypeople. In either case, they are not for you.
- If the organization sells mainly to business people, what types of businesses does it specialize in? If you have unique needs (for example, law office automation or construction job cost estimating), can the personnel provide a reasonable level of support for your application?
- Do the sales people you are dealing with seem to want to sell you the best solution to your problem, or are they pushing the product that will make them the biggest profit? If they are pushing a product, do not try to resist such unprofessional behavior — just avoid it.
- Consider the dealer's clientele. Some stores cater to hobbyists and may not offer you the kind of support that you need for business applications. The store's decor and product displays are a good indicator. If video games are the predominant products, you are probably in the wrong place.
- If you are considering a software purchase, find out whether the software producer provides any direct support. Some software houses provide telephone support that may be better than the typical full-service dealer can provide. Software with this type of support might be a good candidate for purchase from a discount or mail-order dealer.

Remember this maxim: You get *no more than* you pay for. Do not expect more support than you are willing to pay for or than the dealer is prepared to give. If you buy at a discount, the dealer's profit is low and you can expect only limited support.

In general, you should use a commonsense approach to purchasing computer products. A dealer's reputation is one of the best indicators of whether or not you will be served well. Get in touch with other computer users and ask if they have had any experience with the dealer you are considering. Do they know dealers they would recommend?

A local computer user's group is an excellent forum for exchanging gripes and recommendations on dealers. If you have good or bad experiences with a particular dealer, spread the word.

Additional Considerations for Mail-Order Firms

Most mail-order firms do business honestly, but you may have problems getting satisfaction from those who do not. Therefore, you should check out a mail-order firm carefully before you send in your money.

Some important questions to ask are: Does the firm have the items you want in stock? How quickly can it ship after receiving an order? What is the firm's policy on returned merchandise, defective or otherwise?

Most mail-order firms will answer these questions truthfully if they are asked directly. However, your best assurance is the recommendation of other customers. In addition, you might locate some old computer magazines and look for ads. If a mail-order firm has been in business for a year or more, you can be fairly confident that it meets at least minimal standards of legality and fair dealing.

Other Distribution Channels

Computer equipment is now sold in many other places like camera stores and stereo stores. Be wary of buying from these businesses; they are often unable to provide support.

A relatively new phenomenon is the *software store*, which sells only computer programs. Since software stores concentrate on software, they are potentially able to provide more informed advice and better support than many full-service computer stores.

If you deal with a computer consultant, the consultant may purchase hardware and software for you. If the consultant is competent and has good contacts, you will be assured of getting appropriate, reliable products without having to spend your own time studying the market. The consultant may be able to get a better deal than you could, being more technically informed and representing a larger source of business. If the dealer used by the consultant is willing to support you directly, you will have two sources of support to fall back on: the dealer and the consultant.

Many types of computer supplies and accessories can be purchased most readily from *computer supply companies*. Some firms of this type are local; others are national and do most of their business by mail-order catalog.

Some common types of computer supplies, such as paper and diskettes, are conveniently available in many local *office supply stores*. In addition, many computer clubs arrange group purchases of computer supplies and equipment for their members. By buying in large quantities, they can bargain for better prices than an individual could get.

If you are making a large purchase yourself, you can use your own bargaining power to get a better price, better support, or both. You may even be able to buy directly from a distributor or manufacturer if you do not need the support an ISO would normally provide.

Finally, special computer shows around the country attract local dealers who may offer their products at a "show discount." This can give you the chance to meet some of the dealers in your area and compare prices and support. Sometimes the manufacturers of the products attend these shows, and they may sponsor seminars on the use of their products. Manufacturers usually will have someone present who is competent to answer almost any question you might have concerning their products.

CHAPTER 13

Guide to Hardware

This chapter discusses a host of hardware product categories for the IBM PC. We will begin by taking a look at two basic categories of hardware products and some of the special compatibility problems between these products and the PC.

Types of Hardware Products

PC hardware products may be divided into two types: those that go inside the PC's System Unit and those that go outside it.

Most hardware products that go inside the PC are *adapter cards*. These are printed circuit cards that plug into sockets on the System Unit's main circuit board. They give the PC additional features, such as more memory or the ability to control additional devices.

The PC I and PC II System Units have five sockets for adapter cards. These sockets are called *system expansion slots*. Some of the slots are already occupied by adapter cards. At a minimum, there is one card that controls your PC's display and one card that controls the diskette drives. That leaves at most three free slots for new adapter cards.

The PC XT has eight expansion slots for adapter cards. Six of these slots can hold full-length adapter cards; two are located behind the diskette drive and so can hold only half-length cards. The PC XT must be minimally equipped with three full-length cards that control the display screen, the diskette drive, and the Fixed Disk drive. A half-length serial interface adapter card comes with the PC XT as standard equipment. Thus the PC XT leaves as many as four slots available.

Most of the hardware products that go outside the PC are *peripherals*. A peripheral is a device that conveys data from the PC to the outside world, or from the outside world to the PC. The display and printer are two peripherals that you have already encountered. Most peripheral devices require an internal adapter card to interface with the PC.

Hardware Compatibility Considerations

Before purchasing a piece of hardware for your PC, you should make sure that it is *compatible*—that is, that the hardware will work correctly with your PC. For a peripheral device, this is merely a question of what sort of interface the device requires, and whether you have (or can get) an appropriate adapter card. For an adapter card, there are two issues. First, is the card physically compatible with your PC? Second, can your operating system or application programs use the card?

Physical Compatibility

All adapter cards made by IBM will run on all versions of the PC, but not all adapter cards made by other manufacturers will do so. For example, a card that works in the PC XT may not work in the PC I, or vice versa.

Some cards consist of two printed circuit boards sandwiched together. Such a card can hold twice as many integrated circuit chips as a card with one board, and so can provide more features. When such a card is used in the PC XT, however, it may block the slot next to the one it is mounted in, because the PC XT's slots are spaced more closely than the slots on the PC I and PC II.

Software Support

Before buying a non-IBM card, make sure that DOS can operate it. Most manufacturers try to make their adapter cards compatible with IBM's cards, so that DOS can use them.

If a card has features not found on IBM cards, DOS may not be able to support those features even though it supports the IBM-compatible features of the card. Some manufacturers offer programs that add full support for their cards to DOS.

If DOS does not support an adapter card or a feature, a particular application program still may do so. That may or may not be adequate, depending on how you want to use the card. For example, if a card is designed to control a scientific instrument and is used only with programs that operate the instrument, it is sufficient that those application programs support the card. On the other hand, a video display card must have DOS support, or you will not be able to use it to boot the PC.

Even if you know that a certain card works with DOS, you must be sure that it works with *your version*. Different versions of

DOS can cause problems in two ways. First, an early version of DOS may not support more recently developed cards. Second, a *later* version of DOS may not work with an *early* model of a non-IBM adapter card because the card's designers made assumptions about DOS that later ceased to be true.

Careful designers avoid making version-dependent cards by working within IBM's design guidelines, or at least they make their cards easy to update when DOS changes. To be sure a card will work for you, have it demonstrated with the version of DOS that you use on your own PC.

Serial and Parallel Interface Cards

An *interface* is a set of rules for transferring data over a data cable: what voltages are used, what the signals on each wire stand for, and so forth. There are two types of interfaces commonly used on the PC: a *parallel interface* and a *serial interface*.

A *parallel interface*, sometimes called a *Centronics interface*, is usually used to connect the PC to a printer or plotter. Most parallel interface adapters for the PC can only output data.

A *serial interface*, also referred to as an *RS-232C interface*, can both input and output data. It is used to connect the PC to many kinds of peripherals, such as printers, plotters, and modems. The PC XT comes with a serial interface adapter card as standard equipment.

IBM makes adapter cards for both serial and parallel interfaces. Most other manufacturers of serial and parallel interfaces design them to behave exactly like IBM's so that DOS can use them. This leaves little room for choice (or error) in selecting a serial or parallel interface card.

Since a PC has so few free system expansion slots, many companies offer *multifunction cards*, which combine a serial or parallel interface with one or more other features. Common features on multifunction cards are a serial interface, a parallel interface, additional RAM, and a battery-powered clock that can be used to set the system date and time automatically when the PC is booted.

Who Makes Them

The IBM Monochrome Display and Parallel Printer Adapter card contains a parallel interface as well as a controller for the IBM Monochrome Display.

IBM also makes a separate Parallel Printer Adapter card. You can use this card to control a parallel interface printer if you have a Color/Graphics Monitor Adapter instead of an IBM Monochrome Display Adapter card. If you have an IBM Monochrome Display card, you can use the separate Parallel Printer Adapter card to control a second printer.

IBM's Asynchronous Communications Adapter card contains a serial interface.

Other manufacturers of serial, parallel, and multifunction cards include AST, Davong, Quadram, Seattle Computer, and Tecmar.

Control Systems makes adapter cards that contain as many as eight serial interfaces. These are useful for special applications where several users with computer terminals must work with the same PC at the same time. These cards require a special operating system or software support, since DOS cannot support more than two serial interfaces.

Apparat, Inc. makes a card called a Print Spooler that performs a function similar to the PRINT command of DOS 2.0, which is described in Chapter 7. The card contains a parallel port and a 64K RAM buffer. Your PC can write up to 64K characters to the parallel port as fast as it can generate them. The card stores this data in the RAM buffer and then prints it at the printer's normal speed. While the contents of the buffer are being printed, you can use your PC for other tasks.

About Data Cables

A problem that commonly plagues computer users when they purchase new peripheral devices is getting cables that connect the new peripherals properly to their interface cards. This can be a devilish problem for either parallel or serial interfaces.

A parallel interface card for the PC has a 25-pin female socket for data; most parallel interface printers have data sockets with 34 pins or more. Thus you need a special *parallel printer cable* to connect the adapter card to the printer. Such cables are sold by IBM and by many makers of parallel interface cards and parallel interface printers.

A serial interface card has a 25-pin male socket. Most serial devices also use a 25-pin socket, but this fact conceals some complexity in the wiring of the cable. You cannot necessarily use a cable that connects each pin in one plug to the same pin in the other. Worse yet, you cannot even count on using the same cable to attach different devices to the same serial port.

For example, a modem usually works when each pin on the

serial interface card is connected by cable to the same pin on the device. A printer, on the other hand, generally requires that certain pairs of wires on the cable be transposed. Thus you could not use the same cable for your printer and your modem.

Some devices do not even supply all of the signals that the serial interface card expects to receive. To use such a device, you need a cable that connects certain pins on the adapter card's socket in such a way that it tricks the card into thinking that all of the necessary signals are present.

The safest and easiest way to get a data cable that will work with a particular device is to buy a cable designed specifically for that device. Make sure that you get a cable for use with the IBM PC, since this cable might be different from those used with other computers.

If you cannot find a cable designed for a particular device, a technician can wire a cable for you by referring to the IBM PC *Technical Reference* manual and the user's manual for the device.

Monitors

The PC's most important output device is a video display called a *monitor*. A monitor is similar to a television set but is designed for displaying computer data. A monitor adapter card is required to attach a monitor to the PC. Monitor adapter cards are discussed in the next section.

Two kinds of monitors may be used with the PC: IBM's Monochrome Display and a standard computer monitor.

IBM's Monochrome Display must be used with the IBM Monochrome Display Adapter or an equivalent card. It presents a green-on-black image that is unusually sharp.

Standard computer monitors are available from many manufacturers, including IBM. Such monitors must be used with IBM's Color/Graphics Monitor Adapter or an equivalent card. Monitors are available with white, amber, or green monochrome displays, and with color displays.

A standard computer monitor may use either of two types of interfaces to the display card. The *composite video interface* encodes video information in a signal carried by one pair of wires, much as a television transmitter encodes video information in one radio signal. The *RGB* (red-green-blue) *interface* uses three wires to carry video information for the three primary colors that make up a color image. IBM's Color/Graphics card can operate either kind of monitor.

The composite video interface is used by most black-and-white monitors and the lower priced color monitors. More sophisticated color monitors use the RGB interface, which gives more accurate color and better separation between adjacent areas of different colors.

You can use a standard television set as a monitor by connecting the Color/Graphics card to the TV's antenna input through a conversion device called an *RF modulator*. The image quality is poor, however, and in character mode you cannot display 80 characters per line.

What To Look For

If you will do a lot of work with character data, get an IBM Monochrome Display. Its characters are sharper and easier to read than any standard computer monitor.

If you buy a standard monochrome monitor, consider the screen color. Most users are comfortable with a green image like that of IBM's Monochrome Display, but some experts believe an amber image causes less eye strain. The white image has its advocates too.

When buying a monitor, consider the image quality. Is it sharp enough for comfortable viewing over long periods? Are the edges of the image cut off or distorted? Does the surface of the screen produce distracting reflections?

In a color monitor, consider the quality of the color. Do the primary colors converge properly, or are they out of alignment, producing color fringes?

If you want to display color graphics with good resolution, get an RGB monitor. A composite video monitor cannot match the clear, crisp output of an RGB monitor. The lines drawn on a composite monitor may be either smeared together or displayed in incorrect colors. This is a limitation of the composite video interface, and not a reflection on the quality of any particular monitor.

Before you buy a composite video monitor, compare it side by side with an RGB monitor. Perhaps the difference in image quality will change your mind.

A standard monitor can resolve 500 to 700 *pixels* ("picture elements"—the individual points of light that combine to form an image on the screen) in each dimension. The IBM Color/Graphics card displays a 200×640 pixel image in high-resolution mode, so a standard monitor is quite capable of resolving all the detail that that card can display. If you want more resolution, you must get a higher-resolution monitor as well as a graphics card that can display more pixels. Monitors are available with resolutions of 1000 pixels and more, but they cost several times as much as standard ones. The makers of high-resolution display cards can advise you on the features of various monitors and the monitors' compatibility with their products.

What To Look Out For

Some RGB monitors can display colors in only one intensity. That effectively reduces the number of colors that the IBM Color/ Graphics card can display from 16 to 8. For example, such monitors display dark grey as if it were black, and yellow as if it were brown. If you are buying an RGB monitor, be sure to get one with the ability to display all 16 colors if this is important to you.

Do not try to use a television set with an RF modulator as a computer display. The image quality offered by this combination is not good enough for serious use.

Who Makes Them

IBM's Monochrome Display is the only device compatible with the IBM Monochrome Display card and similar cards. Manufacturers of standard monochrome monitors for use with the Color/ Graphics card include Amdek, NEC, Sanyo, and USI.

Micro Display Systems' Genius and Quadram's Quadscreen are display/adapter card sets that can display a full page of single-spaced text (55 lines or more) at a time. The Quadram screen can also display graphics.

Manufacturers of composite color monitors include Amdek, IBM, NEC, Sanyo, and USI. Manufacturers of RGB color monitors include Control Systems, IBM, Princeton Graphic Systems, Quadram, and Sanyo. Manufacturers of very high-resolution color monitors include Control Systems.

Display Cards

To display data, your PC needs an adapter card to control its monitor. This adapter card converts digital signals, which a computer uses to represent data, into signals that will form an image when fed into the cathode ray tube (CRT) of the display.

IBM's Monochrome Display and Parallel Printer Adapter provides a character display 25 lines high and 80 characters wide. It uses a nonstandard video interface that gives an unusually clear display with well-formed characters. Because of this nonstandard interface, this adapter can be used only with the IBM Monochrome Display.

The Monochrome Display Adapter can also display *semigraphics*, which are special character symbols such as boxes, triangles, and lines that can be assembled to form a picture.

IBM's Color/Graphics Monitor Adapter provides a character display of 25 lines by 80 or 40 characters on a standard computer monitor. It has the same character set and semigraphics as the Monochrome Display Adapter, but it can also present *graphics;* that is, it can draw pictures on the display. Text and graphics may be displayed in monochrome or color.

The Color/Graphics card uses *raster graphics*. It forms an image as a television set would; that is, by scanning along a series of raster lines and switching an electron beam on and off to form bright and dark spots on each line. Each pixel may be turned on or off independently.

The Color/Graphics card has two major graphics modes. In *high-resolution mode*, this card displays a one-color image that is 200 lines high and 640 pixels wide. In *medium-resolution mode*, it can display up to four colors simultaneously but uses pixels that are twice as wide, so that the image is 200 lines high and 320 pixels wide.

Display Cards and Software

Most non-IBM display cards are compatible with one or both of those made by IBM. DOS can operate such a card without trouble. If the card has additional features, however, you may need special software to use them.

It is possible to install both a Monochrome Display Adapter and a Color/Graphics Adapter in your PC at the same time. DOS will use the Monochrome Display Adapter to display all system output when you boot. In DOS 2.0, the MODE command can switch the PC's output from one display to the other. In DOS 1.1, a special program can be written to perform this function. Certain application programs can use both displays at once.

With appropriate software, the Color/Graphics Adapter can support a *light pen*, an input device described later in this chapter.

What To Look For

If you expect to do a lot of work that involves character displays, such as word processing or spreadsheet analysis, look seriously at the monochrome display card. Most users find that the graphics card's 80-column display is not sharp enough for long periods of use. If you expect to use character displays a lot but also want graphics, consider getting both cards.

Some non-IBM monochrome display cards can display more data lines and characters than IBM's can. These cards can enhance the usefulness of many programs, particularly word processors and spreadsheets.

Many non-IBM graphics cards offer higher resolution (more pixels) than IBM's Color/Graphics card. Many offer a greater selection of colors. If these extended features of a card are important to you, however, find out how readily you can use them with the software you have.

Graphics cards may have a variety of other features, including *zooming* (that is, expanding part of the display to fill the whole screen), *scrolling* (that is, looking at different parts of a display that is too big to fit on the screen, as though the screen were a movable window), and *paging* (that is, storing the contents of several displays in memory and switching instantaneously from one to another). These features also may need special software support to be useful.

Who Makes Them

Manufacturers of color/graphics cards include Control Systems, IBM, Plantronics, Quadram, Scion, Tecmar, and Universal Research. Many of these products, including those of Tecmar and Scion, offer more resolution than IBM's Color/Graphics card, or more colors, or both.

Control Systems' product has the unusually high resolution of 1024 × 1024 pixels.

Tecmar and Universal Research make adapter cards that can emulate either IBM's Monochrome Display Adapter or Color/Graphics Monitor Adapter. The Tecmar card can also operate in modes that give more resolution than IBM's card, or a greater choice of display colors, or both. If you want both a monochrome display and color graphics but do not need them simultaneously, one of these cards can save you the expense of buying two display cards.

Hercules Computer Technology and Orchid Technology make adapter cards that display both characters and graphics on IBM's Monochrome Display. If you want graphics but do not need color, one of these cards can save you the expense of buying two display units.

Quadram makes a monochrome card and matching monitor

with the unusually large display size of 64 lines by 160 characters. It can also display monochrome graphics, the resolution being 528 lines by 960 pixels.

Light Pens

A *light pen* is a pen-shaped device for use with a monitor. The PC can sense when the pen touches the monitor screen through a switch in the tip of the pen. If the monitor is displaying anything at the point of contact, the PC can sense the pen's approximate position.

You can use a light pen to input data without using the PC's keyboard. For example, you can use it to select an item from a menu of choices displayed on the screen. Some graphics programs allow you to use a light pen to "draw" directly on the screen.

Light pens do not work with the IBM Monochrome Monitor. The Color/Graphics Adapter provides the necessary hardware to support a light pen interface. Any application using a light pen, however, must provide the software to support it.

Manufacturers of light pens include FTG Data Systems and Symtec.

Keyboards

Many PC users are bothered by the differences between the PC's keyboard and standard typewriter keyboards. Some of the PC keyboard's problems are the placement of the left-hand SHIFT key, one key farther left than usual; the ENTER key, which is too small and too far right; and the shapes of the SHIFT, CTRL, ENTER, TAB, and BACKSPACE keys, which have central raised areas higher than the rest of the key surfaces. Users of spreadsheet programs and financial software are bothered by the PC's numeric keypad, which has a nonstandard layout, and by the fact that the numeric keypad cannot be used for numeric entry and cursor control at the same time.

Several manufacturers make keyboards that are electronically compatible with IBM's PC keyboard but offer more conventional layouts. Manufacturers of alternative keyboards include Colby and Key Tronic. The Key Tronic keyboard is available through Qubie' Distributing.

Vertex Systems offers an economical means of improving the IBM keyboard called the Keyfixer, which is a set of collars that can be mounted on several commonly used keys to raise the entire keycap surface to the same height. Keyswapper, a companion piece of software, can change the functions of various keys by modifying DOS. Keyswapper can exchange the functions of the left-hand SHIFT key and the backslash (\) key, putting the PC's left-hand SHIFT key approximately in its normal position. Keyswapper can also make single keystrokes enter strings of two or more characters.

RAM Chips

Your PC has room for a certain amount of RAM on its System Board, although not all of this RAM may be present. Table 13-1 shows the RAM capacity of each type of PC. If your PC's System Board has less than the maximum amount of RAM, you can expand its RAM by plugging chips into empty sockets on the System Board.

IBM sells RAM chips for the PC, but you can buy RAM chip kits for the PC much more cheaply through other sources, such as mail-order houses or computer club group purchases. Just be sure you get the type of chips listed for your PC in Table 13-1.

If you install the RAM chips yourself, carefully follow the instructions that come with them. You will find an *IC insertion tool* for 16-pin integrated circuits (ICs) a valuable aid for inserting the chips without damaging their connecting pins. This tool is available at many electronics supply stores.

Note that you must change the settings of certain switches on the PC's System Board to make the PC aware of the additional RAM. The RAM chip kit should contain specific instructions.

Sellers of RAM chips for the PC include Apparat and Quadram. System 300 sells a kit that may be used to expand a PC I to 256K. The kit contains a circuit board that plugs into the chip sockets on the System Board and holds higher capacity chips like the ones used in the PC II and PC XT.

Type of PC	Minimum RAM on System Board	May be expanded to	Use RAM chip type[1]	Number of chips needed
Old PC I	16K	32K, 48K, or 64K	4116, max. cycle time 200 ns.	9 per 16K to be added
Current PC I	64K	64K	—	—
PC II	64K	128K, 192K, or 256K	4164, max. cycle time 200 ns.	9 per 64K to be added
PC XT	128K	192K or 256K	4164, max. cycle time 200 ns.	9 per 64K to be added

[1] *Cycle time* is a measure of the chip's maximum operating speed. *ns.* stands for "nanosecond," 1/1000 of a microsecond.

Table 13-1.
Expanding RAM on the System Board

RAM Cards

A RAM card gives your PC additional RAM once the System Board is full. By adding one or more RAM cards, you can expand your PC's RAM capacity to 512K bytes or more. This increases the execution speed and capacity of many programs such as word processors and spreadsheets.

IBM makes a RAM card called the 64/256KB Memory Expansion Option. It can add 64K, 128K, 192K, or 256K of RAM to your PC. Some vendors make RAM cards with larger capacities. The most common sizes are 64K, 128K, 192K, 256K, and 512K.

Many vendors make *multifunction cards* that combine RAM with other features. These cards let you use the PC's limited number of system expansion slots more efficiently. Multifunction cards were described earlier in this chapter in the section called "Serial and Parallel Interface Cards."

What To Look For

If your RAM needs may grow in the future, select a card that is expandable. If you buy an expandable 64K RAM card, for example, you can turn it into a 128K, 192K, or 256K card by installing more RAM chips. IBM's Memory Expansion Option is expandable.

Many RAM cards come with a *RAM disk* program that makes DOS treat part or all of the extra RAM as though it were a disk. A program that does a lot of file operations can run many times faster with a RAM disk than with a real disk. But if the PC's operation is interrupted by a power failure or software error before the files in the RAM disk are saved on a real disk, the files will be lost.

Many RAM cards come with *print spooling* software with which DOS can use part or all of the extra RAM to buffer data that is being printed. DOS 2.0's PRINT command performs the same function, but it prints data from files rather than from RAM.

What To Look Out For

If you put more than 320K of RAM in your PC (for example, a RAM card with more than 256K plus the 64K of RAM on the System Board), DOS 1.1's DISKCOPY command will not work. RAM that is used as a RAM disk does not create this problem.

Many hard disk drives are incompatible with the RAM disk programs supplied with RAM cards. Many such drives come with their own RAM disk support, however.

Who Makes Them

Vendors of RAM cards and multifunction cards include AST Research, Computer Technology Innovations, Davong Systems, IBM, Microsoft, Quadram, and Tecmar.

Semidisk Systems offers a RAM card intended primarily for use as a RAM disk, with the unusually large capacity of 1024K.

Note that not all multifunction cards include extra RAM. For example, Tecmar makes cards with various combinations of battery-powered clock, serial ports, and parallel ports, but no RAM.

Printers

There are two major types of printers that can be used with the PC: dot-matrix printers and letter-quality printers. You have already encountered the dot-matrix printer—IBM's Graphic Matrix Printer is an example of it.

Dot-matrix printers offer moderate to high printing speeds, typically 80 to 250 characters per second. The slower printers tend to be small, light, and inexpensive. Modern dot-matrix printers produce output that is easy to read but that is obviously "computer generated" (see Figure 13-1).

A variation on the dot-matrix printer is the *correspondence-quality printer*, which prints more slowly and makes a finer pattern of dots. Correspondence-quality output is comparable to the output of a typewriter with a fabric ribbon, as Figure 13-1 shows.

Many correspondence-quality printers allow you to choose correspondence-quality output at moderate speed or dot-matrix quality output at high speed.

A *letter-quality printer* works much like a typewriter. It strikes the paper with a printing element that carries a set of fully formed characters.

Letter-quality printers run at low to moderate speeds, typically 12 to 50 characters per second. They tend to be larger and more expensive than matrix printers, but they produce very high-quality output, at least as good as an expensive typewriter.

Letter-quality printers use interchangeable type elements, which are available in a variety of styles and character sets. See Chapter 17, "Guide to Supplies," for details.

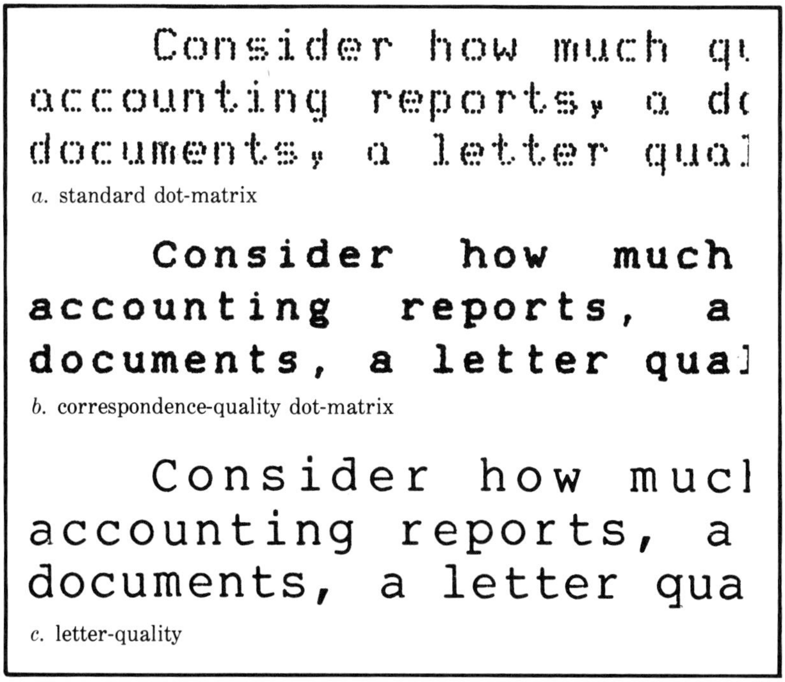

a. standard dot-matrix

b. correspondence-quality dot-matrix

c. letter-quality

Figure 13-1.
Comparison of printer quality

Features of Printers

Some printers, like the IBM Graphic Matrix Printer, have tractor mechanisms and accept only continuous forms. Others have rubber platens like a typewriter and accept only cut sheets. More flexible models have both mechanisms and take both kinds of paper. The tractor may be built in or it may be a snap-on accessory.

Some printers accept wider paper than others. One common width is 9 1/2 inches (8 1/2 inches plus 1/2 inch on either side for edge perforations); that is the greatest width the IBM Graphic Matrix Printer accepts. This width accommodates 80 standard-sized characters per line.

Another common width is 15 inches. Paper 15 inches wide can accommodate lines that are 132 standard-sized characters long, or over 200 characters long if the characters are compressed.

Sophisticated printers can do *bidirectional printing;* that is, they can print alternate lines from left to right and right to left. This reduces the time the print head spends moving without printing, and so increases the printer's effective speed.

Some printers have their own keyboards that can be used for input to the computer. You may find such a printer useful for a special application, but you will need special software to make use of the keyboard.

A very handy feature of some printers (optionally available on many printers) is a *buffer* that holds characters waiting to be printed. A typical printer buffer will hold about 2000 characters, although some hold more than 65,000 characters.

Additional Features of Dot-Matrix Printers

Many dot-matrix printers can print variations on the standard character set: italic and bold characters, extra wide and compressed characters, superscripts and subscripts, and so on. A letter-quality printer, with its fixed characters, can duplicate these features only by swapping the printing elements (see Chapter 17 for more about this).

Some dot-matrix printers can also print graphics. Each pin in the print head is separately controllable, so that each dot position on a line may be printed or not. With special software, such printers can print useful diagrams, graphs, and pictures.

The IBM Graphic Matrix Printer can print graphics. An earlier model, called the IBM Matrix Printer, can print graphics if equipped with an accessory called the Graftrax option.

Additional Features of Letter-Quality Printers

The more sophisticated letter-quality printers can move their print heads in fractions of a character. They can produce *micro-spaced* output in which the right margin is made even by inserting equal amounts of space between all the words on a line. Micro-spaced output resembles typesetting in appearance. Such printers can also raise and lower the carriage by fractions of a line to simulate superscript and subscript characters.

Some letter-quality printers accept *proportional-spaced* print wheels, on which some letters (like *m*) are wider than others (like *i*). This produces an effect even closer to typesetting.

What To Look For

Your applications for a printer determine what features you will need. Consider, first of all, how much quality your output must have. For accounting reports, a dot-matrix printer is fine. For legal documents, a letter-quality printer is indispensable.

Also consider how much speed you need. For example, if you will print a lot of long reports, you will need a faster printer. If you will be printing sales receipts and must produce each one in a few seconds, you may need a fast printer even though it will be idle most of the time. On the other hand, if you print long reports occasionally and you do not care if they tie up the printer for a long time, a slower printer may be satisfactory.

What To Look Out For

Unless your computer use is very specialized, get a printer that can handle both continuous forms and cut sheets. Whichever type of paper you use, you will occasionally want the other.

Do not pay extra for special features like italic printing unless you can anticipate using them. In addition, you should note that all special features like italic printing, microspacing, and proportional spacing require special software support. Before you buy a printer, check whether the word processing program or other software you intend to use can support these features.

Avoid unreliable printers. A printer's moving parts take more punishment than those of most other computer devices, and so printers are more prone to break down. If you feel you cannot judge a particular brand of printer by its reputation or its dealer's reputation, ask people who have owned one for a while.

Be sure the printer's electrical interface is compatible with your PC. If the printer has a parallel interface, you must connect it to the IBM Monochrome Display Adapter, the Parallel Interface

Adapter, or an equivalent card. If the printer has a serial interface, you must connect it to the IBM Asynchronous Communications Adapter or an equivalent card. The two types of interfaces work equally well, but the serial interface requires you to enter two MODE commands each time you boot, as explained in Chapter 7, "Using a Printer." See the section on "Serial and Parallel Interface Cards" in this chapter for more information on printer interfaces.

If you want to use a printer with a keyboard, you must get a serial interface printer and a serial interface adapter. IBM's Parallel Printer Adapter cannot read input. Some other manufacturers' parallel interface adapters may support input, but you will need special software to use them that way, since DOS does not support input through a parallel interface.

Who Makes Them

Manufacturers of dot-matrix and correspondence-quality printers include Anadex, Centronics, Epson, IBM, and Okidata.

Manufacturers and distributors of letter-quality printers include Centronics, Diablo, Leading Edge Products, NEC, Olivetti, and Qume.

Manufacturers of economical letter-quality printers (priced under $1000, with low speed and few special features) include Dynax, C. Itoh, and SCM.

Centronics, Integral Data Systems, and Okidata make correspondence-quality printers that use a special multicolor ribbon and can print color graphics when used with appropriate software.

Graphics Printing Devices

Graphics printing devices fall into three major categories: dot-matrix printers, plotters, and graphics cameras.

Many dot-matrix printers can print dot by dot, as well as character by character. Such printers can readily be used to print graphics output. They produce low to moderate quality output (as illustrated in Figure 13-2), with moderate speed, at low cost.

A dot-matrix printer lends itself naturally to printing a graphics image displayed on a monitor, since the printer's matrix of dots corresponds to the screen's matrix of pixels. In DOS 2.0, the GRAPHICS command enables the IBM Graphic Matrix Printer to do this. Similar programs are available that give other dot-matrix printers the same capability.

A *plotter* produces an image by moving a pen over a sheet of paper. It is connected to the PC through a serial or parallel interface. Plotters generally produce higher quality output than dot-matrix printers, but they cost more and work more slowly.

A plotter moves its pen in increments of a fixed size in one of a fixed set of directions. It renders a diagonal line or a curve as a series of small line segments, as shown in Figure 13-2. The quality of the line depends on the size of the increments of movement. Some plotters use increments too small to be visible to the unaided eye. Most plotters use increments small enough to make lines and curves seem smooth unless they are examined closely.

A *graphics camera* records images on photographic film. It contains a display tube and a camera, and it interfaces to the PC as a monitor would. It uses a special high-resolution tube with a flat

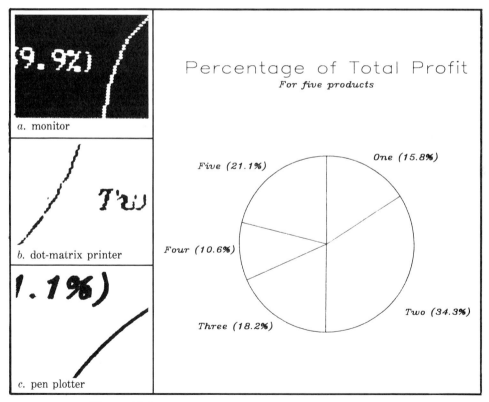

a. monitor

b. dot-matrix printer

c. pen plotter

Figure 13-2.
Comparison of graphics device output: typical business output from a pen plotter

surface to produce a higher quality result than you could get by photographing the screen of an ordinary monitor.

A graphics camera can produce high-quality output when driven by a high-resolution graphics card. Typically, a graphics camera works very fast and is expensive.

What To Look For

The quality of a graphics device's output is controlled primarily by the device's *resolution:* that is, the separation between the closest image points that the device can represent as separate points in its output. For example, a dot-matrix printer that prints 72 dots per linear inch has a resolution of 1/72 inch.

If you wish to use a dot-matrix printer for graphics output, be aware that the printer may not have the same resolution horizontally and vertically. For example, it may print 72 dots per horizontal inch and 60 dots per vertical inch. Your graphics software must be able to adjust to this ratio, or your output will be distorted: a square will print as a rectangle, and a circle will print as an ellipse.

If you print images directly from a graphics display, one printed dot per pixel, your printer should have about the same proportion of horizontal to vertical resolution as your display does. The IBM Color/Graphics Monitor Adapter displays 320 pixels horizontally and 200 pixels vertically. On the IBM Color Monitor, this image is shown in a rectangle whose proportions are about ten inches by seven inches; thus its ratio of horizontal to vertical resolution is about 1.12:1.

For a plotter, resolution is expressed by the size of the *plotting increment,* which is the smallest distance that the plotter can move the pen. Image quality is also affected by whether the plotter can move the pen diagonally. Diagonal pen movements produce a smoother result than alternating horizontal and vertical movements.

Before buying a plotter, consider the maximum size of paper that the plotter can handle. Also consider whether the plotter lets you choose among several types of pens, such as ball-point pens and fiber-tip pens. Such choices give you greater flexibility in the appearance of the plotter's output. Plotters that accept india-ink pens can draw on overhead projector foils.

Some plotters can hold several pens and switch from one to another under program control. This allows you to plot multicolor images.

What To Look Out For

Always confirm that the graphics hardware you buy is compatible with your graphics software. A program may be able to operate one type of device but not another. More subtly, a program may operate a certain device and yet be unable to use a particular feature that you want. The best way to avoid this sort of surprise is to try out the software and hardware together before you buy.

If you try to represent details whose dimensions are about the same as the resolution of the output device, those details will often appear distorted. For example, a diagonal line may appear smooth, jagged, or broken, depending on how it happens to slope. To avoid this sort of distortion, get a device whose resolution is at least three or four times finer than the finest details you want to represent accurately.

If you buy a graphics camera, remember that the camera's resolution can be no better than the graphics card you use to generate the image. If you use IBM's Color/Graphics Monitor Adapter, you will get resolution of 200 × 320 pixels in medium-resolution mode. If the camera is capable of greater resolution, you must buy a high-resolution graphics card to take full advantage of what the camera can do.

Who Makes Them

Anadex and Integral Data Systems make dot-matrix printers that can print colored images with a special multicolor ribbon.

Manufacturers of plotters include Amdek, Enter Computer, Hewlett Packard, Houston Instrument, and Strobe.

Lang Systems and Computer-Mate offer economical color graphics cameras suitable for use with the PC.

Hard Disk Drives

A *hard disk drive* holds much more data than a diskette drive, and can read and write more quickly. It typically stores between 5M and 30M per drive (1M = 1024K), and it runs 5 to 20 times faster than a diskette drive. Hard disk systems cost more than diskette drives (typically $1000 to $4000) but cost less per byte of storage.

The terms *hard disk* and *Winchester disk* are often used interchangeably. "Winchester" actually refers to the particular type of hard disk that is most commonly used on small computers like the PC. A Winchester disk is usually *fixed*—that is, built into the disk drive.

Some hard disk systems can be installed in the PC's System

Unit in place of a diskette drive. Others are separate components that sit under or beside the System Unit.

What To Look For

You will need a disk controller adapter card and software support with any hard disk. Make sure that these are included in the package that you purchase. Furthermore, make sure that it will all work with the version of DOS that you are using.

If your data capacity needs may grow, find out how many drives you can attach to the controller card in the hard disk system you buy. Some controllers can support several drives. In general, only one hard disk controller can be installed in a PC.

Hard disks can be backed up on diskettes, but you may need dozens of diskettes to hold all the data on one hard disk. If your files are large or change often, you will want a backup medium with more speed and capacity. Some hard disk systems have digital tape drives that use special tape cartridges and back up 10M or so in a few minutes. Others have two disk drives, at least one of which uses removable disks.

What To Look Out For

A hard disk drive is inherently more delicate than a diskette drive, and so is more prone to breakdowns if treated roughly. Some brands are less reliable than others. Before you buy, check out the reputation of your dealer, or the brand he or she sells, or both.

Even reliable hard disk drives tend to be easily damaged if not handled with care. If you move your PC around a lot, select a hard disk drive that you can easily disconnect and leave behind.

If you have a PC I or PC II, avoid hard disk drives that mount within the PC. They tend to overheat, since the PC's case and fan are not designed to dissipate the amount of heat these drives generate. This is not a problem with the PC XT, which is designed to hold an internal hard disk and has a more powerful fan.

Who Makes Them

IBM's Fixed Disk is a 10M hard disk and comes as an integral part of the PC XT. You can attach a second Fixed Disk to the PC XT by moving the first Fixed Disk to an IBM System Expansion Unit and installing the second Fixed Disk in the System Expansion Unit's other compartment. You can also install one or two Fixed Disks in a System Expansion Unit connected to a PC I or PC II.

Other manufacturers of hard disk systems include Corona

Data Systems, Corvus Systems, Davong Systems, Genie, Tallgrass Technologies, and Tecmar.

Manufacturers of hard disk systems with removable disks include Genie, Santa Clara Systems, Tecmar, and XCOMP.

Davong, Genie, and Tallgrass Technologies make hard disk systems with a digital tape cartridge drive for backup.

Diskette Drives

IBM's diskette drive is the most common type of flexible disk drive used on the PC. Several other types are available.

Drives compatible with IBM's diskette drives are available from many sources. They are usually less expensive than IBM's drives, and some have additional features. Some of these drives are sold "bare" for installation within the PC's System Unit. Others are sold as a subsystem with their own enclosure and power supply, so that you can use more than two diskette drives on your PC. IBM's Disk Controller Adapter card can support as many as four diskette drives.

Single- and double-sided drives are completely interchangeable. If you have a PC with single-sided drives, you can give it double-sided capability just by replacing the drives.

You can buy drives and controller cards for eight-inch flexible disks. These drives have two advantages over the PC's standard 5 1/4-inch drives. First, they can store more data—as much as 1.6M per disk. Second, they use a generally accepted data recording standard, so eight-inch disks can be exchanged among many different types of computers. No such standard exists for 5 1/4-inch diskettes, so your PC can only exchange 5 1/4-inch diskettes with other PCs and a few other kinds of computers.

You can buy drives that use one of several smaller diameter diskettes. Although not yet common, these smaller diskettes promise to replace 5 1/4-inch diskettes in many compact computers. The envelopes for the sub-5 1/4-inch diskettes are designed to give better protection against scratches and dust than those of 5 1/4-inch diskettes and eight-inch disks.

Several companies make diskette drive adapters. These are largely compatible with IBM's adapter card. Some have additional features, such as serial or parallel interfaces or the ability to control eight-inch drives as well as 5 1/4-inch drives.

What To Look Out For

If you are buying non-IBM 5 1/4-inch drives for economy, be sure the drives you buy are electronically compatible with IBM's drives. Also be sure you know where to get your system repaired with the non-IBM drives in place. IBM and some other repair services will not repair non-IBM components in your PC, and may make you remove them before accepting the PC for any kind of repair.

If you buy eight-inch drives for compatibility with other computers, check what the drives' controller and software can do. You may be able to use the eight-inch drives just as if they were 5 1/4-inch drives, or you may have to use 5 1/4-inch drives for all your work and run a special program to copy files to and from the eight-inch drives.

Different operating systems use different directory and file formats even when they record data the same way. PCDOS is essentially the same operating system that is sold for other computers under the name MSDOS, so eight-inch PCDOS disks should be compatible with most eight-inch MSDOS systems. If you are exchanging disks with a computer that runs a different operating system, you will need a special conversion program to read and write files in the format that the other system expects. Make sure an appropriate program is available.

Who Makes Them

Firms that make diskette drives equivalent to IBM's drives include Tandon and Control Data Corporation (CDC). These firms sell primarily to computer equipment manufacturers and are not equipped to answer inquiries about products or repair from individual users. Expect help only from your dealer if you have problems.

Several firms buy drives from manufacturers and resell them to dealers. Some offer subsystems consisting of a cabinet with one or two drives and a power supply. Resellers of 5 1/4-inch drives and makers of subsystems include Computer Technology Innovations, Datamac, Maynard Electronics, and Percom.

Makers of diskette drive adapters include Maynard Electronics, Computer Technology Innovations, IBM, and Tecmar.

Apparat and Maynard Electronics sell half-height drives that let you mount two disk drives in each of the spaces that IBM intended for one drive. These drives are available in a standard 40-track-per-disk version and an 80-track-per-disk version that stores 800K of data on each disk. The 80-track disks cannot be read or written by standard (40-track) drives, but the 80-track drives can read and write 40-track disks.

Manufacturers of eight-inch drives and adapters include Flagstaff Engineering, Maynard Electronics, and Tecmar. Instor makes an eight-inch disk drive system that connects to the PC—or any other computer—through a serial interface.

Manufacturers of sub-5 1/4-inch drive subsystems include Amdek.

Tape Drives

A *tape drive* stores information on magnetic tape, much like an audio tape recorder. Although audio recorders can be used to record computer data, serious applications demand digital tape drives and tape formulated for digital recording.

Computer tape drives operate at speeds comparable to diskette drives, but digital tapes have much more capacity and cost less than diskettes. Thus tape drives are an important medium for backing up hard disks.

The most common kind of tape drive on the PC and other small computers uses tape that is kept in a cartridge something like an audio tape cassette. There are no widely accepted standards for recording on cartridge tape, so two cartridge drives made by different manufacturers usually cannot read and write each others' tapes.

The most practical medium for transferring large files between computers of different types is 1/2-inch reel-to-reel tape. This kind of tape is widely used on minicomputers and large computers. It is less common on small computers like the PC because 1/2-inch tape drives are often more expensive than the computers themselves.

Three different recording standards are in common use with 1/2-inch tape. They record data at 800, 1600, and 6250 characters per inch, respectively. A tape recorded with one of these standards can be read by any computer with a 1/2-inch tape drive that can use the same standard.

Who Makes Them

Manufacturers of cartridge tape drives include Alloy Computer Products, Davong, Innovative Data Technology, and Tallgrass Technologies.

Corvus makes a device controller called the Mirror that can be used to back up a hard disk on a video cassette recorder. Corvus also makes a tape drive, known as the Bank, which may be used for both backup and on-line storage. It has a capacity of 200MB and allows access to the recorded data anywhere on the tape, much as disk drives do.

Manufacturers of 1/2-inch reel-to-reel tape drives include Alloy Computer Products and Innovative Data Technology.

Co-Processor Cards

The "heart" of a computer—the part that does the actual computing—is called the *central processing unit* (CPU). Your PC's CPU is an integrated circuit called the 8088, made by Intel Corporation.

Different CPUs require computer programs to be represented in different ways in order to be run. The CPU determines what operating system and applications your computer can run. A *co-processor card* gives a computer a second kind of CPU that can run other operating systems and software.

Your PC can be fitted with several brands of co-processor cards, most of which use an older type of CPU, the Zilog Z80. The Z80 can run certain programs that are not yet available for the 8088. For most applications the speed of the Z80 is comparable to the speed of the 8088. The Z80's main limitation is that it cannot use more than 64K of RAM.

The operating system provided with Z80 co-processor cards is Digital Research's CP/M-80.

What To Look For

The convenience and usefulness of a co-processor card depend to a great extent on its compatibility with DOS. The most convenient type of co-processor card lets you run DOS as usual, but automatically uses the Z80 CPU when you run a CP/M-80 program. A less convenient design lets you run only one operating system at a time, and may use a different disk format so that you can pass files between systems only by running a special conversion program.

Most co-processor cards contain 64K of RAM for the auxiliary CPU to use. Check whether this extra RAM is available to PCDOS as well.

Some co-processor cards have their own serial and parallel interfaces. These are nice *if* DOS can use them, or if CP/M-80 can use the PC's regular ports as DOS does. Otherwise, the extra ports are a nuisance, making you move cables around when you switch operating systems.

Who Makes Them

Manufacturers of co-processor cards include Microlog, Byad, and Automated Business Machines.

Sritek makes a group of co-processor cards that use different CPUs, some of which are more powerful than the PC's Intel 8088. Some of these cards can run Xenix, a powerful multiuser operating system sold by Microsoft and based on the popular minicomputer operating system UNIX.

Numeric Data Processors

The PC's System Board has an empty socket where you can plug in an Intel 8087 Numeric Data Processor. The 8087 is an integrated circuit that can perform certain arithmetic calculations in one step that would otherwise take the PC dozens or hundreds of steps. If a program does a lot of calculations, it may run many times faster on a PC with an 8087 than on one without.

In order to take advantage of an 8087, your application programs must be designed to use the 8087's features. Not all programs for the PC can do this. If you want to use an 8087 to speed up a program, check with the maker of the program to see whether it can use an 8087 if one is installed.

If you write your own programs, you can modify them to use the 8087. You will need a language processor designed to compile programs for use with the 8087, or a library of subroutines that you can call to perform 8087 operations. Subroutine libraries for common PC programming languages are often provided by firms that package the 8087 for the PC market.

Packagers of the Intel 8087 and subroutine-library software for the PC market include IBM, MicroWare, and Seattle Computer Products.

Modems

A *modem* is a device that allows your PC to communicate with other computers through the telephone system.

"Modem" is short for "modulator/demodulator." A modem transmits digital data by modulating (encoding) it into an audio *carrier tone*, much as a radio transmitter encodes sound into a radio carrier wave (see Figure 13-3). A modem receives data by demodulating (decoding) it from a carrier tone created by another modem.

Types of Modems

A modem may be either *synchronous* or *asynchronous*. This distinction is based on how digital data is encoded into the carrier tone. Each type of modem communicates only with other modems of the same type.

Asynchronous modems are simple and inexpensive. They are widely used for communication between small computers and in commercial time-sharing systems.

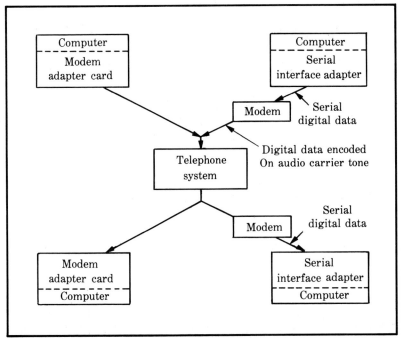

Figure 13-3.
How two computers communicate using modems

Synchronous modems are more complex and expensive, but they are more efficient for transferring data at high speeds. They are often used for communication with the large computers that many big corporations buy for their own use.

A modem also may be either an *acoustic coupler* or a *direct-connect modem*.

An acoustic coupler communicates with the telephone system by holding the ends of a telephone handset in a pair of rubber cups. One cup transmits the outgoing carrier tone to the handset's mouthpiece. The other cup picks up the incoming carrier tone from the handset's earpiece.

A direct-connect modem feeds the carrier tone directly into the telephone system through a cable that plugs into a modular wall jack. It may have a built-in telephone that you can use to dial a call, or it may dial calls itself on command from the PC.

An asynchronous modem may be an acoustic coupler or a direct-connect modem. All synchronous modems are direct-connect.

An asynchronous modem may be a card that plugs into a system expansion slot, or it may be a peripheral that is connected to the PC through a serial interface. All acoustic couplers are serial interface devices. Direct-connect asynchronous modems may be of either type.

A synchronous modem may be a card that plugs into a system expansion slot, or it may be a peripheral that is connected to the PC through a special synchronous interface card. Such an interface card may also be used without a modem to connect the PC by cable to another computer with a synchronous interface, just as a serial interface card may be used to connect the PC by cable to another computer with a serial interface.

Features of Modems

Modems, like serial interface printers, work at particular data rates, or *baud rates*. The least expensive asynchronous modems work at rates of as much as 300 baud (about 30 characters per second). More expensive ones operate at 1200 baud (about 120 characters per second). Some 1200-baud modems can operate at 300 baud as well.

Some asynchronous modems offer data rates of 2400 baud or more. These high-speed modems are expensive and often require special telephone lines. To date only a few computers have them.

Synchronous modems generally operate at rates of 2400 baud and higher. Because of these high data rates, they often require special telephone lines.

Some direct-connect modems have an *auto answering* feature

that allows a computer program to "answer the phone" through the modem. This feature is useful if you want to use your PC for remote computing. For example, you might leave your PC running a special program that fetches information from a data base; you then could use the program by calling the PC from a suitably equipped computer or terminal at another location.

Some direct-connect modems also offer *auto dialing*, enabling a computer program to "dial up" another computer through the modem. With this feature you can run programs that exchange information with other computers automatically. For example, you could program your PC to do its communicating late at night, when telephone charges and time-sharing charges are lower.

How To Use Them

The details of using a modem depend on the particular modem and communication software you are using, and to some extent on the type of computer your PC is communicating with. Here we will give you some general guidelines.

For communication to happen at all, each part of the communication channel between your PC and the other computer must use the same serial interface options. The baud rate must be the same for your modem, your serial interface (if your modem uses a serial interface), and the computer at the other end of the channel. Certain other options like parity, number of data bits, and number of stop bits must also be the same. These options may be set automatically by your communication software, or you may have to set them yourself.

If you are using a serial interface modem, you tell the operating system how to send and receive data with the MODE command just as if you were using a serial interface printer. If your PC has more than one serial interface, you may also have to tell it which one to use.

On the modem, you may have to set the communication options with switches or with commands sent by the PC that the modem captures and uses. If the modem is a PC adapter card, you may be able to set its options with the same commands that you would use to set a serial interface.

You may not have control over the other computer system's options. If you have no control, simply set the PC's serial interface and modem to match what the other system expects.

Once you have set the communication options, you must establish a telephone connection between the PC and the other computer. If you have an acoustic coupler, dial the other computer's number on a telephone and put the phone's handset in the coupler's rubber cups when you hear the other computer's carrier tone. If you have a direct-connect modem, you may dial on the modem's phone, or the communication program may do the dialing for you.

After the telephone connection is established, you may begin using the other computer. What you can use it for, and how, will depend on what software your PC and the other computer are running. Some possible uses are discussed in the section on communication software in Chapter 14.

What To Look Out For

If you have a serial interface modem, you must connect it to a serial interface through a data cable. See the section on "Serial and Parallel Interface Cards" for more information about this cable.

When you buy a 1200-baud modem, be sure that it is compatible with the remote systems you plan to communicate with. There are two kinds of 1200-baud modems in common use. One, called *212A-compatible*, uses a carrier tone standard established by the Bell Telephone 212A modem. The other, *Vadic-compatible*, uses a standard established by Racal-Vadic, Inc. Some modems can use both standards.

Equipping a computer for synchronous communication is a technically complex problem best left to an expert. For starters, there are several kinds of synchronous communication, such as "bisynchronous communication" (BSC), "Synchronous Data Link Control" (SDLC), and "System Network Architecture" (SNA). These may be used over ordinary phone lines, specially dedicated lines (no dialing necessary), plain wires, or coaxial cables. If you need to deal with a computer system that uses synchronous communication, enlist the aid of a consultant or other expert with synchronous communication experience.

Who Makes Them

Manufacturers of asynchronous modems include Hayes, Novation, and Ven-Tel.

Manufacturers of synchronous modems and synchronous interface cards include AST Research, Automated Business Machines, DataSource, IBM, and IE Systems.

Networks

A *local area network* (LAN) is a combination of hardware and software that connects two or more computers and enables them to exchange data very rapidly. A LAN has two uses. First, it enables several computers (called *nodes* in this context) to share an expensive device such as a hard disk drive or a high-speed printer. Second, it permits multiple nodes to share files that are stored on one node.

A LAN typically allows you to use another node's disk, printer, or other device just as if it were attached directly to your PC. If another node is already using a disk you want (or perhaps just a file you want), you are denied access until the other computer is done. If another node is using the printer you want, your output is *spooled* (saved in RAM on a disk) and is printed when the printer is free.

Some LANs provide additional services, such as security (allowing only certain users to have access to certain files) and electronic mail (sending messages from one user to another user).

What To Look For

LANs transfer information at different rates. One LAN for the PC runs at 10 million bits per second (about 1,200,000 characters per second), which is much faster than IBM's Fixed Disk. Another runs at 60,000 characters per second, which is only about twice as fast as a diskette drive.

How fast a LAN you need depends on what you intend to use it for. You might find a slow LAN satisfactory for sharing a printer but not for sharing disk files.

Different LANs put different limits on the number of nodes that may be connected and on the distances that may separate them. Some allow a few dozen nodes, while others allow hundreds. Some allow cables only about 50 feet long, while others allow thousands of feet.

Different LANs use different kinds of cable to connect the nodes. Some use twisted pair cable (two wires twisted together), which is inexpensive and easy to install. Others use coaxial cable, which is costlier and bulkier but which tends to allow higher transmission speeds.

Some LANs serve only a single kind of computer, such as the PC. Others can connect several kinds of computers in one network. If you have or may acquire computers of several kinds, you will find the latter type of LAN more useful.

Some LANs let any node share any other node's resources. Others designate one node as a *master* whose resources others may share. A separate master computer adds to the cost of a LAN, but makes resource sharing easier to manage when many computers are part of the LAN. If there is a master, it may be the same sort of computer as the other nodes, or it may be a special computer that comes with the LAN.

When you evaluate a LAN, consider your probable future requirements. Replacing an outgrown LAN can be troublesome and expensive.

Who Makes Them

Manufacturers of LANs include Corvus, Davong, Orchid Technology, 3COM, and XCOMP.

Expansion Units

An *expansion unit* increases the number of adapter cards you can plug into your PC. The PC I and PC II each have five system expansion slots; the PC XT has eight slots. If you need more than five or eight adapter cards, you can add an expansion unit to your system.

A system expansion unit is typically a box about the size of the PC System Unit, and it is connected to the System Unit by a cable and special adapter card that plugs into one of the System Unit's expansion slots. An expansion unit should contain a power supply large enough to power all of the options that might be plugged into the unit.

Who Makes Them

IBM sells expansion units for both the PC and the PC XT.

IBM's Expansion Unit 5161 Model 1 attaches to the PC. It has eight system expansion slots. One slot is occupied by a card for communicating with the System Unit, and one is occupied by a Fixed Disk Drive Adapter card. The unit also contains a Fixed Disk Drive and has space for a second drive, which must be purchased separately.

IBM's Expansion Unit 5162 Model 2 attaches to the PC XT. It has eight system expansion slots, one of which is occupied by a card for communicating with the System Unit. The System Unit's Fixed Disk Drive Adapter card and Fixed Disk drive may be moved to the Expansion Unit, and a second Fixed Disk drive may be added.

Other manufacturers of expansion units include I-Bus Systems, RCS, and Tecmar.

Other Hardware

Many other devices are available for the PC. Some examples are listed here.

A *joystick* is an input device consisting of a lever mounted on a universal joint. You can indicate motion (usually cursor motion) by swinging the lever in any direction. Joysticks are used by many computer games but have not found much use in business applications. IBM sells a system expansion card called a *Game Adapter* that is used to interface with joysticks.

A *mouse* is an input device that you can move around on a table top or a specially ruled pad. You use it to indicate cursor motion. Most mice have two or three buttons that can be used to invoke actions such as drawing lines, inserting text, and so on. Mice are used by a small but growing number of applications such as text editors, spreadsheet programs, and graphics programs.

A *bar code reader* can be used to read the universal product codes ("bar codes" or UPCs) now printed on the packages of many products. A bar code reader is useful for recording sales of merchandise, for conducting computerized inventories, and for similar purposes.

An *optical character reader* (OCR) reads letters printed on paper. Simple OCRs recognize characters typed with special OCR type elements. More sophisticated OCRs can recognize ordinary typed characters and even hand-printed text.

A *speech synthesizer* enables your computer to "speak." It is useful in applications where the user cannot look at a display because his or her eyes must be directed elsewhere. The size of a synthesizer's vocabulary and the naturalness of its speech depend on the sophistication of the device.

An *analog-digital converter* converts a continuously variable (analog) voltage into a digital signal (that is, a stream of numbers) that a computer can read. A *digital-analog converter* converts a digital signal into a voltage that can be used to control an instrument or tool. These converters are useful in applications such as automatic control of industrial equipment and laboratory instruments.

A *GPIB interface card* lets the PC operate a device with a GPIB (General Purpose Interface Bus) interface, just as a serial interface card lets it operate a device with a serial interface. The GPIB interface is common among scientific instruments that are meant to be computer-controlled. This interface is also known as an IEEE 488 interface.

Other devices too numerous to mention here are available for the PC. Whatever your needs, some supplier is likely to meet them. For suppliers of the products we have just discussed and of others, consult the product guides listed in the "Publications" section of Chapter 15, "Guide to Services," and look over the advertisements in current issues of magazines devoted to the IBM PC.

PC-Compatible Computers

Many companies make computers that they term "PC-compatible." Such computers run most PC software, and many offer features that the PC does not have.

Virtually any computer with an 8088 CPU is PC-compatible in the sense that the MSDOS operating system (essentially the same as IBM's PCDOS) can be made to run on it, and so can most software written for the PC. Some of these machines offer virtually complete software compatibility: they can even run programs that depend on "unique" characteristics of the PC's hardware or software. A few offer complete hardware compatibility: their adapter cards and those designed for the PC are interchangeable.

Some added features found in PC-compatible computers include multiuser operating systems; options such as serial and parallel interfaces built into the System Board; prices lower than IBM's prices for comparable systems; and portability.

Who Makes Them

Manufacturers of PC-compatible computers include Colby Computer, Columbia Data Products, COMPAQ, Corona, and Dynalogic.

Colby Computer makes a kit that converts a standard IBM PC into a portable computer with a nine-inch monochrome display and one diskette drive. The PC's System Board and adapter cards are simply transplanted into the Colby chassis, which contains its own display, power supply, and keyboard.

CHAPTER 14

Guide to Software

Software products may be divided into four basic types: application programs, programming language processors, operating systems, and system utilities.

Application programs *are programs that perform useful tasks such as editing and printing documents, solving statistical problems, or keeping your company's books. Most of the sections in this chapter are devoted to application programs.*

Programming language processors *are programs that support the use of a computer language on a computer system. They are tools for the development of application programs.*

Operating systems *are programs that manage the PC's resources and enable you to run application programs. One section of this chapter is devoted to operating systems.*

System utilities *are special programs that enhance the usefulness of or add capabilities to a computer. A utility might add features to the operating system or perform generally useful services like sorting the contents of a file.*

Evaluating Software

Choosing a software product is, if anything, harder than choosing a hardware product, for software products are more numerous and offer a greater variety of features. Your individual needs and taste will play a great part in your choice.

When you consider buying a software product, ask yourself the following questions:

- What problems do you want to solve? Will this program help you solve them?

- Will this program fit in comfortably with your current working habits, or will you have to change your habits to accommodate it?

- Does this program require any hardware you do not have? Is it compatible with the hardware you have, or must you replace some of your hardware to run it?

- Is this program compatible with the type and version of operating system that you use?

- If you want this program to exchange data with other application programs, is it compatible with them? Can your other programs process data files created by this program? Likewise, can this program process files from your other programs? The box discusses two current trends in software offerings.

- What reputation does this program have? Is it easy or hard to use? Is it reliable or filled with errors? Is it very flexible or limited in scope?

- How good is this program's user's manual? Is it accurate? Well organized? Does it fit your level of experience, or does it talk down to you or over your head? Does it include quick reference aids?

- Does the manufacturer offer support for the program? This is especially important for more complex software like business packages. A toll-free phone line can make the task of initially setting up a piece of sophisticated software much easier. You should also determine whether your dealer can provide any assistance. Are there any introductory classes in your area that provide training for the software product?

Software Families and Integrated Software

Two current trends in software offerings are *software families* and *integrated software*. These should be given serious consideration when you are looking into a major applications need.

A software family is a group of application programs offered by the same manufacturer with the intent of providing full compatibility between the family members. The family approach ensures that you will later be able to purchase software for other applications that will be fully compatible with what you purchase now. An added benefit is that different products in the same family may use the same or a very similar command structure and design philosophy, so that using a second family member feels familiar very quickly.

Integrated software is software that has combined several common applications into one: for example, combining word processing, spreadsheet, and graphics functions into one program. The integrated program provides for quick and easy transition between functions. Since the integrated functions can be intimately tied together, it is possible to support features that are not easily duplicated, even with a software family package.

Here is a useful procedure for choosing a program:

1. Study the features of all the programs you might choose from. Decide which features you need, which you would like, and which you can do without.
2. Eliminate the programs that clearly do not meet your needs.
3. Consider how the remaining programs perform the functions you will use most often. This can affect a program's usability more than all the "nice" features that you will seldom need.
4. Study the remaining products carefully — with hands-on experience if you can get it — and decide which one is best for you.

Word Processors

A word processor is a program that helps you edit and print text files containing such documents as letters, proposals, and contracts.

Most modern word processors use your PC's display as a *window* onto the text. You view a part of a text file on the screen as though you were viewing part of a printed page. Editing commands are entered with function keys or with the CTRL key. The display instantly reflects the effects of the commands on the file.

Two Kinds of Word Processors

There are two basic types of word processing programs. One type displays the contents of your text file on the screen but does not show the file as it will appear when printed; it does not show where lines and pages will end, how paragraphs will be indented, and so forth. You edit the file's contents with function keys or control sequences but you control the file's printed format by storing command lines in the file. You do not see the effects of these command lines until you print the file.

Since this kind of word processor formats the text file when it prints, we will call it a "print-time formatter."

The other type of word processor makes no distinction between the contents of a file and the file's format. It displays your text file as nearly as possible in the way it will be printed, with actual line and page ends and indentations shown on the screen as you edit your text. You format the text with program function key commands or control sequence commands, and you see the effects of the commands instantly.

Since this kind of word processor formats a text file as you edit, we will call it an "edit-time formatter."

Each kind of word processor has advantages. Edit-time formatters tend to be easier to learn and use. The ability to see the effect of a command immediately on your text assists the process of learning; it also eliminates the need to print a file, correct errors, and print the file again.

On the other hand, print-time formatters often allow much more sophisticated formatting commands to be used. This enables you to perform some very powerful formatting operations that an edit-time formatter would give you no way to describe. Thus, if you write documents with complex formats, some print-time formatters may suit your needs better than any edit-time formatter could.

Features

Any word processor has features that help to automate the mechanics of writing and revising a document. The most important of these features are

- *Editing commands.* These allow you to edit natural elements of text, such as words, sentences, and paragraphs, as well as characters and lines.
- *Word wrapping.* As you type, the word processor starts a new line of text automatically when an old line is full. It may *justify* the old line; that is, it may adjust the spacing between words so that the right side lines up with the right margin. If you later make some changes to a portion of the text, you can *reformat* it, causing the word processor to justify the lines again.
- *Pagination.* The word processor divides the text into pages for you. If you add or delete lines, it adjusts page breaks automatically. When you tell the word processor to print the file, it inserts top and bottom margins, and it may add headings, footings, and page numbers to each page.
- *Indentation and tabulation.* You can indent a file's left and right margins. You can set and use tab stops as you would on a typewriter.
- *Print enhancements.* You can underscore and print in boldface sentences, words, or characters. You may also be able to use superscripts, subscripts, and special typefaces if your printer can print these things.

Most word processor programs include support for a limited number of printers. If you have a printer not spported by a certain word processor, you may be unable to use some or all of the printer enhancement features of the word processor. It is thus of prime importance to look at printer support when you are comparing word processors.

Most word processors have additional features that make them especially suitable for certain types of work. Some of these features are

- *Sophisticated formatting features.* If you type a lot of tables or complex indented material, such features can help you format the text the way you want it.
- *Microspacing.* The word processor can justify a line by inserting an equal amount of space between every two words. Microspacing improves the appearance of a file, giving it the appearance of having been typeset. It requires a letter-quality printer.
- *Proportional spacing.* The word processor can print text in which some characters, like *m*, are wider than others, like *i*. Proportional spacing makes a typed file look almost as though it were typeset. It requires a printer that is capable of proportional spacing and a proportional-spaced print element.
- *Automatic paragraph numbering.* If you type a lot of files with numbered paragraphs and subparagraphs, such as contracts, you will find this feature valuable. It will save you the trouble of renumbering your paragraphs by hand whenever you add or delete one.
- *Footnote positioning.* If you use footnotes and want to put them at the bottom of each page, a word processor that can position the footnotes automatically will save you a great deal of time and trouble.
- *Arithmetic processing.* Some word processors can add up a row or column of numbers in a file and insert the sum in the file. Some can do subtraction, multiplication, and division as well.

Who Sells Them

Word processors are among the most numerous software products offered for the PC.

Some word processors that run under DOS are Wordvision, by Bruce & James; EasyWriter II, by Information Unlimited Software; EasyWriter, by Information Unlimited Software (distributed by IBM); Spellbinder, by Lexisoft; Volkswriter, by Lifetree; The Final Word, by Mark of the Unicorn; Benchmark, by Metasoft; WordStar, by MicroPro; WordPlus, by Professional Software; Select, by Select Information Systems; SuperWriter, by Sorcim; and Visi-Word, by VisiCorp.

Mail Merge Programs

A mail merge program can produce personalized form letters by merging a file containing a mailing list and a file containing a letter. The program prints one copy of the letter for each entry in the mailing list, with the data from the mailing list inserted in the letter at points marked by special command codes.

Mail merge programs often have other applications as well. For example, many of them can be used to print customized form letters by prompting you for data to insert at specified points in the letter. Many can assemble and print a document from a list of files containing standard paragraphs.

A mail merge program is usually designed to operate with a particular word processor and is closely integrated with that word processor's document printing function.

One mail merge program is MailMerge, by MicroPro (for use with WordStar). The Select, SuperWriter, and Volkswriter word processors have mail merge features built in.

Spelling Checkers

A spelling checker is a valuable aid for producing a finished document. It scans a text file and compares each word to a dictionary, flagging words that appear to be misspelled.

Many spelling checkers check words for common prefixes and suffixes, so that they will not reject a word like "computers" if only "computer" is in the dictionary. Most have features that let you modify the dictionary or add a supplementary dictionary of your own. This is invaluable if you work in a field that has a specialized vocabulary, such as medicine or law.

Some spelling checkers are designed to work with specific word processors and cannot be used without them. MicroPro's SpellStar is one of these; it can be used only with MicroPro's word processor, WordStar. Other spelling checkers, such as Sorcim's Spellguard, can be used with any word processor.

Spelling checkers include Proofreader, by Aspen Software; EasySpeller II, by Information Unlimited Software (for use with EasyWriter II); SpellStar, by MicroPro (for use with WordStar); The Word Plus, by Oasis Systems; Perfect Speller, by Perfect Software; Spellguard, by Sorcim; and VisiSpell, by VisiCorp.

Grammatik, by Aspen Software, detects typographical and punctuation errors. It also points out overused words, wordiness, and other stylistic problems.

Mailing List Programs

A *mailing list program* lets you enter, update, and print a list of names and addresses. It often lets you store additional information with each name, such as a phone number and a date (for example, the expiration date of a subscription).

Most mailing list programs let you print a mailing list as a report or in one or more label formats. Most programs let you sort and print the labels. For example, you might sort the list according to customer name or ZIP code.

Some mailing list programs let you define additional data fields for your own purposes. You often can use these fields to select a subset of your mailing list for a particular report or label run.

Mailing list programs include First Class Mail, by Continental Software; and the Benchmark mailing list processor, by Metasoft.

Spreadsheet Programs

A spreadsheet program edits and prints tables of numbers ("spreadsheets") much as a word processor edits and prints documents composed of words. A spreadsheet program's power comes from its ability to represent complex relationships among the rows and columns in a table and to use those relationships to recalculate some entries in the table when the values of other entries are changed.

An example will best illustrate how a spreadsheet program works. Suppose you wanted to use a spreadsheet program to compute the cash flow in a business. You would first set up rows of a table to represent units of time, such as months. The columns could then be used to represent various types of income and expenses, cash on hand, and so forth.

After defining the rows and columns, you would define relationships among them. For example, you might define a relationship between sales tax and gross sales such that sales tax was calculated to be 6% of gross sales. After this, whenever a number in the "gross sales" column was changed, the program would recalculate the corresponding "sales tax" value. You might define a formula for growth of sales in a particular product line, so that when one number in that column was changed, the values representing later months' sales, found in the succeeding rows, would be recomputed.

Once you set up the spreadsheet, you could use it to answer questions like the following: If you reduce the price of your product by 10%, thus increasing sales by 5%, and if the increase in volume reduces your unit cost by 5%, what will your cash position be after one year? To answer this, you would only have to change the product price, sales per month, and unit cost (or the formulas used to calculate those values). The spreadsheet program would then recalculate everything else, using the formulas you defined that relate gross income to sales, net income to gross income and expenses, and so forth.

Spreadsheet programs can be used for applications as complex as income tax calculations, loan and mortgage calculations, and investment analysis. Many people use them as the basis for simple accounting systems.

Many spreadsheet programs have additional features, such as the ability to put text as well as numbers in the spreadsheet, to combine two or more spreadsheets into one, and to print charts or graphs from spreadsheet data.

Several companies sell spreadsheet *templates* for a variety of complex applications such as real estate development, accounting, and financial planning. A template is a prewritten set of row and column definitions and relationships for a particular spreadsheet program. Using an appropriate template for an application can save you hundreds of hours of learning time and of programming, testing, and debugging, in the same manner that prewritten application programs save you the time and effort of writing your own programs.

Spreadsheet programs include MicroPlan and GraphPlan by Chang Laboratories; Multiplan, by Microsoft; 1-2-3, by Lotus Development Corporation; CalcStar, by MicroPro; SuperCalc, by Sorcim; and VisiCalc, by VisiCorp. Context/MBA, by Context Management Systems, is a popular spreadsheet/report writer/graphics program that contains its own operating system.

Suppliers of spreadsheet templates include Que and Sofstar.

Planning Aids

You can get many different kinds of programs to help you plan construction projects, business financing, and other activities.

A *time series* is a sequence of numbers that represent the variation of some quantity over time—for example, the monthly income of a business. Several firms make programs that can process time series data statistically. The results of such analysis can help you project trends and prepare charts and graphs depicting these trends. These programs are useful in business financial planning, as well as in other areas like the social sciences.

Time series analysis programs include VisiTrend/PLOT, by VisiCorp. VisiSchedule, also by VisiCorp, uses the Critical Path Method to help you plan the sequence of events in a project with many interdependent parts, such as the construction of a building or the design of a computer program.

Desktop/PLAN, by VisiCorp, is a general business planning package that runs under DOS. It helps you do financial modeling, budgeting, and analysis. It can produce graphs and charts as well as printed reports.

Time Manager, distributed by IBM, is an electronic date book that keeps track of your appointments and helps you schedule your time.

Money Decisions, by Eagle Software Publishing, is a package of programs for doing financial planning and projections.

Business Software

Many companies offer accounting software and other types of business software for the PC. Business software packages for the

PC range from ones suitable for one-person businesses to ones that can meet the needs of moderately large corporations.

An accounting package may perform any or all of the following common functions: general ledger, accounts receivable, accounts payable, payroll, inventory, purchase order entry, and sales order entry. Some packages are modular: you can buy components for one or more of these functions and add more functions later by buying more components.

Before you try to choose an accounting system, analyze your business's needs. Ask yourself the following questions: Which functions do you want to computerize, and in what order? What reports do you need? What level of skill can you count on from the people who must use the system? How many people will be authorized to perform each accounting function (entering payables, making payments, maintaining the chart of accounts, and so forth), and how do you want to control their access to the system? If you are not familiar with accounting practices, you may want to engage an accountant or a computer consultant familiar with accounting applications to help you make these decisions.

In evaluating an accounting package, consider the following points:

- *Is it suitable to your business*? Microcomputer accounting systems have traditionally been designed for small retail firms. Many widely used packages are not appropriate for other types of business, such as manufacturing or professional service. If none of the standard products seem to suit your needs, look for packages designed specifically for your kind of business.

- *Is it adaptable to your needs*? Can the package fit into your business's accounting practices, or must you fit your business to the package? Give particular attention to the reports the package produces. Does it give you the reports you need, with the right amount of detail? Can you modify the report formats to make them as useful to you as they can be?

- *Is it easy to use*? Is the package easy to set up and operate, or might you need the help of a programmer or accountant or both? Does the program provide descriptive prompts to help the user respond with proper input? Is each entry checked for validity upon input? Is the documentation thorough and readable? Does it provide you with information about the formulas and accounting techniques used?

- *Does it conform to good accounting practices*? Does the system produce an acceptable audit trail? Does it let you define passwords and other safeguards that let you control who uses the system for what purpose? Does it prevent "doctoring" accounting data, for example, by modifying posted transactions?

Who Makes Them

Accounting packages include General Accounting, by BPI (distributed by IBM); the EasyBusiness Systems, by Information Unlimited Software; the Peachpak accounting packages, by Peachtree Software (distributed by IBM); Accounting Plus, distributed by Systems Plus; and General Ledger, by State of the Art.

Tax Systems

Several firms offer packages that assist with tax return preparation. Two such packages are Standard Tax (oriented toward tax payers) and Master Tax (oriented toward professional tax preparers), by CPAids.

Personal Accounting Systems

Several firms produce software designed to help you keep track of your personal finances. Many of these packages support functions like tax reporting and personal property inventory.

Personal accounting packages include the Home Accountant and the Home Accountant Plus, by Continental Software; the Financier Personal Series, by Financier; and Money Maestro, by Innosys.

Data Base Systems

A data base management system (DBMS) works like a computerized file cabinet. It stores and retrieves information that can be organized as a set of records. Each record consists of fields containing data.

For example, a DBMS could be used to store information about the customers of a mail-order business. Each data base record would represent one customer. The fields in each record might contain the customer's name, address, date of last order, and so forth.

A DBMS enables you to perform the following functions:

- Define a data base: what fields each record will contain, how long each field will be, and so forth.

- Enter, inspect, and modify data base records.
- Select records from the data base on the basis of the data values in one or more fields.
- Sort records on the values of fields.
- Print reports on the contents of the data base.
- Extract information from the data base to be printed in other useful forms, such as mailing labels.

Relational and Hierarchical DBMS

There are two major types of DBMS on the PC: relational and hierarchical.

A *relational* DBMS organizes a data base like a table. Rows of the table represent records; columns represent fields.

Relational DBMSs are often divided into two categories: data management systems and true DBMSs. A *data management system* can only enter and modify records and print reports on them. A true DBMS has many additional capabilities, the central one being the ability to locate a record by looking up the value of one of its fields in an *index* rather than by reading through the file until the record is found.

A *hierarchical* DBMS organizes a data base into many *data sets*, each of which is like a table. Part of a data set's definition is the fact that it may be "owned" by a record in another data set.

For example, a mail-order house might use a hierarchical DBMS that defines three types of data sets: a customer data set, an order data set, and a line-item data set. There would be one customer data set containing a record for each customer. There would be one order data set per customer, containing a record for each order from that customer. Each order data set would be owned by a record in the customer data set. There would be one line-item data set per order, containing a record for each line-item in the order. Each line-item data set would be owned by a record in an order data set.

Most DBMSs available for the PC are relational. Hierarchical DBMSs are generally more powerful than relational DBMSs, but they are also more difficult to use. They often require the services of an experienced computer programmer to be set up for a useful task.

Menu Driven, Command Driven, And Programmable Data Base Systems

Some DBMSs are *menu driven;* that is, they work by displaying a succession of *menus* from which you choose actions you want to perform. To print a report with a menu driven DBMS, you might respond to a succession of menus asking you to make choices like the following: What data base do you want to print a report from? What field do you want to print in the first report column? How wide do you want the first column to be? What field do you want to print in the second report column?

Other DBMSs are *command driven;* that is, you use them by entering data base commands, just as you use DOS by entering operating system commands.

Menu driven DBMSs tend to be easier to use, since they lead you through the operation you want to perform. Command driven systems require you to learn a new command language. For complex operations, however, some people consider command driven systems easier to use, since the user need not go through many levels of menus to reach the desired goal.

Some DBMSs can interact with a computer program written in a programming language such as BASIC or Pascal, and some have their own built-in programming languages. Such systems let you write computer programs to perform operations that are too complex for the DBMS's commands. Of course, you must learn a programming language to use such a feature.

How to Choose

Choosing a DBMS can be trickier than choosing other pieces of software. The absence of some seemingly minor feature may make a particular DBMS unsuitable for your intended use. For example, you might be unable to use a particular DBMS because it will not let you define as many fields in a record as you need, or because it cannot be made to ignore the difference between upper- and lower-case letters when sorting.

Before you try to select a DBMS, define your application as exactly as you can. Here are some questions you should be sure to answer:

- What data base(s) do you need?
- What fields will be in each data base, what will the fields contain, and how long will they be?
- Approximately how many records will each data base contain?
- What will your reports or other output look like, and where will each piece of data in the output come from?

Take your application description to a person who is familiar with DBMSs and can help you choose an appropriate one. This may be your dealer or a consultant who will help you set up your data base application. Be prepared to make some decisions about how you want to set up your application:

- Do you want a menu driven or command driven system?
- Are you willing to do some programming or pay to have it done?
- How much are you willing to pay for the data base system and any services you need to set up your application?

Who Makes Them

Relational DBMSs available under DOS include QBASE, by Applied Software Technology; dBASE II, by Ashton-Tate; Condor Series 20, by Condor; EasyFiler, by Information Unlimited Software; T.I.M., by Innovative Software; Knowledge Man, by International Software Enterprises; MAG/base, by Micro Applications Group; Selector V, by Micro-AP; InfoStar, by MicroPro; Personal Pearl, by PEARLSOFT/Relational Systems; PFS:FILE for entering data and PFS:REPORT for printing reports, by Software Publishing; and VisiFile, by VisiCorp.

dBASE II is a command driven DBMS that includes a fairly powerful programming language built in as an extension of its command language.

Fox & Geller offers three programs that enhance dBASE II: Quickcode, for generating command files to present menus and print reports; dGRAPH, for producing charts and graphs from dBASE II files; and dUTIL, for combining command files into larger, faster-running files.

Data Base-Plus, by Tominy, is more powerful than most other PC data base systems but also more expensive. It has an optional built-in programming language and interactive report writing package. It is available for use in DOS and is also available on several other computers, including IBM's System/34 and Series/1 minicomputers and the IBM 4300 mainframe computers.

MDBS III, by International Software Enterprises, supports several types of data organization, including relational and hierarchical ones. It can be used with programs written in a variety of programming languages including compiled BASIC, Pascal, and PL/I-86. Compatible versions of the product are available on several other types of computers.

Versaform, by Applied Software Technology, is designed around the concept of entering, filing, and retrieving "forms" that are the electronic analog of the paper forms used in traditional business procedures.

Filing Systems

A *filing system* is similar to a data base management system: it helps you create and search through data files and print reports about their contents. The difference is that a DBMS generally stores data that is divided into fields that have a fixed format and meaning, while a filing system lends itself to storing data that has no particular structure.

Examples of data that you might store in a filing system are notes about customers of your business, a list of errors you have found in computer manuals you use, and reminders of appointments on your schedule.

A filing system lets you enter, modify, display, and print the contents of files. You can search the files for entries that contain certain words or combinations of words.

Filing systems include DataFax, by Link Systems, and VisiDex, by VisiCorp.

Sort Programs

A sort program makes a copy of a file in which the records are arranged in some particular order, such as alphabetical order. An example of an application for a sort program would be the creation of a copy of a mailing list in which the records are arranged by ZIP code.

Most sort programs have some or all of the following features:

- Sorting on particular fields (for example, by the contents of positions 6 through 20 in each record).
- Sorting on fields that are separated by commas, a common way of storing data of variable lengths (see Figure 14-1).
- Sorting on two or more fields (for example, sorting on ZIP code and then sorting records with the same ZIP code on last name).
- Ignoring case, so that "SMITH" and "Smith" will sort the same way. (If case is not ignored, capital letters will normally precede all lowercase letters in the PC's character sequence.)

```
Smith        J.        123 Main St.        Anytown        CA 94900
Topolewsky   Victor    1337 Prospect St.   Emanon         IL 60543
Tremont      Albert    636 Fargo St.       Buffalo Creek  SD 70320

Smith,J.,123 Main St.,Anytown,CA,94900
Topolewsky,Victor,1337 Prospect St.,Emanon,IL,60543
Tremont,Albert,636 Fargo St.,Buffalo Creek,SD,70320
```

Figure 14-1.
**Records with positional fields (top)
and comma-separated fields (bottom)**

- Interpreting fields as numbers, so that 7.0 and 007 will sort the same way.
- Sorting two or more files together into one file.
- Merging two or more sorted files into one file without resorting them.
- Deciding whether to include each input record in the sorted file on the basis of the values of one or more fields.

Sort programs include COMSORT, by Comsen; Info-SORT, by Info-Pros; and QSORT, by Structured Systems.

SORT is a DOS 2.0 filter that sorts lines of text on one fixed-position field. Unlike most other sort programs, it is limited to sorting small files.

Scientific and Mathematical Software

Your PC can be a powerful tool for solving problems in mathematics, engineering, and similar fields.

Statistical problem solving products for DOS include Statistics 5.1, by Basic Business Software; Microstat, by Ecosoft; and NWA STATPAK, by Northwest Analytical.

General mathematical problem solving products include MatheMagic, by International Software Marketing; and muMath, by Lifeboat Associates.

Many programs are also available to help solve problems in specific fields such as electronic engineering, structural engineering, and chemistry. Because of their specialized nature, these programs are generally not sold in stores and are not widely advertised. To find them, study the resource directories listed in Chapter 15, "Guide to Services," and discuss your needs with other computer users who have problems similar to your own.

Communications Programs

A communications program enables you to use your PC to communicate with another computer.

You can use your PC with a modem and a telephone to communicate with a computer at a remote location. You can also communicate with a nearby computer with a serial interface and a data cable. That is a common means of transferring data between computers whose disk data formats are not compatible.

A communications program may be designed to perform synchronous or asynchronous communications. For more information on these types of communication, see the section on "Modems" in Chapter 13, "Guide to Hardware."

Most communications programs can perform *file transfers;* that is, they can copy files back and forth between your PC and another computer.

To transfer a text file you need only have one computer running a communications program that is able to transmit a file and another running a program that is able to receive a file. To transfer a binary file (for example, a DOS COM file), you generally must use the same communications program on each computer. This is because binary data must be encoded by the sender and decoded by the receiver to ensure reliable data transfer, and the two computers must encode and decode the data in the same way.

Specialized programs may apply communications functions to any sort of task, such as collecting data from a group of remote computers; transferring data from a time-sharing system's data base to a spreadsheet program on your PC; exchanging electronic mail with users of other computers; notifying you when some event like the opening of a door occurs at a remote site; or shifting part of a complicated computing task to a larger, faster computer system.

Who Sells Them

General-purpose communications programs include Micro Link II, by Digital Marketing; ASCOM, by Dynamic Microprocessor Associates; PC-Talk, by Freeware; Asynchronous Communications Support, by IBM; MICRO/Terminal, by MICROCOM; and Crosstalk, by Microstuf.

An asynchronous communications program called COMM is supplied free with DOS. It cannot transfer files.

Dow Jones Reporter, a specialized communications program available from IBM, enables you to fetch stock quotations, financial news, and company profiles from the Dow Jones News/Retrieval Service.

Context/MBA, a spreadsheet program sold by Context Management Systems, contains a communications option that can transfer data directly between remote computers and Context/MBA spreadsheets.

Synchronous communications programs are generally packaged with synchronous communications hardware. IE Systems sells synchronous communications software for several brands of modems besides its own. See the section on "Modems" in Chapter 13, "Guide to Hardware," for more information and manufacturers' names.

Programming Language Processors

If you cannot find a commercial program that suits your needs, you may wish to write a program of your own or modify a program someone else has written. In that case you need a programming language processor.

A programming language processor converts a computer program from a form that is easy for a human being to write into a form that a computer can run.

Thousands of programming languages have been developed for different purposes, and many of them are available on the IBM PC.

Low-Level and High-Level Languages

Programming languages are generally classified as either high-level or low-level. Some examples of various languages can be found in Figure 14-2.

A *high-level language* lets you write a program in notation that is close to your natural way of expressing the problem you want to solve. If you are writing a mathematical program, for example, an appropriate high-level language would let you use notation that looked like mathematical equations.

BASIC

```
00620 ANNUAL=ANNUAL+MONTHLY
00630 IF MONTHLY>100 THEN BCOUNT=BCOUNT+1 ELSE SCOUNT=SCOUNT+1
```

COBOL

```
ADD MONTHLY TO ANNUAL.
IF MONTHLY EXCEEDS 100 ADD 1 TO BCOUNT; OTHERWISE ADD 1 TO SCOUNT.
```

FORTRAN

```
      ANNUAL = ANNUAL+MONTHLY
      IF MONTHLY .GT. 100 THEN GOTO 100
      SCOUNT = SCOUNT+1
      GOTO 101
100 BCOUNT = BCOUNT+1
101 CONTINUE
```

PL/I

```
ANNUAL = ANNUAL+MONTHLY;
IF (MONTHLY>100)
THEN BCOUNT = BCOUNT+1;
ELSE SCOUNT = SCOUNT+1;
```

8088 assembly language

```
          MOV      AX,MONTHLY
          ADD      ANNUAL,AX
          CMP      AX,100
          JG       GREATER
          INC      SCOUNT
          JMP      SHORT AFTERINC
GREATER: INC      BCOUNT
AFTERINC:
```

8088 machine language

```
0005 A1 0002
0008 01 06 0000
000C 3D 0064
000F 7F 06
0011 FF 06 0004
0015 EB 04
0017 FF 06 0006
```

Figure 14-2.
Portions of computer programs
in several programming languages

A *low-level language* lets you write a program in a notation that is close to the steps the computer must perform to run the program.

High-level languages are easier to learn than low-level languages. They let you write programs more easily, since you can concentrate on the problem you want to solve and let the language processor take care of the technical details.

High-level languages tend to be more specialized. Many of them are used for writing particular types of programs, such as accounting programs or mathematical programs. High-level languages also tend to produce programs that run more slowly than those written in a low-level language, in some cases by factors of 10 to 100.

High-Level Language Processors: Compilers and Interpreters

High-level programming language processors may be divided into two types: compilers and interpreters.

A *compiler* reads a program you have written in that compiler's *source language* and translates it into your PC's *machine language*. You can store the compiled program in a disk file and run it as you would run a DOS command, which is essentially what a compiled program is.

The compilation procedure is done only during the time when you are creating and debugging the program. Once a compiled program is working, you do not need to compile it any more. Since the compiler translates program statements directly into machine language, the resulting program can be very fast and efficient.

An *interpreter* reads a program that you have written and executes it one program statement at a time. No intermediate step of compiling the program is needed. You simply enter the program and run it. Executing the interpreted program requires the language interpreter to be running on the PC. For example, to run a BASIC program, you must first run the PC's BASIC interpreter, BASIC or BASICA, and then use BASIC to run the program.

A hybrid language processor is the *compiler-interpreter.* It translates a program into an *intermediate language* that is simpler than the source language, but more sophisticated than the PC's machine language. Then it interprets the intermediate-language program.

Compilers tend to produce faster-running programs than interpreters and are more suitable for large, complex programs and programs that will be sold commercially. Interpreters tend to be easier to use, since they can tell you more about what went wrong when your program fails. They also let you modify your program and run it again without the bother and delay of recompiling it.

The compiler-interpreter can provide a high degree of *program portability* (that is, the ability to run a program on different computers) without the run-time penalty of a pure interpreter.

Some Popular High-Level Languages

The most popular language on microcomputers like the PC is BASIC. BASIC is a high-level language that was developed for large multiuser computers in the 1960s and that became popular on early microcomputers because it was easy to implement on simple machines with small amounts of RAM. BASIC is a general-purpose language suitable for most types of programming you are likely to do. Many people criticize BASIC for certain characteristics that tend to encourage bad programming habits and make complex programs difficult to write and maintain.

Pascal, another popular microcomputer language, was first developed as a tool for teaching good programming habits. It has found use in many types of applications because it makes it easy to write programs that are clear, reliable, and easily modified. Its main disadvantage is that it forces you to follow "good" habits that are restrictive to the point that some useful kinds of programs are hard to write at all.

FORTRAN, a traditional language originally developed for solving mathematical applications on big computers, is available on the PC, but it has not been widely used since it has neither the advantages of Pascal nor the overwhelming popularity of BASIC.

COBOL is a traditional big-computer language used for business applications. It too is available on the PC but not widely used. Most COBOL processors are unacceptably slow and lack features that big-computer users are used to. Most business programs for the PC are written in BASIC or Pascal.

PL/I is a language developed by IBM in the late 1960s. It was originally supposed to replace both COBOL and FORTRAN. That has not come to pass, but the language is widely used on big computers for both business and scientific programming. PL/I is available on the PC.

Low-Level Languages

The lowest level language available on any computer is *assembler language*. Assembler language is just a convenient notation for machine language; thus computers with different central processing units (CPUs) actually have different assembler languages.

Assembler language has traditionally been used for writing operating systems, compilers, and similar programs. Advances in computer science have made high-level languages more practical for these applications than they used to be, and assembler language now is used mostly for small parts of programs that must run as efficiently as possible.

C is a "medium-level" language that has seen a recent surge of popularity on the PC. It combines extensive control over how a program runs with many of the advantages of high-level languages like Pascal and PL/I. It is used mainly for writing operating systems, DBMSs, and other highly technical programs, but some of its advocates use it for business and scientific programming as well.

How to Choose a Language

Before you choose a programming language, consider carefully whether you want to learn to program at all. Programming is a time-consuming and often frustrating activity, and the hours you spend programming might better be invested in your job or business.

On the other hand, if you have a real need for a program that does not exist, the benefits of writing it may pay you back manyfold for the necessary investment of time. Also, writing a program to make your PC do exactly what you want can give you a great feeling of satisfaction once it is finished.

In choosing a language, consider the following factors:

- *Suitability.* Is this language suitable for the type of programming you intend to do (business, scientific, game writing, and so on)?

- *Ease of learning.* How hard are you willing to work to master a language? Low-level languages are generally hardest to learn, but high-level languages differ greatly in ease of learning. Different implementations of the same language may differ as well because of factors like language extensions, the quality of error messages, speed of compilation, and so on.

- *Efficiency.* If you plan to write programs that do a lot of calculations, you may find that programs written in an inefficient language are unacceptably slow. In most types of business programs the PC spends most of its time doing I/O operations, making efficiency much less significant.

- *Portability.* How easy would it be to transport programs written on your PC to a different type of computer, or vice versa? If portability is important to you, choose a language that is widely available and an implementation that is fairly standard.

- *Programming tools.* What programs accompany the language processor to make your programming task easier? Some possibilities are a debugger, which helps you see what is happening inside a program to make it produce incorrect results; a syntax checker, which lets you find grammatically incorrect program statements without running the compiler; and an extensive run-time library, which gives you predefined "building blocks" that save you the effort of writing often-used functions for yourself.

If you have difficulty choosing a programming language, ask some experienced programmers for advice. Get several opinions, since programmers tend to have strong opinions for and against certain languages. Ask what languages each programmer has done a lot of programming in. The more languages a programmer knows well, the more likely you are to get informed, unbiased advice.

After you have chosen a language, ask several programmers to recommend a beginner's book on that language. Look over the recommended books in a store and buy at least one. Do not try to learn programming from the user's manual that comes with the language processor you buy. Such a manual is usually intended to be a reference book, and you will have a very tough time learning from it.

Locate a few programmers who are willing to help you when you have problems. Do not run to one of them whenever you have difficulty, though. You will learn better if you solve most of your problems yourself.

Who Sells Them

BASIC is supplied with DOS itself. Two versions are provided: Disk BASIC and Advanced BASIC (command name BASICA). The two versions are very similar, but Advanced BASIC has additional commands for error handling, sound generation on the PC's built-in speaker, and graphics on the Color/Graphics Monitor Adapter. Advanced BASIC requires more RAM than Disk BASIC, but should run comfortably on any PC with 64K of RAM or more.

Yet a third version of BASIC, called Cassette BASIC, is stored in the PC's ROM. The PC runs Cassette BASIC if you boot it without a disk in drive A (and on a PC with a Fixed Disk, if the Fixed Disk has no active partition). Cassette BASIC cannot read or write disk files. It is intended for use on PCs with no disk drives and is of little value otherwise.

Disk BASIC, Advanced BASIC, and Cassette BASIC are all interpreters. A DOS BASIC compiler is available through IBM as a separately priced product.

Digital Research sells CBASIC (an interpreter), a CBASIC compiler, and Personal BASIC, which is intended to be totally compatible with IBM's BASICA.

IBM sells two Pascal products: a Pascal compiler and the

UCSD p-System with Pascal. The UCSD p-System is an operating system that was designed around Pascal by computer science workers at the University of California at San Diego. It is designed to be highly transportable and is available in essentially identical versions on a great number of small computers.

Digital Research sells Pascal/MT+, a compiler, and the Pascal/MT+ SpeedProgramming Package, a set of programming tools.

IBM offers a FORTRAN compiler and a COBOL compiler for DOS. Ryan-McFarland offers a COBOL compiler that is compatible with Ryan-McFarland products under many other microcomputer and minicomputer operating systems.

IBM also offers APL, a mathematically oriented language with powerful features for science and engineering, and Logo, a graphics oriented language that is designed for teaching logic, problem solving skills, and programming concepts to both children and adults.

Digital Research offers PL/I.

IBM offers an assembler for DOS.

C compilers are available from a number of sources, including C-systems, Computer Innovations, Digital Research, Lifeboat Associates (Lattice C), and Telecon Systems. C-Systems also sells C-Window, a debugging package for C that lets you debug the program in source code format rather than compiled format.

Operating Systems

Although DOS is by far the most widely used operating system on the PC, several other operating systems are available. One of them may be more appropriate than DOS for your needs.

There are several reasons for choosing an operating system other than DOS. You may be familiar with it from work on another computer; it may be the standard system on another computer you use; or you may want to run a particular program that can only be used with that system.

On the other hand, using any operating system other than DOS carries certain disadvantages. It gives you less choice of software, since less software is written for an operating system with few users. It also gives you less choice of hardware, since the producer of an uncommon operating system cannot afford to support uncommon devices, and the producer of an uncommon device cannot afford to support uncommon operating systems. For these reasons, when you consider buying an operating system other than DOS, you should determine whether you will be able to use it with software and hardware that you may want to add to your PC in the future.

If you use an uncommon operating system you may also have more difficulty finding consultants to help you with your work or fellow users to share your interests and problems.

About Compatibility

Do not expect any sort of compatibility between different operating systems. They store disk files in different formats and cannot read one another's disks. Thus you will be wise to choose one operating system and stick to it.

Differences between different *versions* of one operating system are subtler, but they can be significant. A new version of an operating system generally offers features that the older one did not. You may have to get updates to some of your application programs to continue using them with a new version of an operating system. You should investigate this sort of incompatibility before buying a new application program *or* a new version of the operating system you have been using.

MSDOS

PCDOS (what we have referred to as simply DOS throughout this book) is based on MSDOS, an operating system sold by Microsoft and available on many computers that use the Intel 8086/8088 family of CPUs.

MSDOS does not run on the PC, but it is so similar to PCDOS that most programs written under PCDOS can easily be adapted to run under MSDOS, and vice versa.

CP/M-86

CP/M-86 is the second most widely used operating system on the PC. It is a product of Digital Research, Inc.

CP/M-86 is available on many small computers besides the PC. It is derived from CP/M-80, a Digital Research operating system that became the de facto standard operating system on computers with the Intel 8080/8085 family of CPUs, just as PCDOS has become the de facto standard system for the PC.

The wide adoption of CP/M-80 and CP/M-86 has freed this system from many of the disadvantages that come with using an uncommon operating system. CP/M *is* a common operating system, although to date it has seen limited use on the PC. CP/M consultants and users are numerous. Many application programs that run under PCDOS also run under CP/M-86, and many hardware manufacturers support CP/M-86 on the PC.

An early version of CP/M-86 for the PC was marketed for Digital Research by IBM. Digital Research's products are now sold only by Digital Research distributors.

Digital Research produces two versions of CP/M-86 for the PC. One, called simply "CP/M-86," has capabilities very similar to those of PCDOS. The other, called "Concurrent CP/M-86," has many additional features. The most notable feature of the Concurrent CP/M-86 is its ability to run up to four programs at once. You can switch the PC's keyboard and display from one program to another with a single keystroke.

Here is a summary of CP/M-86's major technical advantages over PCDOS:

- *Compatibility with other computers.* To date, PCDOS and MSDOS run only one type of CPU: the Intel 8086/8088 family. The CP/M family of operating systems can run on the Intel 8086/8088 family of CPUs (as CP/M-86), the Intel 8080/8085 family of CPUs (as CP/M-80), and the Motorola 68000 family of CPUs (as CP/M-68K). This compatibility can be important if you want to be able to use several kinds of computers or to move programs from one computer to another.

- *File attributes.* CP/M allows you to assign various attributes to individual files. For example, the read-only attribute protects a file from accidental deletion or change. DOS has no comparable feature.

- *Password protection.* Concurrent CP/M-86 allows you to give password protection to individual files or to entire disks. A password-protected file or disk may be used only by a user who enters that file or disk's password when prompted by CP/M. Thus you can let several people use your PC and yet protect sensitive programs or data from use by unauthorized individuals.

- *HELP command.* CP/M has a command called HELP, which you can use to remind yourself about how to run other CP/M commands. HELP can be a valuable aid to beginning and occasional users of the PC.

- *Graphics support.* CP/M-86 for the PC comes with a feature called the Graphics Extension (GSX). GSX provides a set of software facilities for making graphic images, which application programs can use without concern for the type of device the images are to be drawn on. GSX transforms an application program's instructions into whatever form is required by the output device being used. As distributed by Digital Research, GSX supports about a dozen common graphics output devices.

If you have several graphics programs and several graphics output devices, GSX greatly simplifies the problem of ensuring that all the programs can use all the devices. It is sufficient that all of the programs do their output through GSX and that GSX supports all of the devices. Because DOS has no equivalent of GSX, it makes the compatibility problem much harder to resolve: each graphics program that runs under DOS must support each graphics device directly.

GSX support is a standard feature with "plain" CP/M-86. GSX is not presently supported by Concurrent CP/M-86.

Here is a summary of DOS 2.0's major technical advantages over CP/M-86:

- *Disk space use.* DOS uses disk space more efficiently than CP/M. It allocates space to files in blocks of 512 bytes; CP/M uses blocks of 1K, 2K, or more, depending on the total capacity of the disk.
- *Disk capacity.* A CP/M disk may not hold more than 8M. If you have a hard disk larger than that, it must be divided into two or more virtual disks. DOS places no limit on the size of a disk.
- *Sub-directories.* DOS supports sub-directories, a powerful tool for organizing disk files. CP/M has a similar feature, the "user area," but it is more primitive: each disk is divided into 16 numbered areas that may be used somewhat like sub-directories.
- *Time stamps.* DOS supports time stamps for files. "Plain" CP/M-86 does not support time stamps; Concurrent CP/M-86 does.

Some Other Operating Systems

The UCSD p-System is produced by Softech Microsystems and distributed for the PC by IBM. It supports the programming languages Pascal and FORTRAN. It is described in more detail in the "Programming Languages" section of this chapter.

Oasis 16, from Phase One, is available on a variety of computers with 16-bit CPUs, including the PC. Oasis, a similar system, runs on computers with 8-bit CPUs in the Intel 8080/8085 family.

Oasis 16 has several features that make it easy for programmers to develop sophisticated application programs. This has made it popular among companies that develop complete computer-plus-software packages for specialized applications. A limited selection of general-purpose application software has impeded Oasis's acceptance by other kinds of users.

QNX, by Quantum Software Systems, resembles UNIX, a popular minicomputer operating system originally developed by Bell Telephone Laboratories. To a user, QNX appears virtually identical to UNIX. Many UNIX application programs can be adapted to run under QNX with little effort.

When run on a PC equipped with multiple terminals (that is, keyboards and displays), QNX allows several users to run unrelated programs on the same PC at the same time. QNX also has features similar to but much more powerful than DOS 2.0's redirection and pipes. QNX comes with a much more powerful set of filters and other utility programs than DOS does.

Graphics Packages

Graphics packages may be divided into two types: programming aids that help you create graphics with programs you write yourself, and application programs that you can use to create graphics without writing your own programs.

Programming Aids

Many manufacturers of graphics hardware provide software to help you use their products with DOS. This software varies in quality and power, so you should evaluate these products carefully before deciding what device to buy. Be particularly careful not to end up with two or more graphics devices that have no software compatibility. For example, do not get both a display card with software that will not operate your plotter and a plotter with software that will not operate your display card.

Application Programs

Small-computer graphics is such a new field that no leading products exist yet. The best approach to general-purpose graphics software is to look for a product that meets your needs and accept the risk that in a year or two it may become a white elephant.

Several manufacturers of graphics hardware offer application software for their products as well as programming aids. Most often these application programs take a file generated by some other program, such as a spreadsheet processor or a data base system, and use it to generate standard types of *graphic* output, such as pie charts, bar charts, and line graphs.

Some software firms offer similar application programs that use the data files from their other software products to generate a graphic display of the data. The majority of these programs read the files created by a spreadsheet program. For example, Visi-Corp's VisiTrend/Plot can generate graphs from VisiCalc files and print them on a variety of graphic devices. Sorcim's SuperGraph is a similar program for use with SuperCalc. Software Publishing offers PFS:GRAPH, which works with data entered by PFS:FILE or VisiCorp's VisiCalc.

dGRAPH, by Fox & Geller, can create graphs from dBASE II data base files.

Lotus's 1-2-3 and Context's Context/MBA are two spreadsheet programs that have substantial graphics capabilities built in.

Other Software

Many useful programs do not fall into any of the categories discussed above. This section mentions only a few of them. Consult the software directories listed under the heading "Publications" in Chapter 15 for more listings.

Several *disk copying programs* enable you to make backup copies of the copy-protected diskettes that many software publishers use to distribute their products. Note that none of these programs is likely to work with every copy-protected diskette, or even with every protected copy of a particular program product.

Disk copy programs for DOS include Copy II PC, by Central Point Software; and COPYPC, by Nagy Systems.

Mr. Peter Norton publishes The Norton Utilities, a package of DOS utilities that perform useful functions not included in DOS. One valuable program in this package is UNERASE, which can recover a disk file you have accidentally erased if the space occupied by the file has not yet been reused.

CHAPTER 15

Guide to Services

This chapter looks at some of the more important services available to the IBM PC user. Obtaining the services that you need can be as vitally important as selection of the proper hardware and software products for the PC. The topics in this chapter include, among other things, methods of financing equipment, where to turn for programming help, and where to get repair work done on an ailing system.

Repair

The best time to arrange to have your hardware repaired is before it breaks. Do not wait until something goes wrong to find out where you can have repairs done quickly and reliably.

Types of Repair Service

There are three ways to have your PC repaired. *On-site service* is done by a service person who comes to the PC's location. *Carry-in service* is done at a repair center; you must bring the failing component there (or, if necessary, bring the whole system) and pick it up when it is ready. *Ship-in service* is also done at a repair center; you ship the failing component or system to the center, and it is shipped back to you when it has been fixed.

You can pay for service each time you need it, or, for a fixed fee paid in advance, you can purchase a *maintenance contract* that entitles you to as much service as you need over a period of time (usually one year).

Not all service vendors offer all kinds of service or methods of payment. Carry-in and ship-in service may be offered on contract or on a pay-as-you-go basis. On-site service is usually offered on contract only. Also, most service vendors limit on-site service to a certain geographic area.

Some service vendors swap components instead of repairing them. For example, if one of the adapter cards in your System Unit fails, the repair person may simply exchange the card with a working replacement. When your card is fixed, it will be saved until someone else's PC needs it. Swapping service is most commonly offered by an equipment vendor for equipment that it sold.

Choosing a Mode of Service

The type of service that is best for you depends on your needs. A maintenance contract is likely to cost you more over the long run, but it makes your repair expenses predictable and may get you on-site service if you want it. It may also buy you faster service, since many service vendors give their contract customers priority.

If the warranty period has expired on your PC, your PC will have to pass a precontract inspection before the maintenance contract is issued. If a problem is found, you will have to pay to have it fixed before contract coverage can begin. Thus it is important that you do not delay if you wish to get a service contract. Do it while the system is in good working order.

Carry-in service tends to be more economical, but you must make two trips to the repair center to drop your PC off and pick it up. Ship-in service is likely to be attractive only if you live in such a remote area that carry-in service would take hours of your time.

What To Look For

There are advantages to buying repair service from the firm that sold you your computer. You already know the firm, and it knows you. Its personnel should want to service your equipment quickly and well, since they hope you will buy more equipment from them in the future.

Ask a prospective service vendor how fast it will respond to your calls. Most vendors will not make unconditional promises, but will say something like, "We try to respond to every call within one business day." Ask for references if you want to check out this sort of claim.

On-site maintenance is generally done only during business hours, but some service vendors offer extended service hours for an extra fee. Ask about this if it concerns you.

Consider the location of the vendor's service center(s) and the areas they serve. Must a repair person drive two hours to reach you, or can he or she walk over? If you move to another city, is the service vendor likely to have offices there, or will you have to find a new vendor?

What To Look Out For

If you have any doubt about the skills of a vendor's repair people, inquire about their training. Any computer technician with a repair manual can fix a PC, but one who has been trained by IBM or has taken a rigorous in-house training program is likely to do a better job than most others.

If your system has components not made by IBM, ask the vendor whether it will service them all. Try not to depend on different service vendors to repair different parts of your system; you could get into a "finger pointing" situation where each vendor says your problem is in a component it is not responsible for.

Who Does It

A new PC is covered by a 90-day warranty. During this warranty, you may get free carry-in repair service at any IBM Service Center or authorized IBM PC dealer.

When you buy your PC, you can purchase a nine-month Dealer Service Option that effectively extends the 90-day warranty to one year. After the end of the initial 90-day warranty, you may get service only from the dealer who sold you the Service Option.

At any time before expiration of the 90-day warranty or nine-month Dealer Service Option, you may purchase a 12-month Dealer Service Option that gives you carry-in repair service for a year. This option is renewable indefinitely. If you allow the Service Option to expire, though, the dealer is not obligated to renew it.

Most dealers offer service similar to the Dealer Service Option on all equipment that they sell, whether or not it was made by IBM. Some offer on-site service for an additional fee.

Many firms are in the business of repairing computer equipment, and some of them offer service contracts on the PC and some non-IBM adapter cards and peripherals. National firms offering PC service include Sorbus and RCA. RCA offers on-site service at any site in the United States or Puerto Rico.

Consulting and Contracting Firms

Consulting and contracting firms can provide the expertise you may need to get a computer project off the ground. Some of the services offered by these firms include

- Recommending hardware or software
- Writing or modifying software to meet your exact needs
- Installing software and training you or your employees to use it.

The difference between consulting and contracting is ill-defined, and many firms perform both functions. In general, a consultant tells you what you should do or have done; a contractor does these things for you. For convenience, we will refer to both types of firms as "consulting firms."

Consulting firms come in all sizes, from businesses run by one or two professionals to international companies with thousands of employees. If your project is large, a very small firm may not have the resources to handle it. If your project is small, a very large firm will probably not be interested in it. Within those limits, the size of the firm you use is a matter of taste.

Do You Need a Consultant?

When you consider bringing in a consultant, ask yourself what you need to have done. Can you or your employees afford the time to perform the task in question, including the time required to learn how to perform the task, if this is necessary? If not, a consultant may be the answer.

Discuss your needs with your PC vendor and with experienced computer users. Many new users tend to underestimate the technical difficulty of setting up a computer application, particularly if it involves writing software.

You also need to decide whether you want to run the application yourself once it has been set up or whether you would prefer to have someone else run it for you. For assistance in setting up an application, get a consultant. For long-term assistance, you may get a better bargain by hiring a full-time or part-time employee to do the job.

Choosing a Consultant

Once you are convinced that you require the help of a consultant, you need to do some preparatory work. Consulting firms are not mind readers, nor are they in the miracle business. The more information you can give them about your situation, the more intelligent their proposals and accurate their estimates will be.

Perhaps the most crucial task involved in selecting a consulting firm is the job of defining the problem you want solved. A clear and concise problem definition will not only save you time when you sit down with a prospective consultant to discuss your needs, but will also put you in a better position to decide how knowledgeable the consultant is about the area of your need. If you know what you are looking for, the chances are much better that you will be able to recognize firms that cannot deliver it.

When defining your problem, try to devise a standard for judging when the consultant's work has been completed in a satisfactory way. Performance objectives make the best standards. If you need an accounting system, for example, your standard might be something like this: "My bookkeeper will be able to use the system to manage all of my company's financial affairs and prepare a specified set of reports on each month's activity by the sixth working day of the following month. At any time I will be able to get reports on the preceding twelve months' activity in a format helpful for planning my budget over the next year."

Once you have defined your objectives, interview at least one consulting firm. For a major project, you will probably want to interview several. Show the representative of each firm what your problem is and discuss the firm's approach to solving it. In this process you should learn several things:

- How qualified is this firm to do the job? Has the firm had prior experience with this kind of computer application? Does the firm have any specialized knowledge outside the computer field, such as accounting or engineering, that the application will require?

- How long does each firm expect the project to take? How much will it cost?

- Do you trust this firm to do the work competently and efficiently and to be honest in its dealings with you?

- Are you and your employees comfortable with this firm's working style?

- Is your own assessment of the project realistic? If three consultants agree that a job you hoped to have done in two weeks will actually take six months to a year, you probably need to reassess your own analysis.

Get references from each firm you interview, and check them. You are unlikely to get derogatory information from the clients a firm chooses to give as references, but you can find out a lot about how the firm works and whether its background and interests really meet your needs.

Eliminate any firms you consider unsuitable. Ask some or all of the rest to submit a proposal. The proposal may be long or short, formal or informal, depending on the needs of the project. It should be in writing, and it should answer the following questions:

- Who will work on the project? Where and when will the work be done?

- What will be done? How will project completion be defined?

- How will the consulting firm's fee be computed? About how long will the project take and how much will it cost?

When interviews are complete and proposals have been submitted, you should have sufficient information to select a consultant and start the project.

During the Project

Stay in touch with the consulting firm during the project. If the consultants lose sight of your objectives or do unsatisfactory work, it is in your interest to know about it as promptly as possible.

The most important thing you can do as the project progresses is to keep the communication channels open. Consultants cannot work in a vacuum. You and your employees have more detailed knowledge of your needs and habits than consultants can possibly have. The consultants need your suggestions, answers, and feedback to do work that really meets your needs.

What To Look Out For

Computer consultants are not licensed the way attorneys, accountants, and many other professionals are. The computer field is so diverse and changes so fast that licensing is impractical; there is no generally accepted body of knowledge that could be used to define a competent consultant. You must judge the competence of each individual and firm for yourself.

Be wary of people who claim to have all the answers, sometimes before hearing the questions. Many types of projects are hard to estimate accurately—particularly ones that involve programming. If several consultants decline to offer you a guaranteed cost or completion date, the one who does may be the one to watch out for.

Also be wary of unusually low time and cost estimates. The lowest bid may not be the best bargain. A very low bid may come from a firm that does not really understand your problem or from one that is desperate for work and does not honestly expect to do your job for the amount promised.

The computer consulting field attracts technically oriented people who are often not as comfortable dealing with people as they are dealing with machines. But it is essential that a consultant be able to get along with you and your employees, understand your problems, and explain technical issues so that nontechnical people can understand them. Look for these abilities in the people who will be doing the actual consulting work.

Who Does It

Most computer consultants are listed in the telephone directory, usually under a heading such as "Data Processing Service."

A good source of consultants is a recommendation by a business associate whose judgment you trust. If a consulting firm has done good work for someone in the same business as you, you know it has some experience with the customs and problems of your own field.

Your computer vendor may also be able to help. Many vendors know consultants who have done good work for them or their customers in the past and will refer you to several as a courtesy to you.

If you need assistance with a particular software product, try contacting the producer of that product. Some software firms maintain referral lists of qualified consultants.

The Independent Computer Consultants' Association (ICCA), a national professional organization, operates a client referral service for its members. If you send it a brief description of your needs, it will provide a list of members who claim appropriate qualifications, or it will refer you to a local ICCA chapter for such a list. There is no charge for this service.

Information Utilities

An *information utility* uses a large computer to offer information and information-based services to the public. You can connect your PC to an information utility through the telephone system. You will need a modem to transmit and receive data over the phone. (See the discussion of modems in Chapter 13, "Guide to Hardware.")

Information utilities are of three types:

- *Specialized commercial utilities* provide information and other services in specific fields such as law, medicine, finance, and agriculture. They tend to be quite expensive.

- *General commercial utilities* provide information and services of general interest to business and professional people. They tend to be moderately expensive.

- *Personal utilities* provide information and services to the general public. They tend to be economical (under $10 per hour of use). Many of them are not available during business hours because they share equipment that is used by commercial utilities.

Most information utilities are accessible through *communications networks* that let you connect to the computer from most urban areas in the United States for a low hourly fee or at no charge. If you live in an area that does not have a communications network available, you will have to pay for the long-distance phone call as well.

Services Available

Information utilities tend to respond to the market. If a service is wanted by a sufficient number of people, it will soon become available.

One popular group of services involves communications. With *electronic mail*, you can send a message to another person by signing onto the utility, naming the addressee, and typing in the message. When the addressee later signs onto the utility, it displays a notice that "You have mail." The text of all waiting messages can then be viewed at the user's leisure.

Electronic mail has several advantages over both conventional mail and the telephone: first, it can deliver a message instantaneously; second, it gives the addressee a computer-readable copy of the message; and third, it does not depend on someone being near the telephone and free to talk when you send a message.

Another variety of communications is the *electronic bulletin board*, which enables you to "post" a message that any other interested user may read. Many information utilities maintain several bulletin boards for different purposes, such as buying and selling personal property, exchanging gossip about computers and other topics, announcing events, and putting people with common interests in touch with each other.

The flexibility of computers makes many other kinds of communication possible. In *computer conferencing*, for example, you can exchange messages with everyone else in a group of users as though you all were in a conference room. Some services permit you to send Mailgrams and telex messages from your computer, enabling you to communicate with people who are not information utility users themselves.

Information retrieval is another common use for information utilities. Many commercial and personal information utilities have data bases that you can query for information on news events, weather, the stock market, and other topics of general interest. Many specialized commercial services are devoted entirely to this kind of use.

Most information retrieval services have features for automatic data base searching. For example, you could command a service's computer to search a data base of current newspaper and magazine articles for any article that contains the phrase "solar energy" and either of the words "Congress" or "President."

Some information utilities can be used for writing or running computer programs. Since you can run programs for free on your PC, you may never need this service. It is valuable if you want to run large programs or process large amounts of data that will not fit on a computer the size of the PC.

Information Utilities and Your PC

You can use most of the information utilities with a computer terminal alone, but your PC enables you to use these services more effectively. For example, you can use an electronic mail service by composing a message on your PC and then transmitting it in finished form. When you receive a message, you can transfer it to your PC's disk to read, print, or modify at your leisure.

You may be able to take data obtained from an information utility and use it with various application programs on your PC to produce results that you could not get from the utility alone. Several spreadsheet programs, for example, process data that is transferred to your PC from the financial or economic data bases of various information utilities.

Who Has Them

Most specialized commercial utilities are promoted only among the industries that they are intended to serve. You can find out about such specialized utilities through professional organizations and periodicals.

General commercial utilities offering information retrieval services include BRS, with many data bases on science, medicine, and education; Dialog Information Services, with data bases on science, government, and the contents of many newspapers and magazines; CompuServe, with general business information and data bases on stocks and commodities; Dow Jones News/Retrieval, with general business information, data bases on stocks, detailed financial data bases, and general news; and NewsNet, with the full text of many independently published newsletters in a variety of high-technology fields.

Many of the general commercial utilities offer services tailored for personal use as well. Such services are usually restricted to nonbusiness hours and, in some cases, do not offer access to all of the utility's data bases. Utilities offering these types of services include BRS (under the name BRS After Dark), Dialog (under the name Knowledge Index), and CompuServe.

Source Telecomputing offers services aimed primarily at personal users. It includes data bases on government activities and current information from United Press International.

Among spreadsheet programs, Context/MBA can fetch financial information directly from the Dow Jones News/Retrieval service. (Contact Context Management Systems for information.) VisiCorp's VisiCalc can operate on information transferred from several economic data bases maintained by Data Resources, Inc. (Contact VisiCorp for information.)

Communications services such as bulletin boards and electronic mail are offered by BRS, Source Telecomputing, and CompuServe. Source Telecomputing has an electronic mail system that can be used to send Mailgrams. Many local bulletin boards are operated by companies, computer clubs, and individuals, either for profit or as a public service. Lists of bulletin boards are published periodically in the magazine *PC World*. Many bulletin boards offer directories of other bulletin boards.

General computing services, which are used for writing and running computer programs, are available on CompuServe and Source Telecomputing.

Typesetting From Text Files

If you use your PC to write material that must later be typeset, there are several advantages in employing a typographer who can work with your files instead of with printed copy. By eliminating the step of keying in your text on a typesetting machine, you can get faster and more economical service. You can also get more accurate results that require less proofreading, since the content of the typeset copy should be correct if the content of your original text file was correct.

A typographer may accept text files either on PC diskettes or over the telephone via modem or both. Most computer typographers offer you a choice of several predefined file formats. You must include special typographic codes in your text file to change the typeface, indent a margin, and so forth. For complex material like tables, the typographer usually must insert the codes for you.

Typographers who can accept computer files now exist in most large cities. Check your telephone directory under "Typesetting."

Financing Computer Equipment

There are several ways you can finance a major piece of computer equipment for use in your business. The most appropriate type of financing for you will depend on your taxes and financial situation.

Ways to Finance Equipment

The simplest way to obtain equipment is by *outright purchase:* paying for the equipment with your own money or with borrowed money.

A common alternative to outright purchase is a *lease.* A bank or leasing institution purchases the equipment. You agree to make certain payments over a specified period of time, most often two or three years, in return for the right to use the equipment. At the end of the lease, the lessor may take the equipment back but will usually agree to sell it to you for a small sum. A *lease-purchase* is a lease in which the lessor agrees in advance that you can buy the equipment at the end of the lease for a specified sum, usually no more than the equivalent of a couple of monthly payments.

An alternative to buying or leasing equipment is *rental.* You agree to make periodic payments for the use of the equipment, but you are free to return it to its owner at any time. You may be able to apply a portion of your rental payments toward purchase if you choose to buy the equipment instead of returning it.

Factors That Affect Financing

The first factor to consider in selecting a method of financing is *current cost.* How much must you pay when you get the equipment? Can you afford the expense? What effect will it have on your financial position?

Another factor is *future cost.* How much must you pay during the time you have the equipment, and when must you pay it? Is it worth your while to defer payment to a time when you hope to have more money, even if you must pay more in the long run?

The current and future costs of a lease are generally close to those of an outright purchase with a loan. The costs of rental are usually far greater than the cost of a lease. Rental is likely to be attractive only if you are fairly sure that you will not need the equipment for long, or if the owner offers a generous credit toward purchase.

Another factor to consider is the effect of financing on your income tax. Can you *deduct* the cost of using the equipment in the year you incur it, or must you *depreciate* the cost over the equipment's useful life?

The cost of an outright purchase of computer equipment must be depreciated over several years. This defers some of the tax benefits until long after you have spent the money. If you take out a loan to make the purchase, the cost of the loan (that is, the interest you pay) can be deducted in each year that the cost is incurred.

Equipment purchases may be eligible for an *investment tax credit* (ITC), which allows you to subtract a percentage of the cost of the equipment directly from your taxes (*not* from your income used to compute the taxes). This deduction is taken in the year of the purchase. If you rent or lease equipment, on the other hand, you can deduct the full cost of the payments in each year that you incur this expense. However, you cannot claim the investment tax credit since you are not purchasing the equipment. Thus if you have a fairly low income, the worth of the investment tax credit and the ability to defer some of your deductions until future years (when your income might be higher and the deduction will mean more) might tilt the balance in favor of an outright purchase of equipment. On the other hand, leasing or renting might be the best route if you are in a higher tax bracket.

There is no simple way to decide which type of financing is best for you. You must consider the effect of each type of financing on your financial position and your taxes. Businesses often spend thousands of dollars to determine the best method of financing a large equipment purchase. For a purchase worth a few thousand dollars, a rough estimate is sufficient. Consult your accountant or tax adviser for more information.

Who Finances Equipment

Any bank or other institution that makes capital equipment loans is a potential source of financing for a computer purchase. Banks generally will not write leases for small computers, feeling that the cost of the paperwork exceeds the value of the business.

Many computer vendors will lease equipment or will arrange loans or leases when you purchase equipment from them. Evaluate their offers carefully; their terms vary widely. Do not agree to unfavorable lease terms if you can do better with another vendor or another kind of financing.

You may get the best deal by finding a lessor of your own. Many firms lease business equipment this way, but only a few of them will consider transactions as small as a few thousand dollars, and many of them will lease only to governments and corporations. FLC Financial Services is one equipment lessor that will make leases on small purchases and will deal with small businesses. You may locate other such firms by talking to a person with connections in your local financial community, such as your banker, attorney, or accountant.

Companies that will rent you PC systems and peripherals include RCA Service Company, Rent-a-Computer, and United States Data Systems. Rent-a-Computer has offices only in the San Francisco area but will ship to major corporate renters anywhere in the United States.

Insurance for Your PC

Your PC and data are valuable, and damage to them could have serious consequences for your business. You owe it to yourself to insure them adequately.

If you use your PC at home, it may not be covered by your homeowner's or tenant's policy. Such policies generally exclude equipment used in business. Consult your insurance agent; you may be able to extend your policy to cover business equipment, or you may need to buy a separate commercial policy.

If you use your PC in an office but occasionally bring it home, it may not be covered by your commercial insurance while it is in your home. Most commercial policies cover only equipment located at specified sites or in transit. List your home on the policy as a covered location, or make other provisions for home coverage.

Insurance policies exclude many kinds of damage, and some of the exclusions expose your PC to significant risks. The most notable example is damage by an electrical disturbance. Many business policies exclude such damage unless caused by lightning. If an electrical surge caused extensive damage to your PC, such a policy would not cover your loss.

Other common exclusions are damage from malfunctioning plumbing, flood, earthquake, and corrosion caused by humidity or air pollution. Many insurers will extend a policy to cover such risks for an additional fee.

Do not neglect to insure your data. Most policies will compensate you only for the value of your diskettes or other recording media. The information on the media is not covered, although it is of far greater value.

Extra-expense insurance compensates you for the cost of reconstructing and reentering lost data, but it will not compensate you for the value of lost data that *cannot* be replaced. If you feel a need to insure irreplaceable data, get *valuable papers insurance.* To help assure that you are adequately covered, list the items you are insuring and assign a cash value to each one when the policy is written.

You can also get *business interruption insurance,* which compensates you for loss of business income caused by damage to your PC or your data.

One of the best ways to protect your valuable data against loss is to keep a copy of it in a secure place: a safe deposit box or an office in another building. This makes it very unlikely that one incident will destroy every copy of your data.

Many insurance companies are now offering policies that accommodate the needs of small-computer users. Columbia National General Agency and Personal Computer Insurance are two insurance agencies that offer special lines of small-computer insurance. Your insurance agent will have more information.

Publications

Even in this age of electronic communication, one of the best ways of obtaining knowledge about a given subject is through the written word. Books, for example, can explore subjects in greater depth than other sources, while periodicals can present a broad spectrum of information on topics of current interest. In this section, we will look at the various types of publications available for the PC user.

Books

Hundreds of books about the IBM PC and related topics are in print, and more are being published all the time. You can find them in large bookstores and in computer and software stores.

Osborne/McGraw-Hill publishes a series of *Made Easy* books, of which this book is one. Some of the other books in the series address leading software products, such as WordStar, VisiCalc, and SuperCalc.

Periodicals

Several periodicals are published especially for PC users. The two most prominent ones are *PC* and *PC World*. Both contain product reviews, "how to" articles, technical articles, computer programs, news, and advertisements.

Softalk for the IBM Personal Computer, a product of Softalk Publishing, is written more specifically for nontechnical users. You can get a one-year complimentary subscription if you send in your PC's serial number.

Many other magazines serve the small-computer world at large. You can find many of them at computer stores and software stores.

Several weekly and biweekly newspapers serve the general computer community. Two prominent ones are *Computerworld*, oriented mainly toward data processing professionals, and *Info-World*, oriented toward users of small computers with an interest in computer technology or the computer industry.

Some software firms publish periodic newsletters about their products. These contain news and updates, application hints, and information about software problems. These firms include Ashton-Tate (for dBASE II users), Digital Research, Inc. (for CP/M-80 and CP/M-86 users), and Sorcim (for SuperCalc users). Most of these newsletters are free to licensed users.

A newsletter for VisiCalc users called *SATN* is published by SATN Subscriptions. SATN is affiliated with Software Arts, Visi-Calc's original developer.

Directories

Several firms publish directories of PC accessories and other useful products. Some of these include evaluations that will help you choose a product to buy.

One popular directory is the *IBM PC Expansion and Software Guide* by DeVoney, Cobb, and Turenko, published by Que Corporation. It gives brief descriptions of over 2200 programs and hardware products, along with system requirements and the name and address of each supplier.

PC Clearinghouse Software Directory, published by PC Clearinghouse, is a very complete directory of software for all types of personal computers, not just the IBM PC. Most of its information is in tabular form, without text descriptions.

IBM publishes a periodical directory of PC products that it sells, including software developed by other firms and sold through IBM. This directory, called *The Guide to Personal Computer Offerings from IBM*, is available through IBM Product Centers and dealers.

PC World publishes periodic software and hardware guide issues. *LIST* publishes a periodic directory of microcomputer software, much of which runs on the PC. This directory includes many articles of practical use to computer users who are not technically oriented.

IBM User's Manuals

IBM publishes a series of manuals about the PC itself and about PCDOS. Table 15-1 lists these manuals.

Guide to Operations is the central manual in IBM's PC library. It comes with each PC and gives you basic instructions for setting

IBM publication	IBM part no.	Of interest to
BASIC (DOS 1.1)	6025010	Programmers using DOS, particularly but not exclusively those using BASIC
BASIC (DOS 2.0)	6025010*	
Disk Operating System (DOS 1.1)	6024001**	Programmers & users of DOS
Disk Operating System (DOS 2.0)	6024061**	
Guide to Operations	6025000	All users
Guide to Operations Personal Computer XT	6936810	
Technical Reference (IBM PC)	6025005	Programmers and hardware designers
Technical Reference (IBM PC XT)	6936808	Programmers and hardware designers
Programming languages and other program products	various	Users of each program product

* Manual is accompanied by update sheets for DOS 2.0.
** Manual is sold only with program.

Table 15-1.
IBM PC and DOS Manuals

up and operating the PC and the IBM Matrix Printer. The "Problem Determination Procedures" (PDPs) section contains detailed procedures for diagnosing problems with your PC's hardware. The "Options" section has space for the reference manuals accompanying the adapter cards that are installed in your PC or that may be added to it later.

The *BASIC* manual also comes with the PC and contains information about the BASIC programming language. It is an important reference manual if you plan to write programs for your PC in BASIC. If you plan to write programs for your PC in another language, you will also find the *BASIC* manual useful, since it contains a lot of information about how a computer program can use the PC's features.

The *Disk Operating System* manual comes with DOS. It describes DOS commands and application programs packaged with DOS. The manual's appendixes contain technical information of interest to programmers.

The *Technical Reference* manual contains information of interest to programmers and to hardware engineers who want to modify the PC or design accessories for it.

Other IBM manuals describe software products such as the FORTRAN, COBOL, and Pascal compilers. Each manual is packaged with the software product it describes.

User Groups

A *user group* is an organization of computer users with common interests. Most urban areas in the United States now have at least one user group for owners of the IBM PC.

User groups have anywhere from a dozen to several hundred members. Typically, they charge between $20 and $30 a year for membership, publish a monthly newsletter, and meet one evening a month.

Joining a user group can give you the following benefits:

- You will have a place to make personal contact with other users of the PC. Some will be more experienced users who can help you with your problems. Others will have the same interests and problems as yourself, and so will have valuable experiences to share.

- You will hear gossip and rumors that might be important from people who have wide connections in the PC industry.
- You will have access to a library of public-domain programs that many groups collect for their members' use.
- In large groups, you may be able to join subgroups in areas of special interest, such as communications or programming.
- You can save money by participating in group purchases of hardware, software, and supplies. The group's bargaining power enables it to buy products at a substantial discount.

PC and *PC World* periodically print directories of PC user groups. Local PC dealers and software dealers may also be able to tell you about groups in your area.

Many user groups form around areas of interest other than the PC. CP/M groups exist in many areas. There are also groups devoted to particular application programs.

CHAPTER 16

Guide to Accessories

The broad term "accessory" refers to any product that makes the PC more powerful or easier to use. Many common accessories were discussed in Chapter 13, "Guide to Hardware." In this chapter we will look at some accessories that may be a little less common but that can greatly enhance the PC.

Printer Accessories

The printer accessories discussed in this section are divided into three main categories: electronic products that are connected to the computer on one end and the printer on the other, mechanical items that assist in physical tasks like feeding paper to the printer, and other miscellaneous accessories that facilitate the task of working with a printer. See the section on printers in Chapter 13 for more information about these devices.

Electronic Printer Accessories

A *printer buffer* is connected to your PC on one end and to the printer on the other. It can temporarily store extra characters when the PC writes data faster than the printer can print. The buffer lets you finish printing a job and go on to other work while the printer catches up. Thus it is similar in function to a RAM card with print spooling software.

A *parallel-serial converter* takes output from your PC's parallel printer interface and converts it to feed a printer with a serial interface. This lets you use a serial-interface printer without having an Asynchronous Communications Adapter in your PC.

A *peripheral switch* lets you switch your PC back and forth between two or more devices: for example, between a letter-quality printer and a dot-matrix printer, or between a serial-interface printer and a modem. Turned the other way, it can switch one device back and forth between two or more computers.

A 25-wire peripheral switch, sold for use with the RS-232C devices, can be used with the PC and with either serial or parallel interface devices (although not both on the same switch). Use a 25-wire *straight cable* (every pin on one plug connected to the same pin on the other) between the PC and the switch. Use your usual device cable between the switch and each device.

Mechanical Printer Accessories

Many printers have no built-in tractor but accept one as an accessory. Most letter-quality printers are built this way.

Some tractors are *bidirectional:* that is, they can feed the paper backward as well as forward. Others are *unidirectional.* Bidirectional tractors are more expensive and a little harder to load, but they are more versatile and feed paper more smoothly than unidirectional tractors.

A *sheet feeder* automatically feeds sheets of cut paper into a letter-quality printer. It is useful for printing long runs of personalized letters, using paper with your company letterhead if desired. Sophisticated sheet feeders can also feed separate second-page paper stock or envelopes.

CAUTION

Sheet feeders are frequently unreliable and hard to adjust. If you want one, give it a real-life test before you buy.

Other Printer Accessories

Printer stands are of two types. One type is a platform that sits on a table and supports a small dot-matrix printer. A stack of pin-feed paper a few inches high may be placed underneath it.

The other type of printer stand is a piece of furniture that supports a large printer at a convenient height. The printer may be fed paper from a box placed under or behind the stand. Most stands have a basket or tray that stacks the paper after it is printed.

A *sound cover* encloses a printer and muffles the noise it makes when printing. It can be particularly useful with letter quality printers, which tend to be noisy. Some printer stands have sound covers built in.

A *sound absorbing mat* muffles sound that emanates from the bottom of a printer. It is less effective than a sound cover but also costs much less and does not obstruct the printer's controls. It can be particularly useful if the printer rests on a surface that acts like a sounding board.

Who Makes Them

Printer buffers are made by Quadram. A similar device is produced by Apparat in the form of an adapter card.

Parallel-serial converters for several types of serial printers are made by Renaissance Technology.

Peripheral switch makers include Giltronix. Such switches are also sold under house brand names by many computer supply dealers. Giltronix and Tecmar also make peripheral switches that are controlled by software.

Tractors and sheet feeders for a printer are generally made by the manufacturer of the printer.

Printer stands, sound covers, sound absorbing mats, and similar printer accessories are sold by many computer supply firms.

Antistatic Devices

Some of the components in your computer are quite sensitive to static electricity. A static spark can disrupt the operation of your computer, destroy data, and sometimes damage the electronics.

You can get several types of antistatic devices to help deal with this problem. An *antistatic rug* can be installed near your computer over bare floor or carpet. As you walk across it, it disperses the static electricity in your body instead of charging you up.

An *antistatic mat* under your chair performs the same function as you work. The mat is made of a hard plastic material.

You can use *antistatic spray* to add some static protection to existing carpet or tile floor surfaces. The spray is available in both aerosol and plunger spray containers. It is claimed to be nontoxic and nonflammable.

All of these products are available from computer supply firms.

Power Conditioners

As Chapter 11 ("Caring for Your PC") noted, surges and interruptions in the line power can do serious damage to your PC.

Types of Power Problems

There are several types of power-related problems that can damage your PC. Most power conditioners protect against only one or two of these problems. To make an informed decision about the type of protection you want, you must understand what kinds of power problems can occur.

Noise is a signal superimposed on the line power's regular waveform. It can come from radio transmitters, audio equipment, or electrical devices like motors.

A *spike* is a very brief increase in voltage. It lasts only a fraction of a cycle but may peak at 500 volts or more. A *fault* is the reverse of a spike: a very brief decrease in voltage, sometimes down to zero. Spikes and faults occur when a reactive device, like a large electric motor, is turned on or off.

A *surge* is an increase in voltage that lasts, at most, a few cycles. A *dip* is a decrease in voltage that lasts a few cycles. Surges and dips are seldom as intense as spikes and faults, but their longer duration can make them dangerous. They can be caused by any sudden change in electrical load.

A *brownout* is a moderate decrease in voltage that may last as long as several days. It is caused by a demand for power that exceeds the electrical utility's capacity to deliver it at full voltage.

A *blackout* is a complete interruption of power that lasts for any period longer than a few electrical cycles.

The PC's power supply is capable of absorbing most noise, spikes, and faults. It can run on voltage as low as 104 volts, giving the PC protection against most brownouts. It is even capable of carrying the PC through blackouts that last no more than a fraction of a second. If the power in your area is very "dirty," though, you may want the extra protection that a power conditioner can give you. Also, your peripherals may be more sensitive to bad power than the PC is.

Types of Power Conditioners

The characteristics of the major types of power conditioners are summarized in Table 16-1.

A *surge protector* is an inexpensive device that clips voltage surges and spikes to a safe level. It generally provides significant protection against noise.

A *line conditioner* uses an electronically controlled transformer to regulate line voltage. It responds to brownouts, surges, and dips by adjusting the transformer to deliver a constant voltage. Depending on the type of control used, it may or may not respond quickly enough to protect against spikes and faults.

Type of problem	Noise	Spikes	Faults	Surges	Dips	Brown-outs	Black-outs	Typical cost
Effect of surge protector	OK	OK	None	OK	None	None	None	$60-$120
Effect of line conditioner	OK	OK	OK	OK	OK	OK	None	$500-$1000,
Effect of standby power system	None	None	None	None	None	A few minutes	A few minutes	$400 up
Effect of uninterruptible power system (UPS)	OK	OK	OK	OK	OK	OK	Depends on load & battery	$400 up
Effect of motor-generator	OK	OK	OK	OK	OK	OK	A few seconds	n/a
Effect of emergency power generator	None	None	None	None	None	None	Needs time to start	n/a

Table 16-1.
Characteristics of Power Devices

A *motor-generator* uses an electric motor to drive an electric generator, which powers the computer. This device protects the computer from noise, spikes, faults, surges, dips, and blackouts that last no longer than a second or so. Motor-generators are generally "overkill" for the PC, since the PC is too robust to need the very high quality of power that they provide, and even the smallest motor-generators are designed to deliver several kilowatts of power.

A *standby power system* contains a battery and a power inverter that step in to power your computer within a fraction of a cycle if the line voltage drops below a safe level. It can deliver power for several minutes, which is plenty of time to halt your work in an orderly way and turn your PC off.

An *uninterruptable power system* (UPS) is similar to a standby power system, but provides protection against problems like surges and spikes in addition to providing backup power in case of a blackout.

An *emergency power generator* is driven by a gasoline or diesel engine, and so can supply power indefinitely. Since generators that put out "computer-quality" power are made for large computers and are fairly costly, an emergency power generator is not a very practical accessory for the PC.

Who Makes Them

Makers of surge protectors include ICO-RALLY, Panamax, RKS Industries, and SGL Waber. These devices are also sold by many computer supply firms under house brand names.

Makers of small line conditioners include Elgar, Gould, and Sola.

Makers of small-computer standby power systems and UPSs include Control Technology, Cuesta Systems, Elgar, Gould, RKS Industries, SAFT, and Sola.

Power Analyzers

If you are having puzzling problems that you suspect are related to line power, you may wish to get a *power line monitor* to check out your suspicions. A good power line monitor does more than show you whether you have a problem; it tells you what sort of problem you have and when it occurs.

Modern power line monitors record power variations so that you can monitor the power over a period of days and review the results at your leisure. The most popular analyzer is the Dranetz Model 626. It costs several thousand dollars and so is not a reasonable accessory for a PC, but you can rent it from electronic equipment rental companies like United States Instrument Rental. To be useful, the results of a power analyzer should be interpreted by a person familiar with electrical problems and power conditioner technology.

Computer Furniture

If you or your employees will spend a lot of time using your PC, the desk, chair, and lighting you use will have a significant effect on comfort and even health. Poorly designed furniture and poor lighting can cause a variety of troubles, including headaches, eyestrain, fatigue, neck and back complaints, and muscle strain.

Most European countries and some American states have laws governing the sort of furniture that must be provided to people who use computers on the job.

Many office furniture manufacturers have products designed to make a computer user's job more comfortable. Such furniture is advertised as "ergonomically designed." This term is derived from *ergonomics*, the study of how the properties of the human body affect the design of tools and equipment used in work.

The Ideal Working Posture

Figure 16-1 shows the ideal posture for using a computer. You sit with your back vertical and your upper legs horizontal. Your feet are flat on the floor. Your lower legs may be vertical or pushed slightly forward, as you prefer.

Your upper arms should be vertical; your lower arms should be approximately horizontal. There should be a space in front of the keyboard where you can rest your wrists when your arms get tired.

You should tilt your head 15 to 20 degrees below horizontal to view the display screen. Your line of sight should be roughly at right angles to the screen.

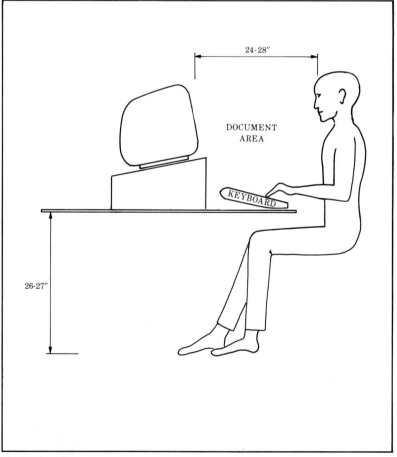

Figure 16-1.
The ideal working position for using a computer

Computer Chairs

Since people come in different sizes and shapes, most computer furniture is designed to adapt to different users' bodies.

A good computer chair has adjustable seat height, back rest height, and back tilt. If the back is spring-mounted, the spring's tension should be adjustable.

The simplest type of chair adjustment is a friction clamp. To adjust the chair, you release a lever or knob that holds it in one position. After making the adjustment you tighten the control, locking the chair in its new position.

Many expensive chairs have a pneumatic control for the seat height adjustment. A gas cylinder supports the weight of the chair so that you can adjust its height with one hand, even while sitting in it. Pneumatic control can be a valuable convenience, since you can easily vary your seat's adjustment as you work. Many ergonomics experts think that being able to adjust the seat from time to time is an important factor in user comfort.

Other characteristics of a good computer chair are a swivel seat, a firm upholstered seat and back rest (to give you effective support but prevent you from slipping out of a good position), and a five-footed base, which is more stable than the four-footed base used on less expensive chairs.

Desks

High-quality computer desks are adjustable. The most common adjustment is keyboard height. Some desks have a support for the display unit that is higher than the keyboard area and that may also be adjustable. Some desks have tilting and turning controls for the display.

Desks, like chairs, are available with friction and pneumatic adjustments. Some desks use a crank adjustment. The most expensive type of control, rarely found in general-purpose computer desks, is electrical.

Other features found on computer desks include special drawers or shelves for computer supplies, under-surface space for computer components like the PC System Unit, and channels for running power and data cables out of sight.

A *work station* is a small desk with just enough surface space for some papers and a terminal or small computer. It has little or no under-surface storage. A work station is suitable for computer activities that involve little or no desk work, such as data entry.

Some companies offer modular desks and work stations. You can buy the frame and storage components you want and assemble them into a customized piece of furniture. If your needs change, you can buy new components and rebuild the furniture as you please.

Who Makes It

Makers of computer furniture include Computer Mate, Dennison National (media storage furniture and supplies), Dennison Monarch (work stations, equipment stands, and related equipment), Tab Products, and Wright Line.

Computer furniture is available at many office furniture stores. It is also sold by most computer supply firms, usually under house brand names.

Williams and Foltz makes a line of high-quality solid oak computer furniture suitable for executive offices and homes. The units can be broken down for moving and can be modified as your needs change.

A Note on Lighting

Good lighting is as important an ergonomic factor as good furniture.

There are three types of light that affect your use of the PC: light on your workspace, general room light, and light reflecting off the screen of your display.

Your workspace light should be bright enough for easy reading, but not so bright that it causes eyestrain or overpowers the image on your PC's display. The light source should not cast heavy shadows on the working surface or create distracting reflections from shiny objects. Large reflector lamps make good light sources. Fluorescent lamps are also good if you like the quality of light they produce.

General room lighting should ideally be somewhat dimmer than the workspace lighting. You should be able to rest your eyes by glancing up from your workspace to the area in front of it. If the room lighting is too dim, however, the contrast between the brightness of your workspace and the background will cause eyestrain.

Arrange your workspace and room lighting to avoid bright reflections off the screen of your display. Tilting or shading the screen may help you shield it from particular sources of light, such as overhead light fixtures and windows. Do not keep the screen in darkness, though, because some reflected light is necessary to keep the image contrast low enough to prevent eyestrain.

Monitor Accessories

The glare and reflections of bright lights or sunlight on your PC's screen may be reduced with a *glare filter*. This is a sheet of polarized material that fits over the surface of the screen. Glare filters are available at many computer stores and from computer supply firms such as Inmac and Misco.

If you do a lot of data input, you may find use for a *copy holder*. It sits next to your keyboard and holds documents upright for easier viewing. Most copy holders have a *line guide* that you can move up and down to mark your place in the document. Some have a motorized line guide that you can advance with a foot pedal, so that you need not take your hands off the keyboard. Copy holders are available from most computer supply firms.

The *PC Pedestal*, a product of Curtis Manufacturing Company, holds the IBM Monochrome Display or Color/Graphics Monitor at a convenient height above a desk top and allows you to tilt it to the angle you find most comfortable. With your display on the Pedestal you can move the PC System Unit off your desk top, freeing more working space on the desk. Curtis also sells extension cables for the keyboard and display, permitting you to move the System Unit several feet away from your work place. A similar device is available from Inmac.

Antitheft Devices

If your PC is in a location that exposes it to theft, you may wish to purchase a device to prevent it from being removed.

One company that makes such devices is Anchor Pad International. The product fastens a PC, printer, or other device to a work surface so that it cannot be moved without a key.

CHAPTER 17

Guide to Supplies

This chapter discusses all the consumable materials that you may use with your PC, such as diskettes and printer paper. It will tell you what varieties of supplies are available, where you can get them, and how to be sure you get what you need.

Diskettes

Many different kinds of diskettes are available today. To get reliable performance, you must buy the right kind of diskettes for your diskette drives.

The major differences among types of diskettes are

- *Size.* IBM diskette drives and compatible drives use 5 1/4-inch diskettes.

- *Sectors.* This term refers to the way a computer detects the position of a rotating disk and finds the beginning of each track of data. IBM drives require *soft-sectored* diskettes.

- *Density.* This refers to the amount of data a diskette can record reliably on one track. For IBM diskette drives and compatible drives, buy double-density diskettes.

  Single-density diskettes work in the PC's drives, but may not perform reliably. Quad-density diskettes work as well as double-density, but with the PC's drives they are unnecessary, and they cost more.

- *Number of sides.* If you have double-sided diskette drives, you will usually want to format double-sided diskettes. Thus you should buy only double-sided diskettes.

  Single-sided diskettes have recording material on both sides, and so can be formatted as though they were double-sided diskettes, but this practice is *not recommended.* Many single-sided diskettes are not properly finished on the reverse recording surface, and will damage your drive's read/write head if formatted as double-sided diskettes.

If you have single-sided drives, buy single-sided diskettes. Double-sided diskettes work equally well, but cost more.

Diskettes are listed in many supply catalogs as *flexible disks.* They are generally sold in boxes of ten. Many computer supply stores will give you a discount if you order several boxes at once.

What To Look For

Buy the highest quality diskettes you can. When you consider the potential cost of losing data, the money you save by buying cheap diskettes is a foolish economy.

Manufacturers of high-quality diskettes test every diskette for errors. Avoid brands that only check samples.

Look for a reinforcing ring around the hub hole in the center of the diskette (see Figure 17-1). This ring is an important factor in diskette life. Many diskettes fail because the hub hole becomes torn or bent, not because the surface of the diskette wears out.

Figure 17-1.
Diskette with reinforcing hub ring

Manufacturer	Single-sided part no.	Double-sided part no.
Dysan	104/1D	104/2D
IBM	6023451	6023450
Maxell	MD1	MD2-D
Memorex	32013417	32013421
3M (Scotch)	744-0	745-0
Verbatim	MD525-01	MD550-01

Table 17-1.
PC-Compatible Diskettes

Many manufacturers claim that their diskettes derive extra reliability and longer life from special dust-absorbing liners built into the diskette jacket. However, since all diskettes have a jacket liner, these claims should not be given too much weight.

Rely on the recommendations of dealers and fellow computer users whom you trust in deciding which diskette brand to use. If you stick to quality brand diskettes, you will rarely, if ever, lose data or programs because of the failure of the disk media itself. Indeed, problems resulting from operator errors and mechanical drive failures far exceed the error rates of quality diskettes.

Who Makes Them

Diskettes are made by many of the major companies that make audio recording tape, as well as by other manufacturers. Several leading brands of diskettes are listed in Table 17-1, along with part numbers for the proper types of diskette.

Hub Reinforcer Kits

A *hub reinforcer kit* applies an adhesive ring to the hub hole in the center of a diskette. This hub ring protects the hole from nicks and tears that can happen when the drive hub clamps the diskette. It helps lengthen the useful life of diskettes that are manufactured without reinforced holes.

A hub reinforcer kit consists of a package of rings and a guide that fits into the hub hole to ensure that each ring is properly centered. Additional packages of rings may be bought separately.

Makers of hub reinforcer kits include Inmac, Uarco, and Misco.

Diskette Organizers

There are a variety of types of diskette organizers on the market. Three of the more common types are files, cases, and vinyl envelopes.

A *diskette file* is a plastic box that operates much like an index card file. It usually has a hinged top and contains several dividers.

A *case* is a plastic box that snaps shut. It generally holds as many as a dozen diskettes. When opened, the case holds the diskettes upright for easy user access. When closed, the case can be stored on a shelf like a book.

A see-through *vinyl envelope* has holes punched along one side so that it can be stored in a standard split-ring notebook. Each envelope holds one or more diskettes (within their paper envelopes) and provides protection from dust. These vinyl envelopes make it convenient for you to store a number of diskettes in a notebook and thumb through them in search of a particular one.

Drive Cleaning Kits

Drive cleaning kits and their use are described in Chapter 11, "Caring for Your PC." The kits are designed to be used on any type of diskette drive of a given size. For the PC, simply purchase a kit for 5 1/4-inch drives.

Makers of drive cleaning kits include Verbatim, 3M, and Inmac.

Printer Paper

There are three basic types of printer paper: roll, continuous form, and cut sheet.

Roll paper is a continuous roll of paper several hundred or thousand feet long. It is not used with the types of printers commonly attached to the PC.

Continuous form paper (also known as *pin-feed paper*) comes in a box of several thousand sheets, joined end-to-end and folded like an accordion. The printer's tractor pins engage a row of holes down each side of the paper, feeding the paper as printing proceeds. This tractor feeding helps keep the paper properly aligned.

Continuous form paper is the kind most commonly used in dot-matrix printers. It is suitable for most kinds of computer printouts. It may be used in letter-quality printers that have tractor attachments.

Cut sheet paper is the type of paper you normally use in a typewriter. It may be used with letter-quality printers and with dot-matrix printers that have rubber platens. It is suitable for correspondence and other printing that is not supposed to look computer-generated. It is not suitable for long computer printouts, since you must either feed each sheet into the printer by hand or purchase a mechanical sheet feeder to do this for you.

Continuous Form Features

Continuous form paper comes in several thicknesses, or *weights*. The heaviest standard weight is 20 pounds, which is comparable to good typing paper or photocopier paper. The lighter weights are 18 pounds (moderately thin) and 15 pounds (quite thin).

The best quality of continuous form paper is called "bond." It is essentially the same as bond typing paper. Somewhat lower in quality and cost is "recycled bond," which is exactly what it sounds like. Lowest in quality and price is "groundwood paper," which resembles newsprint paper. Groundwood paper is not recommended for use with most printers, since it tears and jams easily, and it sheds fibers that can make a printer's moving parts wear out prematurely.

You can get continuous form paper with a preprinted pattern of horizontal bars. This type of form is useful for printing reports, since it helps your eye follow a report line across the page. The most common kind of patterned form is *green bar* paper, with alternating bars of green and white, usually 1/2 inch (three lines) high.

Some continuous form paper comes with perforated margins. You can tear off the margins with the pin-feed holes on them, leaving sheets with a standard *tear-down size* like 8 1/2 × 11 inches. These sheets look like ordinary cut paper except for fuzzy edges where the perforations were.

Also available is continuous form paper with *razor-edge perforations* that leave almost no trace when pulled apart. The very slight "fuzz" left by the perforations is not likely to be noticed unless looked for. This kind of paper is appropriate for correspondence and other applications where the computer-printed appearance of standard continuous forms is undesirable. It can be purchased with your business letterhead preprinted on each sheet.

Razor-edge continuous form envelopes are available to match razor-edge paper. They too may be purchased with a preprinted letterhead.

For the ultimate in continuous form quality, you can buy *tipped-on forms*. These consist of cut sheets (optionally with your letterhead) that are affixed to a continuous backing. After printing, you peel the sheets off the backing. The results are indistinguishable from cut sheets. Tipped-on envelopes are also available for computer addressing needs.

Table 17-2 lists the common sheet sizes of continuous forms.

Other Continuous Form Products

For data processing applications you can make several copies of a printout at once with *multipart forms*, which consist of as many as six sheets folded together with carbon paper in between. You can *decollate* the sheets (pull them apart) after printing. Manual decollation is messy and slow. A *decollating machine* makes it much easier.

Carbonless forms are like multipart forms except that they have no carbon paper. Ink is embedded in the surface of the inside sheets and is released by the pressure of the print head striking the paper. Carbonless forms cost more than carbon-interleaved multipart forms, but they are smudge-proof and they eliminate the messiness of separating carbon sheets from paper sheets.

Type	Size (W × H)	Tear-down size (W × H)	Comments
Paper	14 7/8″ × 11″	—	132 columns @ 10 char/in.
Paper	12″ × 8 1/2″	11″ × 8 1/2″	8 1/2″ × 11″ sideways
Paper	9 1/2″ × 11″	8 1/2″ × 11″	80 columns @ 10 char/in.
Paper	8 1/2″ × 11″	—	80 columns @ 10 char/in.
Label	3 1/2″ × 15/16″	—	Up to 5 lines @ 6 lines/in.
Label	4″ × 1 7/16″	—	Up to 8 lines @ 6 lines/in.

Table 17-2.
Standard Sizes of Continuous Forms

You can buy *continuous form labels*, also called *pin-feed labels*, for computer addressing needs. These labels are self-adhesive and come on a backing with pin-feed holes. After they are printed, they can be peeled off and stuck on envelopes.

Continuous form labels come in several sizes and colors. They may be mounted on the backing sheet in a single column, or in two, three, or four columns. These varieties are often called *one-up* labels through *four-up* labels. Also available are labels with your business name and address preprinted on a portion of the label.

For special applications like printing invoices, you can get *pre-printed forms* with headings and columns already printed on each sheet. Preprinted forms are available to fit the output of many common accounting packages. Some suppliers do custom printing. Special types of business forms, such as continuous checks, are also available from some suppliers.

What To Look Out For

Many computer supply firms consider green bar paper "normal" and blank paper somewhat exotic. If you do not want green bars, be sure to specify "blank forms."

If you plan to use multipart forms, try them with your printer before buying a large quantity. Some printers, particularly dot-matrix printers, cannot print six legible copies. Most printers have a forms thickness control that you can adjust for optimum print quality when you shift from one-part to multipart forms and back.

Who Sells Them

Standard types of continuous forms are sold by all computer supply firms and computer stores and many office supply firms and stores.

Checks To-Go, Moore Business Center, Rediform Office Products, and Nebs Computer Forms sell many kinds of preprinted forms, including business forms that fit the output of many commonly used business software products.

Checks To-Go and Rediform sell tipped-on sheets and envelopes.

Moore Business Center, Nebs Computer Forms, Rediform, and Checks To-Go prepare large and small quantities of custom-printed business forms and continuous checks, razor-edge paper with letterhead imprinting, and related products.

Rediform sells continuous form letterhead paper and related supplies.

Printer Ribbons

Dot-matrix printer ribbons generally come in a single type for each model of printer. Letter-quality printer ribbons have much more variety.

Letter-quality printer ribbons come in two major types: *cloth ribbons* and *multistrike ribbons.*

A cloth ribbon contains a strip of fabric impregnated with ink. It may be used until the ink is exhausted and the printed image becomes unacceptably light.

A multistrike ribbon, also known as a *carbon ribbon* or *film ribbon,* contains a strip of plastic coated with ink on the side facing the paper. It is used once, then discarded. It produces a much sharper image than a cloth ribbon does.

Most letter-quality printers accept both cloth and multistrike ribbons. You may use a cloth ribbon for economy and a multistrike ribbon when you need high quality.

Some printers accept two-color ribbons, which usually come in a red and black color combination. Such printers can switch colors under software control. Two-color ribbons are generally available only in cloth.

You can save money by purchasing recycled ribbons. Ribbon recyclers work either by buying used ribbon cartridges and reloading them, or by reloading your used cartridges and returning them to you.

What To Look Out For

Be sure to buy a ribbon that fits your printer exactly. A great variety of ribbons are on the market. Some have subtle but important differences. For example, one common type of letter-quality printer comes in two variations that use the same ribbon cartridge but contain ribbons that differ in width by 1/32 inch. If you used the narrower ribbon on a printer designed for the wider one, the tops of the printed letters would be cut off, and you might think your printer needed repair.

If you decide to buy recycled ribbons, try out the supplier before making a large purchase. Recycled ribbons vary in quality. Some print light or tend to jam or break.

Who Sells Them

Most printer manufacturers distribute ribbons for their own printers.

Printer ribbons are sold by most computer supply firms and computer stores. The more common types of letter-quality printer ribbons are stocked by many office supply stores.

Ribbon recyclers do local business in many large cities. Look for them in the telephone book under "Data Processing Supplies" or "Office Supplies."

Printing Elements

Virtually all letter-quality printers accept interchangeable printing elements. These elements are named according to their shape: *print wheels* (for Diablo, Qume, and similar types of printers) and *thimbles* (for NEC printers).

NEC's thimble printers and most print wheel printers use plastic elements that are cheap but gradually deteriorate with use. Some print wheel printers use more expensive and delicate metal wheels that last indefinitely if properly cared for. A few printers can accept either plastic or metal wheels.

A great variety of print fonts is available on different elements. The fonts differ in type style (the appearance of the letters), pitch (10 or 12 characters per inch) and character set (the set of alphanumeric, punctuation, or other characters found on the particular element). Printing elements for many printers are available with either fixed-width or proportional-spaced characters.

The most generally useful character set is the standard ASCII set that appears on your PC's keyboard. Some character sets eliminate the more unusual ASCII characters and replace them with other symbols, such as fractions, arrows, the cent sign, and floating accent marks. Special character sets such as Greek and scientific characters are available on some printing elements.

Printing Element Accessories

You can buy holders for most types of printing elements. They can be convenient if you use several different kinds of elements in the course of your work.

Printing element cleaning kits can be used to remove excess ink and debris from an element. They contain either liquid cleaners or sheets of special material that you print on to clean the element.

What To Look Out For

Different printers use different shapes and sizes of elements. Be careful to buy only elements compatible with your brand and model of printer.

Printing elements tend to break at the most inconvenient times. It is wise to keep at least one spare of each kind of element you use. You can often get a discount by buying several elements at a time.

Who Sells Them

Manufacturers of letter-quality printers make printing elements for their own printers. Their selection of type styles and character sets may be limited, though.

A variety of printing elements are sold by most computer supply firms, computer stores, and many office supply stores.

Camwil can modify an existing printing element to produce special character sets by "grafting" characters onto the element. Camwil can also make custom elements, but the cost is high enough to make this service impractical unless you need a large quantity of wheels for a special application.

PART III

Reference Guide For Operations And Problems

_____

_____

_____

_____

_____

_____

_____

_____

_____

_____

Part III will help you through the times when you and your PC are not working in harmony. Whether the problems are a result of hardware failure, software errors, or any other cause, the following three chapters will help you recover and proceed.

The most common problems and their remedies are discussed in this part. Furthermore, many of the problems mentioned in earlier chapters are examined in greater detail. Chapter 18, "Operations and Procedures," Chapter 19, "Problem Determination," and Chapter 20, "Error Messages and Other Messages," present a wealth of information and problem solving methods that can help you develop the knowledge and skill to use your PC effectively.

CHAPTER 18

Operations And Procedures

This chapter is your most important source of reference information about your PC. It is organized in sections that discuss procedures you must perform while using your PC. It explains how to perform each procedure in direct, step-by-step language with a minimum of background explanation.

The PC

This section shows you how to prepare your PC for use, how to handle adapter cards, and how to move your PC. It also describes the use of the keyboard's numeric keypad.

Preparing Your PC for Use

Before you can begin using your PC, its components must be connected. The first few parts of this chapter explain this procedure, in case your dealer did not set up your PC for you.

If your PC has an IBM Fixed Disk, you may have to run two programs to set up the Fixed Disk before you can use it. If you follow the lessons in the tutorial section of this book, you can defer setting up the Fixed Disk until Chapter 3, "Introducing Disks," where you must begin using it.

Where to Put the PC

Assemble your PC where you will use it, so that you will not have to carry it around after it is assembled. If you plan to place it with its back against a wall, you will have to pull it away from the wall or turn it sideways while you set it up. Remember to leave six to eight inches of ventilation space between the back of the PC and the wall.

The System Unit is customarily set up on a desk with the Monochrome Display or color monitor standing on top of it and the keyboard in front of it. If your desk is not deep enough for that, you may place the keyboard and display to the left or right of the System Unit. If you have a System Expansion Unit and printer, you may put them any place where their data cables can reach the System Unit.

Identifying Adapter Cards

Your PC's System Unit contains several *adapter cards* that enable the PC to use disk drives, printers, and other devices. Adapter cards are mounted in *system expansion slots* within the System Unit. Many adapter cards have data cable sockets that face out through slots in the System Unit's back panel (see Figure 18-1). If you have a System Expansion Unit, it contains additional adapter cards.

IBM and many other companies make adapter cards for the PC. Chapter 13, "Guide to Hardware," discusses several different kinds of cards.

To hook up your PC's components correctly, you must know which adapter cards are which. Most adapter cards can be installed in any system expansion slot; therefore, you cannot identify the cards in your PC by the slots they are in. You must be able to recognize each adapter card by its data cable sockets.

The figures accompanying this section show the data cable sockets on IBM's common adapter cards. If your PC has unusual adapter cards or adapter cards made by other companies, you may not be able to identify the cards yourself. In that case, ask your dealer which data cable sockets perform which functions.

Assembling the PC

Gently lift the door on each of your System Unit's diskette drives and slide the protective card out of each drive. Save the cards; you should insert them again if you ever transport the PC as luggage or freight. A good place to store the cards is with the DOS diskette in the *Guide to Operations*.

Figure 18-1.
PC System Unit back panel

Connect the keyboard's coiled cord to the socket near the middle of the System Unit's back panel, shown in Figure 18-1. If you have a plain PC, there are two sockets; be sure to use the one labeled "keyboard." If you have a PC XT, the keyboard socket is the only one in this location.

If you have a Monochrome Display, plug its power cable into the leftmost socket on the back of the System Unit. Find the Monochrome Display Adapter's data cable sockets on the back of the System Unit (see Figure 18-2), and plug the Monochrome Display's data cable into the upper socket.

If you have a color monitor, its data cable may be permanently attached to the monitor. If it is not, plug it in. Consult the monitor's instruction manual if the monitor has more than one socket and you are not sure which one to use, or if you do not know how to set the monitor's controls. Then find the Color/Graphics Monitor Adapter (see Figure 18-3) and plug the other end of the color monitor's data cable into the appropriate socket.

If you have a System Expansion Unit, find the Expansion Receiver Adapter on the System Expansion Unit and connect one end of the System Expansion Unit's data cable there. Find the Expansion Transmitter Adapter on the System Unit and connect the other end of the System Expansion Unit's data cable there.

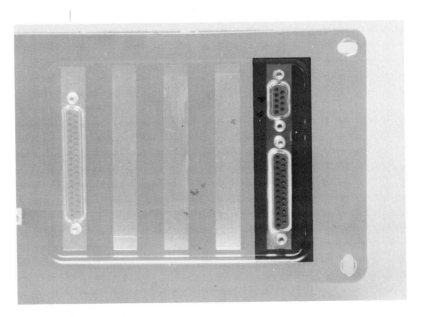

Figure 18-2.
Monochrome Display Adapter cable sockets

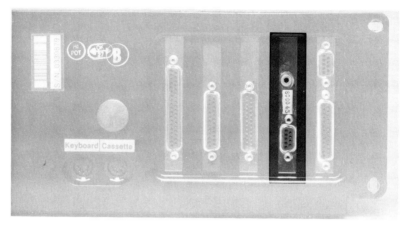

Figure 18-3.
Color/Graphics Monitor Adapter cable sockets

Figure 18-4 shows a data cable socket for either an expansion data transmitter adapter or an expansion data receiver adapter (the two are identical in appearance).

If you have a printer, plug the printer end of its data cable into the appropriate socket on the printer. Consult the printer's instruction book if you are not sure which cable end or which socket to use. Inspect the the PC end of the printer's data cable. If it has a female

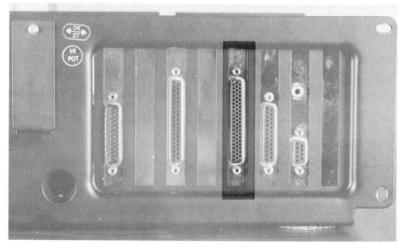

Figure 18-4.
Expansion receiver or transmitter adapter data cable sockets

plug, plug it into the Asynchronous Communications Adapter (see Figure 18-5). If it has a male plug, plug it into the Parallel Interface Adapter (see Figure 18-6) or the parallel interface socket on the Monochrome Display Adapter, as shown in Figure 18-2.

Attach all the power cords to the components they came with, and then to a source of power. You are done assembling the PC.

Notice the pair of bolts on each data cable plug. After you have tested your PC, you may tighten these bolts to ensure that none of the plugs will slip out of their sockets.

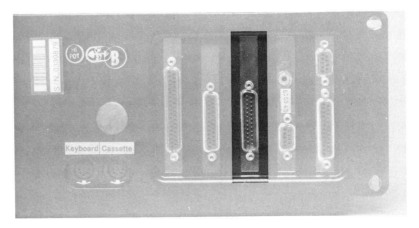

Figure 18-5.
Asynchronous Communications Adapter data cable sockets

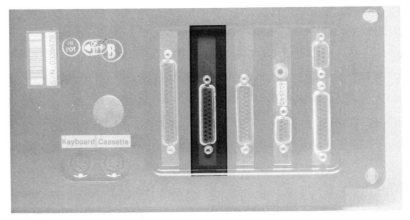

Figure 18-6.
Parallel Interface Adapter data cable sockets

Handling Adapter Cards

If you purchase a new adapter card for your PC, this is how to install it:

1. Read the installation instructions that accompany the card. If they tell you to perform steps that are not mentioned here, decide how to combine those steps with this installation procedure.

2. Avoid building up a static electricity charge in your body while handling the card. You can do this by touching a grounded object *before* you touch the card and at frequent intervals as you are handling the card. Static electricity can cause serious damage to the integrated circuit chips on the card.

3. Turn off the power to your PC and all peripherals before installing or removing an adapter card. This is to protect the card from serious damage as well as to protect you from electric shock.

4. Remove the screws that fasten the System Unit's cover to its back panel, as shown in Figure 18-7. (If you are installing the adapter card in a System Expansion Unit, you may apply these instructions to the System Expansion Unit instead of the System Unit.)

5. Slide the cover forward until its rear edge touches the System Unit's front panel. Here the cover hits an obstruction. Tilt the front of the cover upward and lift the cover free of the System Unit, as shown in Figure 18-8.

6. If you must set any switches on the adapter card, do so before installing it. The switches will be hard to reach after the card is installed. A ball-point pen with the tip retracted

Figure 18-7.
System Unit back panel, showing screws that hold cover in place

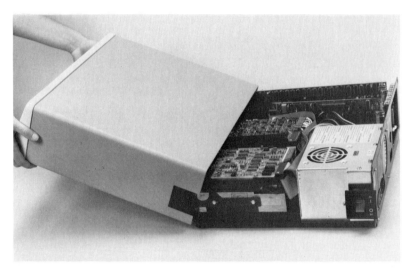

Figure 18-8.
How to lift System Unit cover free of System Unit

is a convenient tool for setting most types of adapter card switches.

7. Select a system expansion slot to hold the adapter card you are installing.

   In general, any card may be inserted in any slot. The PC XT's two rightmost slots are physically unable to hold full-length cards, however; these slots are reserved for short cards like the System Expansion Transmitter card.

   The installation instructions for some adapter cards recommend that the cards be installed in specific slots.

   On the PC XT, certain cards block the slot next to the one in which they are installed. This generally does not happen on the PC I or PC II, whose system expansion slots are more widely spaced.

8. If the card is full-length, a plastic adapter guide may have been supplied with the adapter card. Snap it into the hole provided for it in the System Unit's front panel, as shown in Figure 18-9. This guide prevents cards from touching each other if the PC is bumped. It is very important to use a guide for any card installed next to the speaker.

9. Remove the cover from the rear panel behind the system expansion slot. Save the screw that held the cover in place. (See Figure 18-10.)

Figure 18-9.
System Unit's front panel, viewed from inside

Figure 18-10.
Location of screws on the rear panel behind system slots

10. Place the adapter card above the system expansion slot and carefully press it into the slot. (See Figure 18-11.) Do not touch the bottom surface of the card with your fingers, since the wires that stick out of the card may be sharp enough to puncture your skin.

11. Fasten the adapter card to the System Unit's rear panel with the screw that formerly held the system expansion slot cover in place.

12. Switch sets S-1 and S-2 on the System Board in the PC I or PC II's System Unit, shown in Figure 18-12, tell the PC whether certain adapter cards are installed. The PC XT has a single switch set for this purpose, as shown in Figure 18-13. If you must change the settings of these switches, do so now. Note that each switch is numbered. A label at one end of the switch set shows which setting is "on."

CAUTION

The Monochrome Display may be seriously damaged if you try to use it on a PC whose System Board switches are not set so that the PC knows the device is attached. Follow installation instructions *carefully* when setting the System Board switches!

Figure 18-11.
Pressing the adapter card into the system expansion slot

Figure 18-12.
Location of switches S-1 and S-2 on the PC System Board

Figure 18-13.
Location of the switch on the PC XT System Board

13. Replace the System Unit cover. You must tilt the cover to replace it as you did to remove it. Slide the cover all the way over the System Unit, but wait before you reinstall the screws that hold it in place.

14. Turn your PC on and test the new adapter card. If it does not work, turn your PC off again. Check all connections and switch settings to be sure you installed the adapter card correctly. If you cannot find the problem, seek expert help.

15. When everything works properly, reinstall the screws that hold the cover in place.

Moving the PC

If you need to move your PC, you will have to disconnect its components. The following steps provide guidelines:

1. *If your PC has a hard disk drive not made by IBM*, consult the drive's instruction manual for instructions. Some drives require you to secure the read/write head before moving the drive. If you neglect this step, the disk may get scratched when the drive is moved, causing severe damage. You may have to secure the head by running a special program before you turn the drive off, or by turning a screw or lever *after* you turn the drive off.

   If your PC has a Fixed Disk, you will need to run a head positioning program, which is on the XT diagnostic disk. Follow instructions in the *Guide to Operations*.

2. Remove the diskettes from the diskette drives.

3. If you have double-sided diskette drives, reinsert the cardboard protectors that were in the drives when the PC was bought. These prevent the two read/write heads from knocking together and damaging each other. (If you have single-sided drives, the protectors will not hurt, but they are not needed.)

4. Close the diskette drive doors.

5. Unplug all power cables from the wall and, where possible, from the components they bring power to. Coil and tie all power cables to prevent them from dangling.

6. Unplug, coil, and tie all data cables.

If you are shipping your PC as freight or luggage, pack it carefully. Use the original cartons and plastic foam inserts if they are available. If not, use sturdy cartons and cushion the PC units well on all sides. If you ship your PC often, you may wish to buy special shipping boxes made for it.

The Keyboard

The PC's keyboard is shown in Figure 1-5 in Chapter 1. The functions of the keys are summarized in Table 18-1.

The *numeric keypad keys* on the right side of the keyboard have two sets of functions: they can be used to enter numbers, like the keyboard of a calculator, or they can be used by programs like text editors and spreadsheets to move the cursor around. When they are used in the latter way, they are often referred to as *cursor control keys*.

When you boot, the numeric keypad performs cursor control functions. *To make the numeric keypad enter numbers*, press the NUM LOCK key. To make it perform cursor control functions again, press NUM LOCK a second time, and so forth.

To change the numeric keypad's function temporarily, press either of the SHIFT keys. This changes the keypad's function as long as you hold the SHIFT key down. (The CAPS LOCK key has no effect on the keypad's function.) The SHIFT key also temporarily reverses the effect of the CAPS LOCK key; that is, if you press SHIFT while CAPS LOCK is engaged, the letter keys will enter lowercase characters as long as SHIFT is held down.

Booting

If you want to boot from a diskette, put the diskette in drive A and close the drive door. Turn on your PC's components in the following order:

1. Turn on your Fixed Disk or other hard disk drive, if you have one and if it has a separate power switch. (If you are booting from the hard disk, you may have to wait a few seconds between the time you turn on the hard disk drive and the time you turn on the System Unit. Otherwise the System Unit will finish its checkout and try to boot before the hard disk has come up to speed.)

2. Turn on your monitor or other display device, if it has a separate power switch.

3. Turn on your System Unit.

4. Turn on any other devices.

There is a delay of 10 to 90 seconds while the PC checks out its hardware. After checkout is completed, the PC tries to boot from

Key	Name	Function
F1 through F10	Program function keys	Varies with program being run.
Esc	Escape	Varies with program. Often used to let you "escape" from a program function, menu, or error condition.
⊢← →⊣	Tab	Varies with program. Usually similar to the tab key on a typewriter.
Ctrl	Control	To enter a control character, hold down CTRL and press a typing key. Control characters perform functions that depend on the program being run and the operating system being used. To reboot the PC after power-on, hold down CTRL and ALT and press DEL.
⇧	Shift	Shifts typing keys from lower- to uppercase. Shifts numeric keypad from numeric entry to cursor control functions or back.
Alt	Alternate	Enters various control characters and non-standard data characters. Function depends to some extent on program being run. Hold down ALT and press a typing key. To reboot the PC after power-on, hold down CTRL and ALT and press DEL.
←	Backspace	Backspaces the cursor.
↵	Enter	Ends a line; enters a command. Analogous to "carriage return" on a typewriter.
PrtSc	Print Screen	Used to print information displayed on the PC's screen. See section on DOS for details.
Caps Lock	Caps Lock	Alternately locks typing keys in uppercase and returns them to lowercase.
Num Lock	Num Lock	Alternately locks numeric keypad in numeric entry function and cursor control function. The function of the keypad may be temporarily reversed by SHIFT.
Scroll Lock/ Break	Scroll Lock/ Break	Used to interrupt a running program. See DOS section for details.
0 1 2 3 4 5 6 7 8 9 0 . − +	Numeric keypad/ Cursor control keypad	Used to enter numbers and cursor control commands, depending on status of NUM LOCK and SHIFT.

Table 18-1.
Key Functions on the PC Keyboard

drive A. If it fails, it tries to boot from the IBM Fixed Disk, if one is attached. If there is no Fixed Disk, or if the Fixed Disk is not ready or has no active partition, the PC runs a BASIC processor that is in ROM. BASIC displays the following prompt:

```
The IBM Personal Computer Basic
Version C1.10 Copyright IBM Corp 1981
62940 Bytes free
Ok
```

If this happens, correct the problem (if any) and reboot.

Starting DOS

When the system checkout is complete, the PC boots DOS from the diskette or Fixed Disk.

If there is no file named AUTOEXEC.BAT on the disk from which DOS booted, DOS prompts you for the date and time. You may press ENTER to accept the date or time DOS displays, or you may enter a new date or time. DOS accepts the date and time in many different formats. The following formats work for all versions of DOS:

Enter new date: **7-4-1983{ENTER}**   *(for "July 4, 1983")*

Enter new time: **13:30{ENTER}**   *(for "1:30 p.m.")*

Rebooting Without Turning the PC Off

To reboot the PC without turning it off, hold down the CTRL and ALT keys, and press the DEL key.

In rare cases, CTRL ALT DEL does not work. If this happens to you, turn your System Unit off, wait a few seconds, and turn the System Unit on again.

Adjusting the Display: The MODE Command

If you are using a Color/Graphics Adapter card, you can use the MODE command to manipulate the way the PC displays information on your monitor. *If you are using both a Monochrome Display Adapter card and a Color/Graphics Adapter card,* you can also use MODE to switch back and forth between the two displays.

When MODE is used for these functions, it expects up to three parameters:

A>**mode 40,L,T{ENTER}**

- The first parameter indicates the kind of character display you want. Use one of the following values:

    "40" gives you a display with 40-character lines on the Color/Graphics Display Adapter and monitor.

    "80" gives you a display with 80-character lines on the Color/Graphics Display Adapter and monitor.

    "BW40" gives you a black-and-white display with 40-character lines on the Color/Graphics Display Adapter and monitor.

    "BW80" gives you a black-and-white display with 80-character lines on the Color/Graphics Display Adapter and monitor.

    "CO40" gives you a color display with 40-character lines on the Color/Graphics Display Adapter and monitor.

    "CO80" gives you a color display with 80-character lines on the Color/Graphics Display Adapter and monitor.

    "MONO" directs output to the Monochrome Display.

    If you omit the first parameter, MODE does not change the current type of display.

- The second parameter shifts the Color/Graphics display left or right for greatest readability. It serves no function for the Monochrome Display. Use one of the following values:

    "L" shifts the display left one character (on a 40-character display) or two characters (on an 80-character display).

    "R" shifts the display right one character or two characters.

    If you omit the second parameter, MODE does not shift the display.

- If the third parameter is "T," MODE displays a test pattern after shifting the display; then it asks you if the display is properly aligned. If you respond **N** for "no," MODE shifts the display again, displays the test pattern, and reprompts you.

For example, this MODE command sets the display to the Color/Graphics Adapter with an 80-character color display:

A>**mode co80{ENTER}**

The following MODE command sets the display to the Color/ Graphics Adapter with an 80-character display. The color/black- and-white mode is not changed. The display is shifted two charac- ters to the left:

`A>mode 80,L{ENTER}`

The following MODE command does not change the display mode. It shifts the Color/Graphics display left, and then displays a test pattern and prompts you to determine whether to shift the dis- play again:

`A>mode ,L,t{ENTER}`

General Information About DOS

PCDOS is the disk operating system described in this book. This section summarizes many of the files and conventions used by DOS.

Device Names

DOS associates a *device name* with each I/O device on a PC. DOS's standard device names are shown in Table 18-2.

To redirect all output intended for a printer (LPT*n*) *to an Asynchronous Communications Adapter* (COM*n*), use MODE:

`A>mode Lpt1:=com1{ENTER}`

- The first parameter names the device whose output is being redirected. It is followed by a colon.
- The equal sign (=) separates the two parameters.
- The second parameter names the device that output is being redirected to. Thus, the example above redirects LPT1's out- put to COM1. The second parameter is *not* followed by a colon.

To use a device for I/O with a command that expects a file, use the device name instead of a file's name as a command line parameter. This technique also works with the commands expected by many — but not all — application programs.

Device name	Meaning when used as input device	Meaning when used as output device
CON:	Keyboard. Press F6 ENTER to indicate end of input data.	Screen
AUX: or COM1:	1st Asynchronous Communications Adapter port (see chapter on Printers for more information)	
COM2:	2nd Asynchronous Communications Adapter port	
LPT1: or PRN:	None	1st Parallel Printer port
LPT2:	None	2nd Parallel Printer port
LPT3:	None	3rd Parallel Printer port
NUL:	Dummy device. Returns an immediate end-of-data indication.	Dummy device. Accepts any amount of data and discards it.

Table 18-2.
Standard Device Names

COM and EXE Files

Any file with the extension COM or EXE represents a command or an executable computer program. ("Command" and "program" are the same thing from a user's point of view.)

When you enter a command, DOS searches the default disk for a file with the command as its filename and the extension COM. If it cannot find such a file, it searches for the same filename with the extension EXE and then with the extension BAT. If it cannot find those file specifications either, it displays the error message "Bad command or file name".

To run a command from a drive other than the default drive, put the drive name before the command name:

A>**b:chkdsk{ENTER}**

The COM and EXE files present on IBM's DOS disks are shown in Table 18-3.

Command	Version*		Type	Function
	1.1	2.0		
ASSIGN		X	COM	Change drive letter assignments (see IBM *DOS* manual)
BACKUP		X	COM	Back up Fixed Disk files to diskettes
BASIC	X	X	COM	BASIC processor
BASICA	X	X	COM	Advanced BASIC processor
BREAK		X	Internal	Controls operation of CTRL BREAK
CHDIR CD		X	Internal	Changes current directory
CHKDSK	X	X	COM	Display disk status; check and fix file structure
COMMAND	X	X	COM	DOS command processor; not normally entered on a command line
COMP	X	X	COM	Compare two files
COPY	X	X	Internal	Copy files
DATE	X	X	Internal	Set date
DEBUG	X	S	COM	Debug a COM or EXE file (see IBM *DOS* manual)
DEL	X	X	Internal	Erase a file (a synonym for ERASE)
DIR	X	X	Internal	Display disk directory
DISKCOMP	X	X	COM	Compare two diskettes
DISKCOPY	X	X	COM	Copy a diskette; format target diskette if necessary
EDLIN	X	X	COM	Line-oriented text editor
ERASE	X	X	Internal	Erase a file
EXE2BIN	X	S	EXE	Create a COM file (see IBM *DOS* manual)
FDISK		X	COM	Set Fixed Disk partitions
FIND		X	EXE	Filter; find lines containing a given string

*"S" indicates this file is on DOS 2.0 supplementary disk.

Table 18-3.
Standard DOS Commands

| Command | Version* | | Type | Function |
	1.1	2.0		
FORMAT	X	X	COM	Format disks
GRAPHICS		X	COM	Enable SHIFT PRTSC to print graphics
LINK	X	S	EXE	Create an EXE file (see IBM *DOS* manual)
MKDIR MD		X	Internal	Create sub-directory
MODE	X	X	COM	Set display mode; set LPT assignment; set asynchronous interface parameters
MORE		X	COM	Filter; display a file in screen-sized sections
PATH		X	Internal	Set and display search path
PRINT		X	COM	Queue text files for printing
RECOVER		X	COM	Recover data from corrupted or damaged disks
RENAME REN	X	X	Internal	Rename a file
RESTORE		X	COM	Restore Fixed Disk files from diskettes
RMDIR RD		X	Internal	Remove sub-directory
SORT		X	EXE	Filter; sort lines in alphabetical order
SYS	X	X	COM	Copy DOS to a copy-protected distribution diskette
TIME	X	X	Internal	Set time
TREE		X	COM	List a disk's sub-directory structure
TYPE	X	X	Internal	Display an ASCII file
VER		X	Internal	Display name and version number of DOS
VERIFY		X	Internal	Control verify-after-write feature
VOL		X	Internal	Display a disk's volume name

*"S" indicates this file is on DOS 2.0 supplementary disk.

Table 18-3.
Standard DOS Commands (continued)

Halting and Restarting Programs

To halt a program temporarily, enter CTRL NUM LOCK. To restart the program, press any typing key.

To halt a DOS command permanently, enter CTRL BREAK. You should get DOS's command line prompt unless the program has disabled CTRL BREAK.

To halt an application program permanently, use that program's "end and return to DOS" command. This command will make the program end in an orderly way and ensure that any files the program has used are left in a usable state.

If an application program has no special "end" command, or if that command does not seem to work, you can often terminate the program by entering CTRL BREAK.

Special Files on the DOS Disk

Table 18-4 lists several files that may be present on your DOS disk and have special meanings to DOS.

You should not erase or modify one of these files unless you understand the function of the file and the effect your action will have on DOS. Consult the discussions of those files in the appendixes of this book and in IBM's *Disk Operating System* manual for more information.

File's name	DOS versions	Created by	Function
COMMAND.COM	All	FORMAT/S	DOS command processor
AUTOFILE.BAT	All	*you*	Batch file DOS will run automatically when you boot
CONFIG.SYS	2.0	*you*	Controls aspects of DOS operation such as whether BREAK defaults on or off
ANSI.SYS	2.0	DOS	Enables DOS to use certain sequences of "displayed" characters for cursor control. Needed only if CONFIG.SYS contains a line saying DEVICE=ANSI.SYS

Table 18-4.
DOS Disk Files With Special Meanings to DOS

Batch Files

A *batch file* is a text file that contains DOS commands. It must have the filename extension BAT. You run it by entering its filename (and its disk name, if necessary) as though it were a command.

One batch file may run another, but DOS will never return from the second batch file to the first. If the first file has any commands after the command that starts the second batch file, they will never be executed.

Parameters in Batch Files

To create a batch file that uses one or more parameters, put a parameter symbol (%) at each point in the file where you want a parameter to be used when the file is run. Use "%1" to represent the first parameter, "%2" to represent the second, and so on, up to "%9". Use "%0" to represent the filename of the batch file.

For example, if you create a batch file named COPYDIR.BAT containing the following commands,

```
copy %1 %2
dir %2
```

and you run the batch file like this,

A>**copydir a: b:{ENTER}**

DOS processes the batch file as though it contained this:

```
copy a: b:
dir b:
```

When DOS substitutes parameter values for parameter symbols, it simply inserts a string of characters. If this produces an invalid command line, the error is not revealed until that command line is run.

To use the character "%" in a batch file command line, put %% in the file. You must do this because a single % in a batch file signals the beginning of a parameter symbol.

If there are more parameter symbols in the batch file definition than parameters in the command line that runs it, DOS substitutes null parameters (zero characters long) for the excess parameter symbols. If there are more parameters in the command line than parameter symbols in the batch file, the excess parameters are ignored.

Halting a Batch File

To halt a running batch file, enter CTRL BREAK. This halts the currently running command in the batch file unless that command has disabled CTRL BREAK.

If CTRL BREAK does halt the command, DOS displays the following prompt:

```
Terminate batch job (Y/N)?
```

To halt the entire batch file, press the Y key. To proceed to the next command line in the batch file, press the N key.

AUTOEXEC Files

An *AUTOEXEC file* is a batch file named AUTOEXEC.BAT. If DOS finds an AUTOEXEC file in the root directory of the boot disk when you boot, it runs that file before giving you its "A>" prompt.

If DOS finds an AUTOEXEC file, it does not prompt you for the date and time. *To set the date and time with an AUTOEXEC file*, you must include the DATE and TIME commands in the file, as described in the following sections.

Special Commands Used in Batch Files

DOS contains several commands that are intended mainly for use in batch files. Some of these commands can only be used in batch files; they are sometimes called *subcommands*. Others may be run directly from the keyboard.

Table 18-5 lists the DOS commands that are intended mainly

Command	Enter from keyboard?	Function
CLS	Yes	Clear screen and move cursor to upper left corner
ECHO	Yes	Control display of command lines run from batch file and of command line prompts
FOR	No	Apply one command to several files
GOTO	No	Change order of running batch file lines
IF	Yes	Run a command if a condition is true
PAUSE	Yes	Suspend running of a batch command until a typing key is pressed
REM . (dot)	Yes	"Remark;" performs no function
SHIFT	No	Enable batch file to process more than 10 parameters

Table 18-5.
Commands Intended Mainly for Use in Batch Files (DOS 2.0 Only)

for use in batch files. The most useful of these commands are described in the following sections.

DATE and TIME

DATE and TIME set the date and time, respectively, that DOS uses in time stamps for files. You enter them like this:

```
A>date 3-15-1983{ENTER}
A>time 13:33{ENTER}
```

- DATE and TIME accept their parameters in a variety of common formats. The formats shown here are accepted in all versions of the DOS.
- If DATE or TIME is run with no parameter, it displays the current date or time and prompts you to enter a new value. You may enter a value or just press ENTER to accept the value displayed. These are the forms of DATE and TIME normally used in a batch file.

To set a precise time, run the TIME command and enter a time a few seconds in the future. Wait for the time you have entered and press ENTER.

PAUSE and REM

PAUSE halts your PC's operation and displays the message "Strike any key when ready". REM (remark) presents a message like PAUSE, but it does not halt the PC. The REM command may begin with the word REM or with a period.

```
A>pause Insert the data diskette in drive B;{ENTER}
A>REM Each program should run about 12 minutes.{ENTER}
A>.Each program should run about 12 minutes.{ENTER}
```

- Any text that follows PAUSE, REM, or the period (.) on the command line is displayed as part of the command line.

If the PAUSE command above were run in a command file, it would display this on the screen:

```
A>pause Insert the data diskette in drive B;{ENTER}
Strike a key when ready . . . _
```

ECHO (DOS 2.0 Only)

The ECHO command controls whether DOS displays the command lines as it runs them. The ECHO command can also display a message on the screen.

```
A>echo off{ENTER}
A>echo on{ENTER}
A>echo Disk directories follow{ENTER}
```

- OFF makes DOS stop displaying its command line prompt and the command lines it is running. It does not affect information displayed by commands, such as error messages or directory listings.
- ON makes DOS resume displaying its command line prompt and the command lines it is running.
- Any other text following the command name is displayed on the screen. Unlike REM, ECHO displays its text even when ECHO OFF is in effect.

If you run the third ECHO command with echoing on, you will see this:

```
A>echo Disk directories follow{ENTER}
Disk directories follow
```

If you run the command with echoing off, you will see the message alone:

```
Disk directories follow
```

CLS (DOS 2.0 Only)

The CLS (clear screen) command erases the PC's screen and moves the cursor to the upper left corner:

```
A>cls{ENTER}
```

FOR (DOS 2.0 Only)

Use FOR to run a command once for each of a list of file specifications:

```
for %%f in (a:.com b:.dat c:.txt d:) do dir %%f
```

- "%%f" is a symbol that represents a file's name, much as "%1" represents a parameter symbol. The filename symbol must consist of two %s (%%) followed by a letter.
- "in (. . .)" defines a set of filenames.
- "do dir %%f" defines a command, which in this example is "dir %%f". If FOR is to be useful, the command must refer to the filename symbol at least once.

DOS runs the command once for each file name in "in (. . .)". Each time the command is run, one file name from the set is substituted for "%%f".

For example, running the command above would have the same effect as running the following commands:

```
A>dir a:.com{ENTER}
A>dir b:.dat{ENTER}
A>dir c:.txt{ENTER}
A>dir d:{ENTER}
```

If you use a global filename character in one of the file names in the set, DOS expands the name into as many matching file names as it finds on the disk. For example, if you use the following command

```
for %%f in (a:*.com) do dir %%f
```

DOS runs the following commands:

```
A>dir a:command.com{ENTER}
A>dir a:format.com{ENTER}
A>dir a:chkdsk.com{ENTER}
          .
          .
          .
```

If you enter a global file specification that does not match any filenames, DOS "runs" a command line with nothing on it, as though you had pressed ENTER at the keyboard.

You can use "in (. . .)" to list parameters other than file names, but DOS interprets the characters * and ? as global filename characters whether you intend the parameters to be file names or not.

FOR may be used only in batch files.

IF (DOS 2.0 Only)

Use IF to run a command if a certain condition is true, and skip the command if the condition is false. In the following examples, extra spaces emphasize the separation between different parts of each command:

```
if    %1 == b:index.txt    dir b:index.*
if    errorlevel 2    echo Warning, backup failed!
if    exist b:dogstory.txt    dir b:dogstory.*
```

- The first example compares two strings and runs the following command if the strings are equal. Either string may be a parameter symbol, a sequence of characters, or a combination of both.

   DOS considers upper- and lowercase characters to be unequal in an IF comparison. For example, the condition "b:index.txt == B:INDEX.TXT" is false.

- The second example runs the following command if DOS's

current error level is equal to or greater than the specified number (2 in this example).

The *error level* is a code that a program can set to indicate whether it ran normally or encountered some sort of error.

Internal commands leave the error level unchanged. All external commands set it. Some commands always set it to zero. Others set it to a nonzero value at the end of an unsuccessful run, with a higher number generally indicating a more serious problem. Error level codes set by standard DOS commands are shown in Table 18-6.

- The third example runs the following command if the specified file exists.

  You may use global filename characters in the file specification. The EXIST condition is true if at least one file fits the file specification.

  IF, unlike FOR, may be entered directly through the keyboard.

NOT reverses the effect of an IF condition. It may be used with any form of IF:

```
if    not %1 == b:index.txt    dir b:index.*
if    not errorlevel 1    echo Backup successful.
if    not exist b:dogstory.txt    dir b:dogstory.*
```

- The first example compares two strings and runs the following command if the strings are not equal.

- The second example runs the following command if DOS's current error level is less than the specified number.

- The third example runs the following command if the specified file does not exist.

Error Level	Meaning
0	Successful completion
1	No files found to back up or restore
3	Run terminated by user entering CTRL BREAK
4	Run terminated due to I/O error or hardware error

Table 18-6.
Meaning of Error Level Values for BACKUP and RESTORE

Command Labels and GOTO (DOS 2.0 Only)

A *label* is a line that gives a name to a certain point in a batch file. It is always preceded by a colon (:). A label may be any length, but only the first eight characters after the colon are meaningful. Thus it is good practice to limit labels to eight characters or less.

Use GOTO in a batch file to make DOS "go to" a label and begin running command lines at the first line after the label.

For example, the following batch file uses labels and GOTO commands:

```
echo off
backup b:/m
if not errorlevel 1 goto ok
echo ******************************
echo *Error in backup of disk b!!!!*
echo ******************************
goto end
:ok
echo Backup complete.
:end
echo on
```

After setting ECHO OFF and running BACKUP, DOS tests the error level. If the error level is not 1 or greater, DOS goes to the label OK, echoes "Backup complete.", and sets ECHO ON. If the error level is 1 or greater, DOS displays a prominent warning message, goes to the label END, and sets ECHO ON.

DOS considers upper- and lowercase characters to be the same in labels. Thus, ":loop", ":LOOP", and ":Loop" are all the same label, and "goto loop", "goto LOOP", and "goto Loop" are all the same command.

SHIFT

The SHIFT command makes each parameter symbol in the current batch refer to the next parameter to the right. SHIFT has no parameters:

```
shift
```

For example, consider this very simple batch file:

```
type %1
shift
type %1
shift
type %1
```

Suppose this batch file were run by the following command line:

```
A>type3 x.txt y.txt z.txt{ENTER}
```

The first TYPE command would type X.TXT. The first SHIFT command would make "%1" refer to the second parameter and "%2" refer to the third. Thus the second TYPE command would type Y.TXT. The second SHIFT command would have the same effect as the first SHIFT command, so the third TYPE command would type Z.TXT.

To make a batch file perform the same operation on each of a variable number of parameters, use SHIFT inside a loop. The following example runs a program named RCVE and a program named CRCC on each of its parameters:

```
:loop
  if %1. == . goto end
  rcve %1
  crcc %1
  shift
  goto loop
:end
```

The IF tests the value of the first parameter. If the parameter is not null, RCVE and CRCC are run on it. Then SHIFT makes "%1" refer to the second parameter and GOTO LOOP makes the process repeat. After the last parameter has been processed, SHIFT makes "%1" refer to a "parameter" that does not exist, and the next time through the loop, IF goes to END.

Notice the trick that this IF uses to express the idea "if %1 is absent, go to END." It compares "%1" with a dot added to the end to a dot alone. If the two are equal, "%1" must be empty (that is, absent). There is nothing magical about the dot; it is just a placeholder that prevents IF from thinking that it should compare "%1" to "goto". Any other character would work as well.

BASIC Programs

BASIC is the most commonly used programming language on many microcomputers, including the PC. If you exchange public domain programs with other PC users, most of the programs you get will be written in BASIC.

A BASIC program is kept in a file with the filename extension BAS. To run a BASIC program, use the BASICA command:

```
A>basica b:samples{ENTER}
```

- The parameter gives the disk name and filename of the program to be run. BASICA assumes the filename extension is BAS, so you need not enter it.

Some BASIC programs run other BASIC programs automatically. To use a BASIC program that does this, you generally must keep all of the programs to be run on the default disk.

You can usually interrupt a BASIC program by entering CTRL BREAK. This returns you to BASIC's command prompt, "Ok".

When you see BASIC's command prompt, you may enter any BASIC command. Some useful commands are

- SYSTEM to return to DOS.

- RUN to restart the program at the beginning.

- CONT to restart the program at the point where it was interrupted.

BASIC and BASICA

DOS has two main BASIC processors: *Advanced BASIC*, which is run by the command BASICA, and *Disk BASIC*, which is run by the command BASIC.

BASICA has features that BASIC lacks, but BASIC consumes less RAM, allowing you to run a larger program. If your PC has only 64K of RAM, you may have to run some programs with BASIC so that they will have enough RAM to run on your PC. If you have 96K of RAM or more, this should seldom or never happen to you.

Library Disks

Many computer clubs offer their members diskettes filled with programs that are in the public domain. These disks are called *library disks* because they come from the club's "program library." If you get such a disk, here's how to use it:

1. List the disk's directory with the DIR command. Look for a file with a name like README. Type or print this file. It should explain what the other files on the disk are and how to use them.

2. Any file with the extension DOC or TXT is a text file. Type or print it to get instructions for using the programs on the disk.

3. Any file with the extension BAS is a BASIC program. Run it with the BASICA or BASIC command, as explained in this chapter's discussion of BASIC programs.

4. Any file with the filename extension COM or EXE is an executable program. Run it by entering its filename as a DOS command.

Environment Strings (DOS 2.0 Only)

DOS reserves an area in RAM, called the *environment*, for storing information that tells various programs how they are to work. The environment may contain a variable number of *environment strings*, each of which consists of a name, an =, and a value. A program uses the environment by scanning it for the environment strings that concern it.

Lesson 10-2 in Chapter 10 provides a more detailed introduction to environment strings. You may wish to refer to that discussion as you use the guidelines that follow.

The SET Command

To store an environment string in the DOS environment, use the SET command:

```
A>set texdrivers=c:\tex\drx{ENTER}
A>set texdrivers={ENTER}
A>set{ENTER}
```

- The first example assigns a value to an environment string, creating the string if it did not previously exist. SET forces the name to uppercase, but leaves the value in lowercase if you enter it that way. This example would assign the value "c:\tex\drx" to the environment string TEXDRIVERS.
- The second example removes an environment string from the environment.
- The third example displays the current contents of the environment.

Managing the Environment

DOS recreates the environment each time you boot. If you want to set certain environment strings every time you boot, use SET commands in the AUTOEXEC.BAT file. Certain CONFIG.SYS commands create environment strings, too, as discussed in the following section.

You can increase the size of the environment by adding a string or lengthening the value of a string until you run a command that loads a new part of DOS into RAM. PRINT, GRAPHICS, and some forms of MODE do this. When you run such a program, it puts the new part of DOS immediately after the environment, preventing you from increasing the size of the environment further except under the following conditions:

- DOS reserves 127 bytes for the environment when you boot, so you can always expand it up to that size.

- You can add or lengthen a string after deleting or shortening a string, as long as the total size of the environment does not increase.
- If you reboot, you can expand the environment freely until you enter PRINT, GRAPHICS, and so forth again.

Table 18-7 lists several environment strings that have special meanings to DOS. Some application programs use other environment strings for their own purposes; consult your programs' user's manuals for more information.

The CONFIG.SYS File

If DOS finds a file named CONFIG.SYS in the root directory of the boot disk when you boot, it sets certain characteristics of DOS according to the contents of the file. Thus, you can use a CONFIG.SYS file to control certain aspects of DOS's operation.

CONFIG.SYS must be a text file with one configuration command per line. You may create it with EDLIN or your preferred text editing program.

To make DOS check for CTRL BREAK whenever a program asks DOS for service, put the configuration command BREAK in CONFIG.SYS. BREAK looks like this:

BREAK=ON

The opposite command, BREAK OFF, makes DOS check for CTRL BREAK only when the program that is running tries to do an

Environment string name	Set by	Meaning
PATH	PATH; also by DOS when you boot	Defines directory paths to be searched when a command name is not found in the current directory
COMSPEC	DOS when you boot	Directory and name of the file containing DOS's command processor
PROMPT	DOS; also by the PROMPT command	Defines DOS's command prompt. The prompt may be redefined to include time stamp, DOS version number, etc.*
BREAK	—	Setting BREAK ON has the same effect as running the DOS command BREAK ON.

*See the discussion of the PROMPT command in IBM's *Disk Operating System* manual for more information.

Table 18-7.
Environment Strings Set and Used by DOS

I/O operation on the screen, keyboard, printer, or serial interface. If CONFIG.SYS contains no BREAK command, DOS assumes BREAK OFF.

To change the name or location of the command processor DOS is to use, put the configuration command SHELL in CONFIG.SYS. SHELL looks like this:

```
SHELL=A:\COMMAND.COM
```

For "A:\COMMAND.COM", substitute the drive, path, and file name of the command processor you want to use.

The effect of SHELL is to change the value of the COMSPEC environment string. Set COMSPEC with the configuration command SHELL, not with the DOS command SET. SHELL makes DOS use the desired command processor as soon as you boot, so that you need not keep a copy of COMMAND.COM just to run a SET command.

To change the initial search path, put the configuration command PATH in CONFIG.SYS. The format of the operand field in the configuration command PATH is the same as in the DOS command PATH. For example:

```
A>path \com;\wp;\ {ENTER}
```
                                                   DOS Command

```
PATH=\COM;WP;\
```
                                                   CONFIG.SYS command

Diskettes

This section provides information about diskettes: how to change diskettes in a drive; how to format diskettes and make backup copies; how to make a bootable diskette by copying DOS to it; and how to deal with diskette errors.

Changing Diskettes

It is safe to change the diskette in a drive whenever you see DOS's command line prompt. When you change the diskette, DOS automatically sets that drive's current directory to the new disk's root directory.

You may put a data diskette (one that does not contain a copy of DOS) in drive A after you have booted DOS. DOS prompts you to reinsert the DOS disk when necessary.

CAUTION

Never change a diskette in either drive when a command is running unless the command directs you to do so. If you fail to observe this rule, the command may destroy data stored on the new diskette by writing data intended for the old diskette on top of it.

Formatting a Diskette

You must format a diskette before you use it with any command except DISKCOPY. Formatting a diskette consists of writing a special pattern of data over the entire recording surface. FORMAT erases any data stored on the diskette being formatted.

To format a disk, run FORMAT:

```
A>format b:{ENTER}
A>format b:/s/v{ENTER}
```

- The parameter names the drive you will use to format the diskette.
- The /S (system) option makes FORMAT copy DOS from the boot disk to the diskette being formatted.
- The /V (volume name) option makes FORMAT prompt you for a volume name to give this diskette. If you omit it, FORMAT does not give the diskette a volume name (*DOS 2.0 only*).
- The /1 (one side) option makes FORMAT format a single-sided diskette, even if the drive being used is a double-sided diskette drive. Use this option to format a diskette that a single-sided drive can read.
- The /8 (eight sector) option makes FORMAT format an eight-sector-per-track diskette. Use this option to format a diskette that DOS 1.1 can read (*DOS 2.0 only*).

FORMAT prompts you to insert a diskette in the specified drive. Insert a diskette and press any typing key to make FORMAT begin formatting the diskette.

If you used the /V option, FORMAT prompts you for the volume name to give the diskette. You may enter a name that is as many as eleven characters long. The valid character set is the same as for a filename or a filename extension. All letters are treated as uppercase.

After formatting the diskette, FORMAT prompts you to press the Y key to format another diskette or the N key to return to DOS.

Diskette Format Compatibility

Table 18-8 shows all DOS diskette formats and the versions of DOS that can process them. In general, DOS adjusts automatically to the format of any diskette it can process at all. DISKCOPY is an exception: it always leaves the target diskette with the same format as the source diskette. It automatically reformats the target diskette if necessary.

FORMAT normally formats a diskette of the type listed in the "Normally reads/writes" column of Table 18-8. You can get a different type of diskette by running FORMAT with options such as /1 or /8, as described above.

Backing Up a Diskette

To back up a diskette, run DISKCOPY. DISKCOPY creates an exact copy of the source diskette on the target diskette. It formats the target diskette first if necessary:

```
A>diskcopy a: b:{ENTER}
```

- The first parameter is the name of the drive in which you will put the source diskette.
- The second parameter is the name of the drive in which you will put the target diskette.

DISKCOPY prompts you to insert the source and target diskettes in the appropriate drives. Press any typing key to make DISKCOPY begin copying the source to the target.

DOS version	Can read/write	Approx. capacity	Files per diskette	Normally reads/writes
1.0	1 side, 8 sector	160K	64	1 side, 8 sector
1.1	1 side, 8 sector 2 side, 8 sector**	160K 320K	64 112	1 side, 8 sector* 2 side, 8 sector**
2.0	1 side, 8 sector 2 side, 8 sector** 1 side, 9 sector 2 side, 9 sector	160K 320K 180K 360K	64 112 64 112	1 side, 9 sector* 2 side, 9 sector**

*On single-sided drives.
**On double-sided drives only.

Table 18-8.
Diskette Format Compatibility

If the source and target diskettes go in the same drive, DISKCOPY prompts you to insert the source disk and the target disk in turn until it has copied all the data on the source to the target. The number of times you must switch diskettes will depend on how much RAM your PC has.

After copying the source diskette, DISKCOPY prompts you to press the Y key to copy another diskette or the N key to return to DOS.

Managing Backup Diskettes

To ensure that you will always be able to find your backup diskettes when you need them, you should:

- Label the diskettes clearly.

- Store all of the backups in one place: either together with the diskettes they back up or in a separate backup area. You may want to keep additional backups of some or all data in another location to protect yourself against loss by fire, theft, or other misfortune.

It is not a good practice to make two consecutive backups of a disk on the same target diskette. If anything should happen to your PC while DISKCOPY is making the second backup, neither the first nor the second backup will be usable. The simplest way to avoid this possibility is to keep two backup diskettes for each data diskette or two sets of backup diskettes for your hard disk, and to use them alternately.

A more sophisticated technique involves keeping a pool of backup diskettes. The backup pool technique is illustrated in Figure 18-14. It works like this: create a backup pool containing a few more diskettes than you will need at any one time. Keep the backup diskettes in a box with the oldest one in the front.

When you make a backup, use the oldest diskette in the pool. After making the backup, return the preceding backup diskette, which it replaces, to the pool. When you return a diskette to the box, put it in the back.

Put an identifying label on the paper envelope of each backup diskette, not on the diskette itself. When you make a backup, put the new backup diskette in the labeled envelope and put the old backup diskette in an unlabeled envelope from the pool.

The backup pool technique ensures that an old backup will not be overwritten until it works its way to the front of the pool. That gives you the added safety of a grace period during which you can recover the old backup from the pool if necessary.

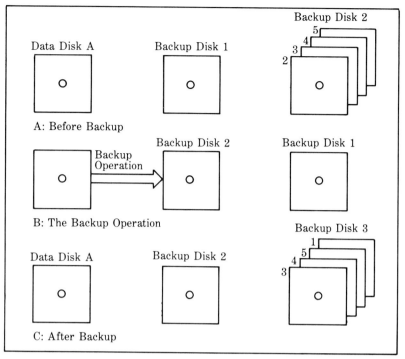

Figure 18-14.
Organizing a backup diskette pool

Copying DOS to a Program Diskette: The SYS Command

Some application programs are *copy-protected* to prevent purchasers from making unauthorized copies. *Copy-protection* means that the protected programs cannot be copied to another diskette, although they may be run from the diskette on which they are stored.

To run a copy-protected program from drive A, you must first make it "bootable"; that is, you must copy DOS to the diskette program.

To copy DOS to a diskette containing a copy-protected program, run SYS:

`A>`**`sys b:`**`{`**`ENTER`**`}`

- The parameter gives the drive name of the drive containing the diskette to which DOS is to be copied.

When you run SYS, you must have a bootable diskette in drive

A so that SYS has a source from which it can copy DOS. If the diskette in drive A is not bootable, SYS prompts you to change it.

After you run SYS, copy any special DOS files you will need from your regular DOS diskette to the program diskette. You will need COMMAND.COM; you may also need CONFIG.SYS and ANSI.SYS.

You cannot use SYS to change one of your own diskettes from nonbootable to bootable, since SYS can only operate on a diskette with space reserved for DOS before the first file on the diskette.

Dealing With Diskette Errors

If you use diskettes, sooner or later you are going to have difficulty reading or writing to one. Diskette errors may be revealed by data that is *corrupted* for no apparent reason. You may find garbage in a text file, or you may find that one copy of a COM or EXE file ceases to work.

The most common symptoms of diskette problems are the following messages:

```
Disk error reading drive x
Abort, Retry, Ignore? _

Disk error writing drive x
Abort, Retry, Ignore? _

File allocation table bad, drive x
Abort, Retry, Ignore?.
```

The meanings of the first two messages are self-evident. The last one means that something bad has happened to the part of the diskette that is used to keep track of the location of each file on the diskette.

After each message, DOS waits for you to respond:

- *To retry the operation that produced the error*, press R. This is the appropriate response if you have noticed and corrected some condition like an open drive door or an unwanted write-protect tab on a diskette. In other cases, pressing R usually produces the same error again, but it does no harm and so it is always worth a try.

- *To ignore the error*, press I. If the operation is a read, DOS simply tries to read the next part of the file. This is seldom an appropriate response, since it makes an application program read or write an incomplete version of a file without knowing it.

- *To halt the program that is running* and return control to DOS, press A for "abort." This is generally the appropriate response when you get a diskette error while running a program and R does not work.

CAUTION

Do not remove a disk from the drive when you get a disk error. If you do, DOS may corrupt the *next* diskette that you insert in the drive. You may change disks *after* you press A and see DOS's command line prompt.

Causes of Diskette Errors

To respond appropriately to a diskette error, you must know what caused it. The major possibilities are:

- The diskette drive or diskette drive adapter has failed and cannot read from or write to the diskette even though the diskette itself is OK.
- The disk drive or adapter has failed and has corrupted the diskette by writing invalid data on it. Nothing is physically wrong with the diskette, but the data on it is damaged or inaccessible.
- The diskette has been damaged or has worn out so that it can no longer store data reliably.

The last cause is the most common, but the first two are potentially more serious, so you should suspect them first when a diskette I/O error occurs.

Identifying a Malfunctioning Diskette Drive

To check out the diskette drive, you need a test diskette that contains data and that you know is in good condition. Select a diskette that is replaceable, since a malfunctioning drive may corrupt a diskette even when it is only supposed to read from it.

If you are using DOS 2.0, run VERIFY ON. This will help you catch additional errors if they occur. The VERIFY command is described in Chapter 10; you can look there for more information on its use.

Put your test diskette in the drive where the error occurred. Do something that exercises the drive thoroughly, such as copying the diskette to a second diskette.

If errors occur, the diskette drive or its adapter is probably failing. Arrange to have it repaired. Do not try to use your PC until the repair is done. If no errors occur, the diskette that gave you problems is probably worn or damaged, and nothing is wrong with the drive.

Identifying Alignment Problems

A common cause of diskette errors is a misaligned drive: that is, a drive that does not position its read/write head the same way as other drives.

To see if you have a misaligned diskette drive, format a diskette on the suspect drive. Then run some programs that exercise the drive thoroughly with that diskette. For example, copy another diskette (from another drive) to the suspect drive, and then copy the newly created diskette to a third diskette (also on another drive). If the suspect drive passes this test but cannot use diskettes formatted on other drives and cannot format diskettes that other drives can use, misalignment is likely to be the problem.

Identifying Borderline Hardware Problems

Sometimes a failing drive produces errors so seldom that it can usually pass the tests just described even though it is regularly corrupting disks. Then your PC seems to be OK, except that you keep getting I/O errors on various disks.

If you suspect this sort of problem, reformat and reuse some of the diskettes that seem bad. If they give no more problems than any other diskettes, you probably have a borderline hardware problem.

Repairing Corrupted File Structure (DOS 2.0 Only)

Malfunctioning programs or hardware can corrupt the file structure of the diskette, so that some parts of the diskette do not appear to belong to any file and yet are not marked as free. Parts of a diskette may also appear to belong to two or more files at once.

When these problems occur, CHKDSK displays warning messages about invalid file structure and reports a smaller than usual amount of total disk space. If you are running a program that habitually corrupts a diskette's file structure, the diskette's total space may decrease gradually through use. Invalid file structure may also come to your attention through problems such as disappearing data.

Before you try to repair any corrupted diskette, back up the diskette with COPY (by copying all files on the diskette to an empty diskette) and again with DISKCOPY. Some measures you take to repair a diskette may corrupt it further. Having these backups will give you the freedom to recover from such unsuccessful experiments. If you cannot recover data from one kind of backup diskette, you may be able to recover it from the other.

To repair a diskette's file structure, run CHKDSK:

`A>`**`chkdsk b:/f/v{ENTER}`**

- The parameter identifies the drive containing the diskette to be repaired. If it is omitted, CHKDSK processes the default drive.
- The /F option makes CHKDSK *fix* the file structure of the diskette. CHKDSK reports each file structure error that it finds and prompts you for permission before fixing the error. If you omit the /F option, CHKDSK reports file structure errors but does not try to fix them.
- The /V option makes CHKDSK display more detailed information about its progress as it checks the diskette than it normally does.

Note that CHKDSK repairs a diskette so that its file structure is valid again, but it does not necessarily return the diskette to its condition before the file structure was corrupted. Information about what is on a diskette is often lost when the file structure is corrupted and cannot be recovered.

If CHKDSK finds an area on the diskette that is neither marked as free nor is part of a file, it puts that area in a file so that you can inspect the data and retrieve it if you want to. CHKDSK names such files FILE0000.CHK, FILE0001.CHK, FILE0002.CHK, and so forth. After running CHKDSK, look for these files and inspect them if they are present. You may delete them after retrieving any text from them that you want to keep.

Repairing a Corrupted Directory (DOS 2.0 Only)

Malfunctioning programs or hardware can corrupt a diskette's directory so that none of the files on the diskette can be found, even though the information in the files may be intact.

This problem manifests itself through an apparently empty directory on a diskette that should contain files, or through I/O errors when you try to run DIR on a diskette.

To reconstruct a diskette's directory, run the RECOVER command:

`A>`**`recover b:{ENTER}`**

- The parameter identifies the drive holding the diskette to be processed.

RECOVER constructs a new root directory containing all the files on the diskette. The files are named FILE0001.REC, FILE0002.REC, FILE0003.REC, and so forth.

RECOVER cannot tell exactly where each file should end, so the size of each file is a multiple of the unit that DOS uses to allocate file space. You must edit each text file to eliminate spurious data that appears at its end.

Retrieving Corrupted Files

Malfunctioning hardware can corrupt a diskette's format so that one or more parts of the diskette cannot be read from or written to. It is somewhat as if these parts of the diskette were not formatted. This problem reveals itself through I/O errors when you try to read or write data on the affected part of the diskette.

To retrieve a corrupted text file, first use the COPY command to copy the file to a good disk. When you get DOS's I/O error message and prompt, press I for "ignore." DOS will try to read the next part of the file. You may get many error messages representing unreadable parts of the file.

When COPY is done, the copy of the file includes as much of the corrupted file as can be read. You may fill in the missing parts of the file with a text editor. You can usually retrieve most of the missing parts from your backup disk.

If you are using DOS 2.0, you can use the RECOVER command to retrieve data from a partly unreadable text file. RECOVER is easier to use for this purpose than is COPY, because it does not give you a time-consuming message and prompt each time it encounters a diskette error. Here is an example of RECOVER being used to retrieve a corrupted file:

```
A>recover b:elephant.txt{ENTER}
```

• The parameter names the file that you want to retrieve.

RECOVER reads the text file and marks any corrupted parts so that DOS will never again try to use them. This effectively makes the corrupted parts disappear from the file and prevents DOS from trying to reuse the corrupted areas on the disk. You may then copy the file to a good disk without getting error messages.

Both file recovery techniques can theoretically be used to retrieve nontext files such as COM or EXE files. Since there is seldom any way to repair the damage to such files, though, the "retrieved" files are useless. You can only restore such files from your most recent backup.

Retrieving Files From a Damaged Diskette (DOS 2.0 Only)

A diskette can become worn or physically damaged, so that some parts of it cannot hold data.

The symptoms of this problem are the same as the symptoms of corrupted format, except that you get more diskette errors when you try to reformat the diskette, or else the errors quickly return.

You deal with this problem the same way you would deal with corrupted format, except that you should discard the worn or damaged diskette instead of trying to reuse it.

In principle, you could run the RECOVER command on a worn or damaged diskette and then continue using the diskette *without* reformatting it. Since RECOVER takes the damaged areas of the diskette out of circulation, it effectively turns a damaged diskette into an undamaged diskette with somewhat reduced capacity. Using RECOVER in this way is unwise, though. A worn or damaged diskette often has some areas that are not affected badly enough to fail immediately but will fail after some further use. It is foolish to entrust your data to such a diskette. The cost of the diskette is trivial compared to the value of the data stored on it.

Hard Disks

DOS 2.0 can operate the IBM Fixed Disk. Most other manufacturers of hard disks provide software enabling most disk procedures to work the same way with their products as with IBM's Fixed Disk. You should consult your dealer or your hard disk's instruction manual, however, before following the directions given here for IBM's Fixed Disk.

Most of the following directions do not apply to any hard disk supported under DOS 1.1, since IBM did not provide any form of hard disk support in that version.

Setting Up the IBM Fixed Disk (DOS 2.0 Only)

Like a diskette, the Fixed Disk must be formatted before it can be used. Formatting a Fixed Disk is somewhat more elaborate, though. This section describes the formatting procedure as well as the preparation that must precede formatting.[1]

---

[1]Your Fixed Disk may have been formatted for you by your dealer. You can tell whether or not the Fixed Disk has been formatted by trying to list its directory. If you get a directory listing, the disk has been formatted; if you get an error message, it has not.

Your Fixed Disk is designed to let you use it with more than one operating system. You can do this by dividing the Fixed Disk into as many as four *partitions*. Each operating system sees one partition as a smaller Fixed Disk and ignores the other partitions.

You create the DOS partition with the DOS command FDISK. If you want to create partitions for other operating systems, you must use commands in those other systems to do so. No operating system can create a partition for another operating system or use files in another system's partition.

Each partition occupies a fixed portion of the Fixed Disk. A partition's boundaries are defined by the first and last *cylinder* it occupies on the disk. A cylinder is the part of a hard disk that can be read from and written to with the read/write head in one position. The IBM Fixed Disk has 305 cylinders, numbered 0 through 304. Each cylinder can hold 32K bytes of data.

At any time, one of the Fixed Disk's partitions may be the *active partition*. When you try to boot with no diskette in drive A, the PC boots its operating system from the Fixed Disk's active partition.

To use the Fixed Disk with DOS, you must perform the following steps:

1. Create a DOS partition.
2. Format the partition.
3. If you want to boot DOS from the Fixed Disk, store DOS in the partition.

Using FDISK to Manipulate Partitions

The FDISK command lets you set your Fixed Disk partitions as you want them.

To define the DOS partition, run FDISK:

```
A>fdisk{ENTER}
```

FDISK presents a menu of functions that it can perform. Each function is numbered, and you select a function from the menu by entering its number. The items on the menu are

1. Create DOS Partition.
2. Change Active Partition.
3. Delete DOS Partition.
4. Display Partition Data.
5. Select Next Fixed Disk Drive.

Item 5 will appear only if your PC has two Fixed Disks. We will look at each option below.

Creating a DOS Partition

To create a DOS partition, select FDISK's option 1. If the Fixed Disk contains no partitions yet, FDISK asks you if you want to create a DOS partition that includes the entire disk. If you answer N for "no," FDISK prompts you for the size and starting cylinder that the DOS partition is to have. Then FDISK creates the DOS partition and returns to DOS.

If the Fixed Disk already contains partitions, FDISK displays their boundaries in a table with the following entries:

- *Partition:* the partition's number, 1 through 4.
- *Status:* A for active, N for nonactive.
- *Type:* DOS or non-DOS.
- *Start, End,* and *Size:* the boundaries and size of the partition, all in cylinders.

If your PC already has a DOS partition, FDISK beeps and displays a message instructing you to press ESC to return to the option menu. FDISK will not allow you to define more than one DOS partition on a disk.

If your PC does not yet have a DOS partition, FDISK prompts you for the size and starting cylinder of the partition you want to create. Then it creates the partition and returns FDISK's option menu.

Changing the Active Partition

FDISK makes the DOS partition active automatically when you create the partition. If your Fixed Disk has two or more partitions and you want to change the active partition, you can do so with FDISK.

To change the active partition, select FDISK's option 2. FDISK displays the boundaries of the existing partitions in a table like that displayed by "Create DOS Partition." Then it prompts you for the number of the partition you want to make active. When you enter the number, FDISK makes that partition the active partition and returns to its option menu.

Deleting the DOS Partition

To delete the DOS partition, select FDISK's option 3. You might want to delete the DOS partition in order to create a new DOS partition that is a different size or on a different part of the disk.

FDISK displays the boundaries of the existing partitions. Then it warns you that deleting the DOS partition will destroy all data in the partition and prompts you to confirm that you want to do this.

If you respond Y for "yes," it deletes the partition. Then it returns to DOS.

Displaying Partition Data

To display the current partitions, select FDISK's option 4. This option presents a display like that of "Create DOS Partition" but performs no other function before returning to DOS.

Selecting the Next Fixed Disk Drive

If your PC has two Fixed Disks, you can *make FDISK act on the second drive* instead of the first (that is, on DOS drive D instead of drive C) by selecting FDISK's option 5. This option leaves you in the FDISK menu so that you can select another function.

Formatting the Fixed Disk (DOS 2.0 Only)

To format the DOS partition of the Fixed Disk, run FORMAT just as you would to format a diskette:

```
A>format c:/s/v{ENTER}
```

The /S and /V options have the same functions for the Fixed Disk as for diskettes. The /1 and /8 options are meaningless and should not be used.

Storing DOS on the Fixed Disk

You store DOS on the Fixed Disk by formatting the Fixed Disk with the /S option.

You must also store any commands and programs you want to be able to run from the Fixed Disk. At a minimum, you need COMMAND.COM, which is placed on the Fixed Disk automatically by the FORMAT command when it is used with the /S option. If you do not want to copy all the files on your DOS diskette to the Fixed Disk, the following minimum set is recommended:

BACKUP.COM
CHKDSK.COM
CONFIG.SYS   (If you have defined this file on diskette)
EDLIN.COM   (Or another text editor of your choice)
FORMAT.COM
MODE.COM
PRINT.COM
RESTORE.COM
TREE.COM

It is *strongly recommended that you use sub-directories* to separate different groups of files on your Fixed Disk. Using sub-directories is the only practical way to keep control when you accumulate hundreds of files for dozens of applications. The use of sub-directories is discussed in Chapter 8 and also later in this chapter. Chapter 8 contains suggestions for organizing your disk with sub-directories.

Backing Up the Fixed Disk (DOS 2.0 Only)

Use the BACKUP command to back up the Fixed Disk. BACKUP copies files from the Fixed Disk to one or more diskettes in a special format that enables it to store files too big to fit on a single diskette. To use files backed up with BACKUP, you must restore them to the Fixed Disk with RESTORE.

See the discussion on "Managing Backup Diskettes" earlier in this chapter for more information.

Getting Ready

Before running the BACKUP command, set aside as many diskettes as you will need to back up the Fixed Disk. BACKUP, unlike DISKCOPY, cannot format its target diskettes; thus you must format all the diskettes before running BACKUP if they have not already been formatted for use with DOS.

To estimate the number of diskettes you will need, run CHKDSK against the Fixed Disk and note how many bytes of disk space are occupied by files. Divide this number by 360K (the capacity of a double-sided diskette with nine sectors per track) and add one or two for safety's sake. If your Fixed Disk is completely full, you should need 28 diskettes.

Running BACKUP

To back up files stored on the Fixed Disk, run the BACKUP command:

```
A>backup c: a:{ENTER}
```

- The first parameter is the drive name of the Fixed Disk.
- The second parameter is the name of the drive in which you will insert the target diskettes.

BACKUP prompts you to insert a diskette in the diskette drive. Insert a formatted diskette and press any typing key. BACKUP erases any files already on the diskette and then begins backing up the files that are on the Fixed Disk.

If one diskette cannot hold all the files, BACKUP prompts you to insert another diskette when the first one is full. This continues until all the files are backed up.

Making a Partial Backup

A *partial backup* includes only some of the files that match BACKUP's first parameter. A partial backup is a time-saving technique that you can use when only a few files have been changed since the last full backup.

```
A>backup c: a:/d:7-4-1983{ENTER}
A>backup c: a:/m{ENTER}
```

- In the first example, the /D option makes BACKUP *back up only files that have been created or modified on or after the specified date.*

- In the second example, the /M option makes BACKUP *back up only files that have been created or modified since BACKUP was last run.*

If you use the first form of BACKUP with the date of the day after the most recent full backup, you can restore the Fixed Disk completely by restoring the most recent full backup and then restoring the most recent partial backup. (This presumes that no files were changed between the time the full backup was run and the start of the next day, and that you always enter an accurate date and time when you boot.)

If you use the second form of BACKUP, you can restore the Fixed Disk completely by restoring the most recent full backup and then restoring all subsequent partial backups, oldest first.

CAUTION

If you make partial backups with /D, be aware of the following pitfalls in the design of DOS:

- If you create or modify any files after making a full backup and before the system's date changes, those files will not be included in subsequent partial backups.
- COPY and some other DOS commands create and modify files without setting their time stamps. COPY gives a new file the same time stamp as the file from which it is copied. You can force COPY to give a new file a current time stamp by putting "+,," after the "from" file's name:

```
A>copy a:example.txt+,, c:{ENTER}
```

Restoring Files Saved With BACKUP

To copy files from a BACKUP diskette to a Fixed Disk, run the RESTORE command:

```
A>restore a: c:{ENTER}
```

- The first parameter names the drive from which RESTORE is to read the backup diskettes.
- The second parameter names the Fixed Disk to which you want to restore the data that is on the backup diskettes.

RESTORE prompts you to insert the first backup diskette in the diskette drive. Insert the diskette and press any typing key. RESTORE begins restoring files from the backup diskette to the Fixed Disk.

If there are several backup diskettes to restore from, the command RESTORE prompts you to insert each one in turn. Always insert the backup diskettes in the order in which they were created.

Unlike BACKUP, RESTORE does not erase all files from the target diskette; it adds the restored files to the files that are already there.

Restoring Partial Backups

If you have made a partial backup with the /D option, you can restore the entire contents of the Fixed Disk by restoring the most recent full backup and then restoring the most recent partial backup. (Note the exceptions listed in the "Caution" above.)

If you have made partial backups with the /M option, you can restore the entire contents of the Fixed Disk by restoring the most recent full backup and then restoring all subsequent partial backups, oldest first.

In either case, the Fixed Disk will end up containing any files that you erased after the full backup, since BACKUP has no way of recording the fact that a file has been erased.

Saving and Restoring Specific Files

BACKUP and RESTORE let you save and restore specific files by including a file's name or global filename specification in the parameter that represents the Fixed Disk:

```
A>backup c:ar83??.dat a:{ENTER}
A>backup c:file.ext a:{ENTER}
A>restore a: c:*.dat{ENTER}
A>restore a: c:file.ext{ENTER}
```

Using BACKUP with a file's name is a useful way of making a copy of a file to transport from one PC to another. Using RESTORE with a file's name is useful for restoring a particular file that has been deleted or modified by mistake.

How BACKUP and RESTORE Use Sub-Directories

BACKUP normally saves files only from the directory that you name in the first parameter or from the current directory if you name none. *To save files from the named or current directory and all of its sub-directories*, use BACKUP with the /S option:

```
A>backup c: a:/s{ENTER}
```

To save all the files on a disk, make BACKUP save the root directory with the /S option:

```
A>backup c:\ a:/s{ENTER}
```

Similarly, RESTORE normally restores files only to the directory that you name in the second parameter or to the current directory if you name none. *To restore files to the named or current directory and all of its sub-directories*, use RESTORE with the /S option:

```
A>restore a: c:/s{ENTER}
```

To restore all the files on a disk, use RESTORE to restore the root directory with the /S option:

```
A>restore a: c:\/s{ENTER}
```

When you run RESTORE with /S, it automatically creates any sub-directories that are needed to restore the requested files. When you run RESTORE without /S, it does not create sub-directories. If you want to restore files to a particular sub-directory, you must first create that sub-directory with MKDIR if it does not already exist.

BACKUP records the directory from which each saved file came. RESTORE will only restore a file to its original directory. For example, if you save all the files on a disk with BACKUP and then restore them to the root directory with RESTORE, omitting /S, only the root directory's files will be restored. If you save the files in directory \X and try to restore them to directory \Y, like this,

```
A>save c:\x a:{ENTER}
A>restore a: c:\y{ENTER}
```

no files will be restored, because none of the files on the backup diskette came from directory \Y.

I/O Errors on Hard Disks

I/O errors can occur on hard disks as well as on diskettes. The symptoms of I/O errors are generally similar on both hard disks and diskettes.

Most hard disks are permanently sealed in a dust-free plastic shell. Because of this, problems with the disks themselves are actually less common than are problems with their adapter cards, which are no less reliable than any other adapter cards.

When I/O errors occur on a hard disk, you may use the same data recovery techniques that were described for diskettes earlier in this chapter. Boot from a diskette before trying to recover data if you suspect the hard disk is malfunctioning. After recovering your data, have the disk drive or its adapter card repaired.

Files

Files are the basic unit of disk storage. Files hold collections of related data on a disk, much as a file folder holds related information. This section shows how to name files, how to manipulate them, how to set up sub-directories, and how to use I/O redirection.

Naming Files

A file is identified by a *file specification*. We commonly but informally refer to the file specification as the *file's name*.

A file's name has three parts:

B:EXAMPLE.TXT

- The *drive specification* or *drive name*, which identifies the disk drive that holds the disk that contains the file. The drive name is a letter followed by a colon.
- The *filename*, a one- to eight-character name describing the file's contents. We always spell "filename" as one word to distinguish it from a "file's name," our informal name for a file specification.
- The *filename extension*, an optional one- to three-character name describing the *type* of the file's contents. If present, the filename extension is separated from the filename by a dot.

Valid and Invalid File Specifications

Some examples of valid file specifications are shown in Table 18-9. In general, you may use any of the following characters in a filename or filename extension:

Capital letters, A to Z

Lowercase letters, a to z (DOS treats them as capitals)

Numerals, 0 to 9

Punctuation symbols, ! @ # $ % & ( ) - _ { } ' '

The following punctuation symbols are *not* allowed in a filename or extension:

^ * = + [ ] ; : " \ | , . / ? < >

In addition, certain filename extensions have special meanings to DOS, and they should be used only for files that conform to DOS's expectations. Table 4-1 lists the standard filename extensions and their accepted meanings.

Global Filename Characters

To write a file specification that refers to a group of files, use global filename characters in the filename or filename extension.

DOS recognizes two global filename characters: the question mark (?) and the asterisk (*). The ? matches any character. When used at the end of a filename or extension, it may also match no character. The * is used only at the end of a filename or extension. It matches any number of characters.

Table 18-10 shows several examples of file specifications that contain global filename characters.

File's name	Drive name	Filename	Filename extension	How file's name is read
example	default	EXAMPLE		EXAMPLE
example.txt	default	EXAMPLE	TXT	EXAMPLE dot TXT
b:example.txt	B	EXAMPLE	TXT	B colon EXAMPLE dot

Table 18-9.
Some Valid File Specifications

File specification	Meaning
JULY??B.COM	Matches JULY01B.COM, JULY02B.COM, JULYXQB.COM, JULY_B.COM, etc.
JULY????.COM	Matches any file with a filename beginning "JULY" and a filename extension of "COM": JULY01B.COM, JULYXY.COM, JULY−.COM, JULY.COM, etc.
JULY∗.COM	Equivalent to JULY????.COM.
∗.COM	Matches any file with a filename extension of "COM".
JULY.∗	Matches any file with the filename "JULY" and any extension (or no extension).

Table 18-10.
Some File Specifications With Global Filename Characters

Listing Files With the DIR Command

To list the names, sizes, and time stamps of the files on a disk, run the DIR command:

```
A>dir{ENTER}
A>dir b:{ENTER}
A>dir b:july.dat{ENTER}
A>dir b:july{ENTER}
A>dir b:.dat{ENTER}
```

- If there is no parameter, as in the first example, DIR lists all files on the default disk.
- If the parameter is a drive name, as in the second example, DIR lists all files on that drive.
- If the parameter is a file's name, DIR lists that file. Global filename characters may be used to list a group of files.
- If the parameter is a filename (with no dot and extension), DIR lists every file with that filename and any extension.
- If the parameter is a dot and extension (with no filename), DIR lists every file with that extension and any filename.

To list file specifications only, five per display line, use DIR with the /W (wide) option:

```
A>dir *.com/w{ENTER}
```

To prevent a long directory list from scrolling off the screen before you can read it, use the /P (pause) option:

A>**dir/p{ENTER}**

Copying a File

To copy a file, run COPY:

A>**copy scooba.dat b:dooba.dat{ENTER}**
A>**copy scooba.dat b:{ENTER}**
A>**copy a: b:{ENTER}**

- The first parameter names the file to copy *from.*
- The second parameter names the file to copy *to.* If a file with this name already exists, it is replaced; COPY gives no warning.
- If the file's name is omitted from the second parameter, as in the second form, COPY gives the *to* file the same name as the *from* file.
- If the file's names are omitted from both parameters, as in the third form, COPY copies every file on the *from* disk to the *to* disk.

To copy two or more files at once, use global filename characters in the first parameter. If you do this, you may use corresponding characters in the second parameter to *change the names of the files in a systematic way.* For example, to copy every DAT file on drive B to a file with the same filename and the extension DA2, run

A>**copy b:*.dat b:*.da2{ENTER}**

COPY normally assigns the target file the same time stamp as the source file. *To give the copied file a current time stamp*, append "+,," to the source file's name:

A>**copy b:fit?a.dat+,, b:form?.dat{ENTER}**

Renaming a File

To rename a file, run the RENAME command:

A>**rename b:scooba.dat dooba.dat{ENTER}**

- The first parameter identifies the file to rename.
- The second parameter is the new name to be used. RENAME ignores the drive name if one is used.

If the new name describes a file already on the disk, RENAME gives a warning message and does not rename the file.

To rename two or more files at once, use global filename characters. Use corresponding characters in the second parameter to change the names of the files in a systematic way. For example, to rename every DAT file on drive B to the same filename with the extension DA2, run

```
A>rename b:*.dat b:*.da2{ENTER}
```

Erasing a File

To erase a file, run either the ERASE or the DEL command (the two are identical):

```
A>erase b:scooba.dat{ENTER}
A>del b:scooba.dat{ENTER}
```

- The parameter names the file to erase.

To erase two or more files at once, use global filename characters. If you enter "erase *.*", ERASE prompts you to be sure you want to erase all files on the disk before it does so.

Sub-Directories (DOS 2.0 Only)

A *sub-directory* is a file on a disk that contains directory information. In this context a disk's basic directory is known as the *root directory*.

A sub-directory may hold both data files and other sub-directories; thus sub-directories can be nested inside other sub-directories. It is customary to view a disk's directory structure as a *tree* whose "root" is the root directory, whose "branches" are sub-directories, and whose "leaves" are files. Such a tree is illustrated in Figure 18-15.

Using Sub-Directory Names With File Specifications

The sequence of sub-directories leading to a particular file is often called a *path*. Paths are written like this:

```
A>type b:\a2\b2\c2\file.dat{ENTER}
A>type b:c2\file.dat{ENTER}
A>type b:..\x1.dat{ENTER}
A>type \autoexec.bat{ENTER}
```

- The drive name, if used, precedes the path name.
- In each example, the backslash (\) separates sub-directory names from each other and from the file's name.
- In the first example, the \ before the path name means that the first sub-directory, A2, is to be found in the root directory.
- In the second example, the absence of a \ before the path name means that the first sub-directory, C2, is to be found in the *current directory* (that is, the directory DOS will refer to if you enter a file's name alone).

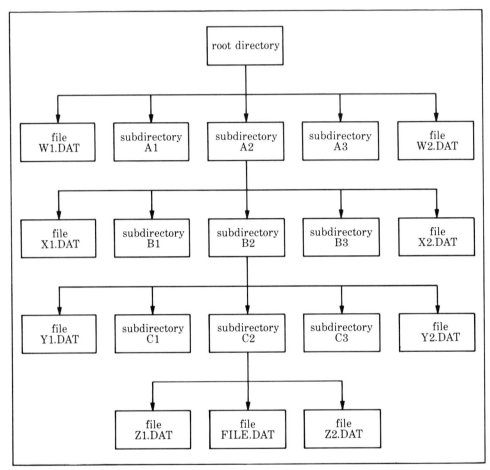

Figure 18-15.
Structure of a disk with sub-directories

- In the third example, the directory name .. refers to the *parent* of the current directory. If the current directory were B2, for example, .. would refer to directory A2.
- In the fourth case, the path \ refers to the root directory. Use this form of path name to refer to a file in the root directory when some other directory is current.

If a command will accept a parameter that refers to a disk rather than a file, it will generally accept a path name that leads to a sub-directory rather than a file. For example, to display the contents of the sub-directory \A2\B2, you would run

```
A>dir \al\b2{ENTER}
```

And to display the contents of the root directory on drive B, run

```
A>dir b:\{ENTER}
```

Creating a Sub-Directory

To create a sub-directory, run the MKDIR (make directory) command:

```
A>mkdir b:al{ENTER}
A>mkdir b:\b2\c2{ENTER}
```

- The parameter gives the path to the sub-directory being created.

A sub-directory may only be created in an existing directory. Thus you must build up the directory structure from the root directory one level at a time.

The rules for naming a sub-directory are the same as the rules for naming a file: the name may be one to eight characters long, followed by an optional dot and an extension of one to three characters. The characters allowed in sub-directory names are the same as those allowed in file's names.

Changing and Displaying the Current Sub-Directory

To change or display the current sub-directory on a disk, run CHDIR:

```
A>chdir b:b2\c2{ENTER}
A>chdir b:\a2\b2\c2{ENTER}
A>chdir b:\{ENTER}
A>chdir b:{ENTER}
```

- The parameter gives the path to the sub-directory that is to become current on the designated disk.
- The parameter \ makes the root directory current.
- If the parameter is omitted, CHDIR displays the path of the current directory on the designated disk.

When you put a new diskette in a diskette drive, DOS automatically sets that drive's current directory to the root directory.

Removing a Sub-Directory

To remove a sub-directory, run the RMDIR (remove directory) command:

```
A>rmdir b:\al\b3{ENTER}
```

- The parameter is the path to the sub-directory to be removed.

You cannot remove a sub-directory from a disk if it contains files or lower level sub-directories or if it is the current directory.

CAUTION

Do not try to remove a sub-directory with the ERASE command. ERASE cannot remove a sub-directory, but if the sub-directory contains files, it will delete them all.

Displaying the Contents of a Sub-Directory

To list the contents of a sub-directory, run DIR:

```
A>dir b:{ENTER}
A>dir b:\r1{ENTER}
A>dir b:\r1\*.dat
```

- The parameter names the disk and sub-directory to be listed.
- If no path is given, as in the first example, the current directory is listed.
- Filenames or partial filenames, as shown in the description of DIR in the section "Listing Files with the DIR Command," may be used with sub-directory names. The /W and /P options may be used.

When DIR is run on a directory that contains sub-directories, it lists each sub-directory with "<DIR>" after its name. File names are also shown, as in any DIR listing.

When DIR is run on a sub-directory, it lists entries named "." and "..". These entries represent the current directory and the current directory's "parent," respectively.

Displaying the Sub-Directories on a Disk

To display the sub-directories on a disk, run TREE:

```
A>tree b:{ENTER}
```

- The parameter names the drive holding the disk you want to display.
- The /F (files) option makes TREE list the files in all the directories in addition to listing the directories themselves.

Searching for Command Files

A *search path* is a sub-directory that DOS uses to search for any command name not found in the current directory.

Search paths help you separate your programs and data. Keep your programs in one sub-directory and your data files in another. When you are using the programs, make the data files' sub-directory the current sub-directory and define a search path to the program files' sub-directory. You can run the programs on the data without ever having to enter a path in a command line.

To define one or more search paths or display the current search paths, run PATH:

```
A>path \pgms{ENTER}
A>path b:\wp;c:\pgms{ENTER}
A>path b:\{ENTER}
A>path ,{ENTER}
A>path{ENTER}
```

- Each parameter defines one search path. DOS will search the paths in the order in which you specify them.

- If you run PATH with more than one parameter, as in the second example, you must separate the parameters with semicolons (;), *not* spaces.

- Refer to the root directory as \. Thus the third example tells DOS to search the root directory of the disk in drive B.

- If you run PATH with at least one parameter, PATH replaces all previously defined search paths with the path(s) you specify.

- If you run PATH with a null parameter, as in the fourth example here, PATH cancels all current search paths without defining new ones.

- If you run PATH with no parameters, as in the fifth example, PATH displays the current search paths but does not change them.

Search paths do not go away when you change disks, but they do go away when you boot. If you want them to take effect automatically, you should put a PATH command in an AUTOEXEC.BAT file when you boot.

Dealing With Overlay Files

Many users like to keep all of their programs in one directory and set a search path to that directory. This permits them to keep one copy of each program on a disk and yet to run any program from any directory.

This technique generally works well, but it creates a problem with application programs that use overlays. An *overlay* is a part of a program that is kept in a file different from the COM or EXE file that contains the program itself. The program loads overlays into RAM only when it needs them. Large programs reduce the amount of RAM they need by loading several overlays into the same part of RAM.

If an application program does not know how to find its overlay files through the search path, you must store copies of those files in each directory you want to run the programs from, even though you need to store the program itself in only one directory.

The following batch file illustrates a convenient way to deal with this problem. You can adapt this batch file to work with each application program you use.

The batch file tests to see whether an overlay file needed by a hypothetical application program already exists in the current directory. If the file does not exist, the batch file copies it from the directory where it is stored, runs the program, and then deletes the file. If the file does exist, the batch file simply executes the program.

This batch file lets you store copies of a program's overlay files in certain directories where you use the programs a lot. In those directories the batch file will run the program without the delay caused by copying the files first.

```
if exist example.ovr goto itshere
  copy \com\example.ovr
  example
  erase example.ovr
  goto end
:itshere
  example
:end
```

Displaying a File With the TYPE Command

To display a file, run TYPE:

A>**type b:scooba.dat{ENTER}**

- The parameter names the file to display.

To make TYPE pause while you view the screen, enter CTRL NUM LOCK. Press any typing key to make TYPE resume.

To halt TYPE before it displays the whole file, enter CTRL BREAK.

I/O Redirection (DOS 2.0 Only)

DOS lets you *redirect* a command's displayed output to a disk file instead of to your PC's printer and redirect the program's source of input from a file instead of from the keyboard.

Redirecting a Command's Input and Output

To redirect a command's displayed output to a file, put the greater-than sign (>) and the file's name at the end of the command line:

```
A>tree b:/f >datadisk.tre{ENTER}
A>tree c:/f >>datadisk.tre{ENTER}
```

- Any character (nongraphic) output that the command would normally show on the display is directed to the file instead. Thus the first example stores disk B's sub-directory structure, complete with file names, in a file on disk A named DATADISK.TRE. It is not shown on the display, as it would normally be.
- If an identically named file already exists, > makes DOS replace it; >> makes DOS append to it.

To redirect a command's keyboard input source to a file, put the less-than sign (<) and the file's name at the end of the command line:

```
A>sort <datadisk.tre{ENTER}
```

- Any input that the command would normally read from the keyboard is read from the file instead.

Filters: SORT, FIND, and MORE

A *filter* is a command that reads text from the keyboard (or more commonly, reads redirected input from a file) and displays it (or writes it to a file) after changing it in some systematic way.

DOS has three filter commands: SORT, FIND, and MORE.

To sort lines in alphabetical order, run SORT:

```
A>sort <datadisk.tre{ENTER}
A>sort/r/+10 <datadisk.tre{ENTER}
```

- SORT's input source is the keyboard. Input is normally redirected to a file, as in these examples.
- SORT's output is the display (unless redirected).
- The /R (reverse) option makes SORT sort in descending alphabetical order. If it is omitted, SORT sorts in ascending order.
- The /+n option makes SORT sort only on text from the nth character of each line to the end of the line. You may substitute any number you want for n. If the option is omitted, SORT sorts on the entire line.
- The most input that SORT can process is 63K bytes.

To display or count all lines containing a specified sequence of characters (a *string*), run FIND:

`A>find "EXE"/c/v <datadisk.tre{ENTER}`

- FIND's input source is the keyboard. It is normally redirected to a file, as in the example above.
- FIND's output goes to the display (unless redirected).
- FIND looks for lines containing the string inside the quotation marks. Represent a quotation mark in the string by a pair of quotation marks.
- The /C option makes FIND display only the number (count) of lines containing the string. If /C is omitted, FIND displays each line.
- The /V option makes FIND count or display all lines that do *not* contain the string.

To display a file one screenful (24 lines) at a time, run MORE:

`A>more <datadisk.tre{ENTER}`

- MORE's input source is the keyboard (unless redirected to a file).
- MORE's output is the display (unless redirected).
- MORE displays a screenful of text followed by the message "—More—". When you press a typing key, MORE displays the next screenful of text, and so forth.

Pipes

A *pipe* is a direct connection between the display output of one program and the keyboard input of another. *To use a pipe,* put two commands or more on the same line with the | symbol between them:

`A>dir b: | sort{ENTER}`

- DOS runs the first command and redirects its display output to a temporary file created for this purpose.
- Then DOS runs the second command and redirects its keyboard input source to the same temporary file.
- After running the second command, DOS erases the temporary file.
- You may join three or more commands with pipes.

Examples of Filters and Pipes

Here are some simple but useful applications of filters and pipes. Each example is shown twice: first with separate command lines and I/O redirection, and then with a single command line and pipes.

To display a directory listing of a disk, sorted in filename order, run

```
A>dir b: >diskb.dir{ENTER}
A>sort <diskb.dir{ENTER}

A>dir b: ¦ sort{ENTER}
```

To display a directory listing of a disk, sorted in descending order by file size (the file size field in a DIR listing line begins in column 13), run

```
A>dir b: >diskb.dir{ENTER}
A>sort/r/+13 <diskb.dir{ENTER}

A>dir b: ¦ sort/r/+13{ENTER}
```

To display only those lines of a directory listing that contain the string "AR♭" (where the symbol ♭ represents "blank"), run

```
A>dir b: >diskb.dir{ENTER}
A>find "AR " <diskb.dir{ENTER}

A>dir b: ¦ find "AR "{ENTER}
```

These commands could be used as a more powerful alternative to the global filename character ? to display all files whose filenames end in "AR", no matter how long each filename is.

To display only those lines of a directory listing that do not contain the string "♭COM♭", run

```
A>dir b: >diskb.dir{ENTER}
A>find " COM "/v <diskb.dir{ENTER}

A>dir b: ¦ find " COM "/v{ENTER}
```

Using a Printer

This section discusses how to set up a serial interface printer for use with the PC, and how to use the printer with DOS and with programs running under DOS.

For information about how to set up and load IBM's Graphic Matrix Printer, see Chapter 7, "Using a Printer."

Preparing the PC to Use a Serial Interface Printer

To prepare the PC to operate a serial interface printer, you must

1. Connect the printer to your PC's Asynchronous Communications Adapter or other serial interface adapter. Note that the PC needs a differently wired cable than most other computers to operate a serial interface printer. If your printer cable is not intended for use on a PC, *it will not work.*

   In technical terms, the PC's serial interface adapter is configured as data terminal equipment rather than as data communication equipment. It must be connected to the printer by a special kind of cable called a *null modem.* Table 18-11 shows how to wire a printer cable that works with the PC and most types of serial printers.

2. Determine how your printer expects to receive data over the cable. The variable factors and their possible settings are

   - *Baud rate:* 110, 150, 300, 600, 1200, 2400, 4800, or 9600.

   - *Parity:* none, odd, or even.

   - *Data bits:* 7 or 8.

   - *Stop bits:* 1 or 2.

3. After you boot, use MODE to set the PC's serial interface to communicate with the printer:

   `A>mode device:baud,parity,data,stop,P{ENTER}`

Connect this pin at one end...	...to this pin at the other end	Connect this pin at one end...	...to this pin at the other end
1	1	6	20
2	3	7	7
3	2	8	8
4	5	20	6
5	4		

Table 18-11.
A Printer Cable for Most Serial Interface Printers With the IBM PC

- For *device*, substitute the device name of the serial interface adapter that is connected to the printer. If your PC has only one serial interface adapter, it is COM1. If your PC has two serial interface adapters, it may be COM1 or COM2. Try both names if you are not sure which adapter is which.

- For *baud*, substitute the proper baud rate.

- For *parity*, substitute N for none, O for odd, or E for even. If you omit this parameter, it defaults to E.

- For *data*, substitute the number of data bits. If you omit this parameter, it defaults to 7.

- For *stop*, substitute the number of stop bits. If you omit this parameter, it defaults to 2 for a baud rate of 110 and to 1 for any higher baud rate.

- The P makes DOS continue to try to send data to the printer indefinitely if it returns a "not ready" indication. You can stop the retries by canceling a program with CTRL BREAK. If you omit P, DOS will retry P for a short interval and then give an error message.

For example, to set COM1 to 1200 baud, no parity, 7 data bits, and 1 stop bit, enter

```
A>mode com1:1200,n,7,1,p{ENTER}
```

If you are unsure of the proper setting for *parity*, *data*, or *stop*, let the parameter assume its default value. This value is appropriate for most printers.

4. Next, use MODE again to redirect the PC's printed output from the device name LPT to the device name of the printter's serial interface:

```
A>mode lpt1:=device{ENTER}
```

- *device* has the same value as it does in the first MODE command.

Printing With PRTSC

To print the contents of the screen, enter SHIFT PRTSC. In DOS 1.1, this works with alphanumeric information only. In DOS 2.0, you can make SHIFT PRTSC work with graphic information as well

by entering the GRAPHICS command, provided you have IBM's
Graphic Matrix Printer or an equivalent printer.

To print a text file, enter CTRL PRTSC to slave the printer to the
screen. Then display the file with any command such as TYPE:

```
A>type b:dogstory.txt{ENTER}
```

Enter CTRL PRTSC again to unslave the printer.

This technique will work with most commands and programs
that display output a line at a time.

Printing With PRINT (DOS 2.0 Only)

To queue a file for printing so that you can run other commands
while DOS prints the file, run the PRINT command:

```
A>print b:dogstory.txt b.txt{ENTER}
A>print b.txt/c{ENTER}
A>print/t{ENTER}
```

- PRINT accepts a variable number of parameters. The files
  named by the parameters are queued for printing in the
  order they are named. As many as ten files may be in the
  queue at a time.
- PRINT with no parameters displays the current contents of
  the print queue.
- The /C (cancel) option removes one or more files from the
  print queue. /C affects all filenames from the one that *precedes* it to the end of the command line. Thus, in the second
  example, the file B.TXT would be removed from the print
  queue.
- The /T (terminate) option removes all files from the print
  queue.

Before you queue a file for printing, be sure that your printer is
on-line and ready for use. If you have a serial interface printer, run
the MODE commands that make the PC send its printed output to
the serial interface.

The first time you use PRINT after booting, it displays the
prompt:

```
Name of list device [PRN]: _
```

Enter the device name you want queued files to be printed on.
To print files on PRN (a synonym for LPT1, your PC's first or only
parallel interface), press ENTER alone.

Once you have queued a file for printing, you may not remove the disk containing the file or erase or modify the file until it has been completely printed or removed from the queue.

When DOS finishes printing a queued file, it sends a form feed character to the printer. This separates the printouts and makes the printout of each file start at the beginning of a new page.

CHAPTER 19

Problem Determination

This chapter contains explanations of some common problems that cannot be explained in Chapter 20, "Error Messages and Other Messages," mostly because they have symptoms other than error messages. The problems are grouped by the activity you are likely to be engaged in when they occur, such as booting, printing, using a diskette, and so on.

Since there is no way to organize these problems neatly in alphabetical order, we suggest that you read the chapter quickly to familiarize yourself with its contents. Then, when you have a problem, you will be better prepared to find the solution.

Problems Associated With Booting

SYMPTOM: when you turn the PC on, it displays an error code in the upper left corner of the screen. The system may either continue to boot, display a message instructing you to take some action, or halt.

PROBLEM: the PC's power-on diagnostics have detected an error. This may be due to malfunctioning hardware, improper switch settings in the System Unit, or other causes.

SOLUTION: consult the "Problem Determination Procedures" section in the IBM *Guide to Operations* manual. This section tells you how to interpret and handle many common power-on error codes.

Error codes can be caused by turning on system components in the wrong order. Always turn on your external hard disk drive or System Expansion Unit, if any, before you turn on the System Unit.

If your system boots normally despite the error code, you may not need to take any corrective action. Look up the code, but do not be concerned if its explanation makes no sense or you cannot make the code stop occurring.

If you cannot resolve the problem with the aid of the *Guide to Operations*, seek advice from the firm responsible for servicing your PC.

SYMPTOM: when you try to boot, the PC displays a boot message beginning "The IBM Personal Computer Basic".

PROBLEM: you forgot to insert the DOS diskette, or you inserted it incorrectly. Review the instructions for inserting the diskette in Chapter 2.

If you have two diskette drives, you may have inserted the DOS diskette in the wrong drive. It goes into drive A, the *left* drive.

If you have a Fixed Disk, this symptom also indicates that the Fixed Disk does not have an active partition.

SOLUTION: insert the DOS diskette properly in drive A and close the drive door. Reboot the PC by holding down CTRL and ALT and pressing DEL.

SYMPTOM: the PC boots from the Fixed Disk when you intended it to boot from a diskette.

PROBLEM: you forgot to insert the DOS diskette, or you inserted it incorrectly. Review the instructions for inserting the diskette in Chapter 2.

If you have two diskette drives, you may have inserted the DOS diskette in the wrong drive. It goes into drive A, the *left* drive.

SOLUTION: insert the DOS diskette properly in drive A and close the drive door. Reboot the PC by holding down CTRL and ALT and pressing DEL.

SYMPTOM: upon booting, DOS does not prompt you for the date and time and may spontaneously execute some commands.

PROBLEM: your DOS disk has an AUTOEXEC.BAT file.

SOLUTION: eliminate the AUTOEXEC.BAT file or add the DATE and TIME commands to it. See Chapter 9 for more information.

If your PC has an adapter card with a battery-powered clock, the AUTOEXEC.BAT file may run a special command that sets the current date and time automatically when you boot. This makes the DATE and TIME prompts unnecessary.

SYMPTOM: CTRL ALT DEL does not reboot the PC.

PROBLEM: a hardware or software error has corrupted the part of DOS that is kept in RAM to read the keyboard and perform elementary functions like rebooting when CTRL ALT DEL is pressed.

SOLUTION: turn the PC off. Wait at least ten seconds, and then turn the PC on again.

SYMPTOM: you power the PC down and back up, but it does not boot automatically, and you may not be able to boot it with CTRL ALT DEL.

PROBLEM: you did not give the PC time to "settle down" in the *off* state.

SOLUTION: after turning the PC off, wait at least ten seconds before turning it on again.

Problems Associated With the Display

SYMPTOM: you are using a Color/Graphics Monitor Adapter, and one of the edges of the image is cut off.

PROBLEM: the adapter has not been set up to align text properly for your monitor.

SOLUTION: use the MODE command to adjust the image. See Chapter 18, "Operations and Procedures," for details.

SYMPTOM: when you display a text file with TYPE (or with a similar command that copies the file to the screen), it appears to contain Greek letters and other unexpected symbols.

PROBLEM: a part of each byte that is not normally used to store character data contains data in this file. The PC interprets the whole byte as a character value and displays nonstandard characters. If the file is a data file used by a program like a word processor, the program is probably using this part of each byte to record information about the text in the file, such as where each paragraph ends.

SOLUTION: use the program that created the text file to display it correctly.

Problems Associated With Disks

SYMPTOM: under DOS 1.0, the PC stops running when programs are loaded from a certain diskette; alternatively, text files stored on a certain diskette appear to be missing large sections of text.

PROBLEM: you are trying to read a double-sided diskette. DOS 1.0 does not support double-sided diskettes.

SOLUTION: read this diskette under DOS 1.1 or a later version. If you must run DOS 1.0 for some reason, copy the files to a single-sided diskette.

SYMPTOM: the diskette directory appears to contain many "file names" that are nonsensical or entirely blank.

PROBLEM: you are trying to read a nine-sector diskette (created with DOS 2.0) with DOS 1.0 or 1.1, which can only handle eight-sector diskettes.

SOLUTION: *do not* give DOS a chance to store information on the disk; it can only do damage! Boot DOS 2.0 *immediately.*

If the earlier version of DOS tried to modify the diskette, check all files to see if their contents have been corrupted. If any files are corrupted, see Chapter 18, "Operations and Procedures," for instructions on how to recover data from a corrupted diskette.

SYMPTOM: you receive disk I/O errors, usually indicated by one of DOS's "Abort, Retry, Ignore?" messages.

PROBLEM: there is no diskette in the diskette drive; the diskette is incorrectly inserted; or the drive's door is open. If none of these is true, the diskette is worn or damaged, or the diskette drive is malfunctioning.

SOLUTION: see Chapter 11, "Caring For Your PC," or Chapter 18, "Operations and Procedures," for a discussion of this problem.

Problems Associated With Printing

SYMPTOM: the printer does not print when it should; the printer's "on-line" or "ready" light is off.

PROBLEM: the printer is not ready to print for some reason. The entire PC may "freeze"; that is, it may not respond to any input. Check the following possibilities:

- The printer is not plugged in or turned on.
- The printer's "on-line" control, if any, is not properly set.
- The ribbon is broken, jammed, or not installed.
- For a letter-quality printer with a multistrike ribbon, the ribbon is used up.
- If raising the printer's cover puts the printer off-line, the cover is up. If the cover has been raised and lowered again,

the "reset" button (if any) has not been pressed to put the printer back on-line.

- The paper is not properly loaded, or it is jammed. Note that on some printers it is possible to load paper so that it does not pass through the "out of paper" sensor. In that case the sensor does not detect the presence of paper, even though the paper is loaded and seems to be feeding properly.

SOLUTION: correct the problem and press the printer's "reset" button or "on-line" control. If the PC "froze" when data was sent to the printer, it should now unfreeze and the printer should begin printing immediately.

If you correct all apparent problems and the printer still does not go on-line, ask a more experienced person for help.

SYMPTOM: the printer does not print when it should; the printer's "on-line" or "ready" light is on.

PROBLEM: the printer is not receiving data from the computer. Check the following possibilities:

- The printer's data cable is not connected to the PC or is connected to the wrong data socket.
- The printer's data cable is not properly wired for connecting this printer to the PC. Be sure the cable is specifically wired for connecting an IBM PC to the type of printer you have through the appropriate interface (serial or parallel).

If you have a serial interface printer, remember that the PC's serial interface adapter is designed in an unusual way. In technical terms, the serial interface adapter is configured as data terminal equipment (DTE) rather than as data communications equipment (DCE). A cable that connects the printer to most other types of computers *will not work* without modifications.

- If you have a serial interface printer, you failed to assign LPT1 to COM1 using the MODE command. (If your PC has two serial ports and you are using the second one, assign LPT1 to COM2 instead of to COM1.)
- If you have a serial interface printer, the serial interface parameters are not set to the same values on the printer and on the PC's serial interface.
- If you have a serial interface printer, you used the MODE command to set the IBM Graphic Matrix Printer's line spacing or character pitch. This form of MODE automatically resets DOS's printed output to LPT1, the parallel printer interface.
- If you are using the PRINT command, you entered the

wrong device name in response to PRINT's "list device?" prompt.

SOLUTION: correct the problem and restart the printing operation. Use the MODE command if necessary to reassign LPT1 or to set your PC's serial interface parameters or both. You may have to put the printer back on-line when you are done.

If you correct all apparent problems and the printer still does not work, ask a more experienced person for help.

SYMPTOM: the printer prints nonsense.

PROBLEM: if you are using a serial printer, your PC's serial interface is not configured to match the printer's interface.

SOLUTION: set your PC's serial interface and the printer's serial interface to the same parameters. Use the MODE command to set the PC's serial interface parameters. See the section on printers in Chapter 18, "Operations and Procedures," for details.

SYMPTOM: the printer stops in the middle of a printout and the PC freezes.

PROBLEM: the printer has entered a "not ready" state because it ran out of paper or for a similar reason.

SOLUTION: correct the problem and put the printer back on-line.

SYMPTOM: your printer prints strange characters or starts printing characters in a strange manner (for example, double-spaced, very large).

PROBLEM: your PC sent the printer special control characters or character sequences that instructed it to do what it is doing.

SOLUTION: to reset any mode changes, turn your printer off, wait a few seconds, and turn the printer back on. Try printing a file that you know is straight text (without control characters). If it works, the strange results were probably caused by a file that contains control characters. If the printout is still not correct, your printer is improperly adjusted or is malfunctioning. Consult your printer's instruction book or ask a more experienced person for assistance.

If you trace the problem to control characters in a data file, look for another way to print the file. If the file was produced by a word processor, spreadsheet program, or another application program of this type, print the file using the "print" function provided with the program.

If you are already trying to print the file with the program that created it, that program is probably making incorrect assumptions about the type of printer you have; thus it is sending printer control characters that have inappropriate effects. You may be able to correct this problem by running an "install" command that modifies the program to make it operate your printer correctly. See the program's user's manual for details.

SYMPTOM: your serial printer does not print all of the characters that the PC sends to it. It may print a few lines correctly before it starts missing characters.

PROBLEM: early PC I's have several errors in the ROMs. The most serious error prevents DOS from detecting a "not ready" signal from a serial interface device.

If your PC sends data faster than the printer can print, the printer's buffer fills up. Then the printer sends the PC a "not ready" signal. The PC ignores this signal and continues sending data that the printer cannot accept, and so characters are lost.

You can tell if your PC's ROM contains this error by entering the DEBUG command (not mentioned elsewhere in this book because it is meant for use by programmers) and inspecting a date stored in the ROM. Place the DOS diskette in drive A and enter the following:

```
A>debug{ENTER}
-d f000:fff5 fffc{ENTER}
```

If DEBUG displays the following, you have an early ROM that contains the error:

```
F000:FFF5   30 34 2F-32 34 2F 38 31              04/24/81
```

If DEBUG displays a line containing a later date, as shown here, your ROM does not contain the error, so something else must be wrong:

```
F000:FFF5   31 30 2F-31 39 2F 38 31              10/19/81
```

To leave DEBUG, enter

```
-q{ENTER}
```

SOLUTION: several fixes can be tried, including the following:

- Mr. Peter Norton sells a program called COMPROM that corrects the erroneous code after it has been copied into RAM during booting. You can correct the problem by running this program each time you boot DOS. Mr. Norton's address is given in Appendix B, "Index of Manufacturers."
- Reduce the baud rate on your printer and serial interface adapter to a rate no greater than the speed at which the

printer can print. This prevents the printer's buffer from filling up and so prevents the problem from occurring.

- Avoid the problem by using a parallel interface printer.
- Use a parallel-to-serial converter (described in Chapter 16, "Guide to Accessories") to connect your serial printer to the PC through a parallel interface.

Miscellaneous Problems

SYMPTOM: the PC displays error messages or error codes indicating that you are getting memory data errors in RAM.

PROBLEM: if you are using a monitor not made by IBM, it may be producing radio emissions that are strong enough to disturb your PC's memory.

SOLUTION: move the monitor a foot or more away from the System Unit.

SYMPTOM: when you run CHKDSK, it says that your PC has a different amount of RAM from the amount that you know is installed.

PROBLEM: the switches in the System Unit that tell DOS how much RAM the PC has are set incorrectly.

SOLUTION: set the switches correctly. See the installation instructions for your RAM card.

SYMPTOM: when running under DOS 1.1 on a PC with more than 384K of RAM, DISKCOPY never finishes running.

PROBLEM: an error in this program prevents it from running correctly under these conditions.

SOLUTION: buy DOS 2.0. As an interim solution, use COPY instead of DISKCOPY or reset the switches on the PC's System Board to make DOS think you have only 320K of RAM. The instructions that come with your RAM card tell you how to set the switches.

CHAPTER 20

Error Messages And Other Messages

This chapter contains the error messages and other messages that are produced by DOS and the DOS commands described in this book. Messages are listed in alphabetical order. Each message is followed by possible explanations of its cause.

Much of the information within this chapter may also be found in the IBM *Disk Operating System* (DOS) manual. Messages relating to commands not discussed in this book (such as LINK, EXE2BIN, and DEBUG—all used primarily by programmers) can be found in the *DOS* manual.

Notice that some of the messages in this chapter are accompanied by the prompt "Abort, Retry, Ignore?". These messages usually indicate an unsuccessful attempt to read from or write to a device, such as a disk drive or a printer. In these instances, DOS expects you to respond by entering the first letter of the action you would like to take:

- **A** for Abort. DOS will halt the program that requested the read or write operation and give you the DOS prompt.
- **R** for Retry. DOS will attempt to read from or to write to the device again. This gives you an opportunity to "fix" any problem before you enter **R** (for example, by putting a disk in the drive).
- **I** for Ignore. DOS pretends the error did not occur and allows the program to continue running. If the operation is a read, DOS tries to read the next part of the file. If the operation is a write, DOS discards the information it was to have written. This is seldom an appropriate response to an error, since it allows an application program to read or write an incomplete version of a file without knowing it.

Note that error messages do not always accurately reflect the problem that is occurring. For example, you might receive any of the device error messages just presented if you attempt to use a double-sided diskette in a single-sided drive, or if you use a nine-sector diskette with a version of DOS earlier than 2.0. The specific message you receive in this instance will depend on what you try to do with the diskette.

Try to use a commonsense approach to solving a baffling error message. Think about what you are doing. Is the error message you got a message that you might expect in this situation? Skim through both this chapter and Chapter 19, "Problem Determination," for ideas about what might be wrong. Check Chapter 18, "Operations and Procedures," for more ideas.

A

All files canceled by operator

PRINT. This message is for your information only and does not indicate an error. PRINT displays this message when you cancel the printing of all queued files via the /T parameter.

All specified file(s) are contiguous

CHKDSK. This message is for your information only and does not indicate an error. None of the files you named are fragmented.

Allocation error for file, size adjusted

CHKDSK. A filename precedes this message. An invalid sector number was found in the file allocation table. The file was truncated at the end of the last valid sector.

Attempted write-protect violation

FORMAT. The diskette being formatted cannot be written to because it is write-protected. You are prompted to insert a new diskette and press a key to restart formatting.

B

Backing up files to diskette xx

BACKUP. This message will be followed by a list of files that were backed up on the indicated diskette.

Backup file sequence error

RESTORE. A file to be restored was backed up onto more than one diskette. You did not insert the diskette with the first part of the file. Rerun RESTORE and start with the correct diskette.

Bad call format error reading/writing $device$
Abort, Retry, Ignore?

DOS and commands. There is an error in the software that controls the indicated $device$. Enter **A** to return to the DOS command line prompt. Ask the dealer who sold you the device to help you correct the problem.

Bad command error reading/writing *device*
Abort, Retry, Ignore?

DOS and commands. There is an error in the software that controls the indicated *device*. Enter **A** to return to the DOS command line prompt. Ask the dealer who sold you the device to help you correct the problem.

Bad command or file name

DOS. The command just entered is not a valid command to DOS. You should check your spelling and reenter the command. If the command name is correct, check to see that the default drive (or the drive you specified) contains the external command or batch file you are trying to execute.

Bad or missing command Interpreter

DOS. The disk that DOS is being started from does not contain a copy of COMMAND.COM, or an error occurred while the disk was being loaded. If rebooting fails to solve the problem, copy COMMAND.COM from a backup diskette to the root directory of the disk that failed.

This message also appears if COMMAND.COM has been removed from the directory that it was originally in when DOS was started, or if the COMSPEC= parameter in the environment points to a directory not containing COMMAND.COM, and DOS is attempting to reload the command processor.

Bad or missing *filename*

DOS. This message appears only at startup and indicates that a device driver named in a DEVICE=*filename* parameter in the CONFIG.SYS file was either not found or set a break address that was out of bounds for the machine size, or that an error occurred while the driver was being loaded. That driver is not installed by DOS.

Bad unit error reading/writing *device*
Abort, Retry, Ignore?

DOS and commands. There is an error in the software that controls the indicated *device*. Enter **A** to return to the DOS command line prompt. Ask the dealer who sold you the device to help you correct the problem.

Batch file missing

DOS. DOS was unable to locate the batch file that it had been processing. The file may have been erased or renamed by one of the steps within it. Batch processing stops and the DOS prompt appears.

C

Cannot do binary reads from a device

COPY. You have used the /B parameter with a device name while attempting to copy from the device. The copy cannot be performed in binary mode because COPY must be able to detect the end of the file from the device. You should omit the /B parameter or use the /A parameter after the device name.

Cannot edit .BAK file - rename file

EDLIN. All .BAK files are considered to be backup files, with more up-to-date versions of the files assumed to exist. Therefore, .BAK files should not be edited.

If it is necessary to edit the .BAK file, either rename the file or copy it and give the copy a different name.

Cannot load COMMAND, system halted

DOS. While attempting to reload the command processor, DOS determined that the area in which it keeps track of available memory has been destroyed or that the command processor could not be found in the path specified by the COMSPEC environment parameter. You should restart DOS.

Cannot start COMMAND, exiting

DOS. While attempting to load a second copy of the command processor, either the FILES= parameter in the configuration file was found to contain too small a value, or there is insufficient available memory to contain the new copy of COMMAND.COM.

COMn:$bbbb,p,d,s,t$ initialized

MODE. The Asynchronous Communications Adapter has been initialized. The values represent

n	adapter (COM1 or COM2)
$bbbb$	baud rate
p	parity
	e even
	o odd
	n none
s	stop bits (1 or 2)

t type of serial device

     p   serial printer (serial timeouts will be retried)

     —   other serial device (serial timeouts will not be retried)

Contains invalid cluster, file truncated

CHKDSK. The file whose name precedes this message contains an invalid pointer to the data area. The file is truncated at the last valid data block if the /F parameter was used.

Contains xxx non-contiguous blocks

CHKDSK. The file whose name precedes this message is not written contiguously on disk; instead, it is written in xxx pieces on different areas of the disk. This is only an information message and does not indicate a problem on the disk. Since fragmented files take longer to read, you should consider copying badly fragmented files to another disk. This will record the files sequentially, resulting in better system performance when the files are read.

Convert directory to file (Y/N)?

CHKDSK. The directory whose name precedes this message contains enough invalid information that it is no longer usable as a directory. If you reply **Y**, CHKDSK will convert the directory to a file so that you may examine it with DEBUG. If you reply **N**, the directory is not changed.

Convert lost chains to files (Y/N)?

CHKDSK. If you wish to recover the data in the "lost" blocks found by CHKDSK, reply **Y**. If you reply **N**, CHKDSK will free the blocks up so that they can be allocated to new files.

Copy another (Y/N)?

DISKCOPY. If you wish to copy another diskette, enter **Y**; DISKCOPY will prompt you to insert the next source and target diskettes. If you do not wish to copy another diskette, enter **N**.

Copy complete

DISKCOPY. The contents of the source diskette have been successfully copied to the target diskette.

Copying x sectors per track, n side(s)

DISKCOPY. The n will be either 1 or 2, indicating the number of sides that DISKCOPY has successfully read from the first track of the source diskette. The x will be 8 or 9, indicating the number of sectors per track found on the source diskette.

D

Data error reading/writing *device*
Abort, Retry, Ignore?

DOS and commands. DOS cannot read/write data on the indicated *device*. This usually means that a bad spot has developed on a disk or a failure has occurred in a disk drive or disk drive adapter card. *Do not change disks until you have resolved the problem.* See "Dealing with Diskette Errors" in Chapter 18, "Operations and Procedures," for further instructions.

Disk boot failure

DOS. An error occurred while DOS was being loaded into memory. If subsequent attempts to start the system also fail, place a backup DOS diskette in drive A and restart your system.

Disk error reading/writing *device*
Abort, Retry, Ignore?

DOS and commands. DOS cannot read/write data on the indicated *device*. This usually means that a bad spot has developed on a disk or a failure has occurred in a disk drive or disk drive adapter card. *Do not change disks until you have resolved the problem.* See "Dealing with Diskette Errors" in Chapter 18, "Operations and Procedures," for further instructions.

Disk error writing FAT *x*

CHKDSK. A disk error was encountered when CHKDSK was attempting to update the file allocation table (FAT) on the specified drive. *x* will be 1 or 2, depending on which of the two copies of the file allocation table data could not be written. If this message appears twice, for FATs 1 and 2, the disk should be considered unusable.

Disk full — write not completed

EDLIN. An End Edit command ended abnormally because the disk does not have enough free space to save the entire file.

Some of the file may be saved on disk, but the portion in memory that is not saved is lost.

Disk not compatible

FORMAT. The drive you specified cannot be used by the FORMAT command. It is not supported by the IBM device interfaces that FORMAT requires.

Disk unsuitable for system disk

FORMAT. A defective track was detected where the DOS files were to reside. The diskette can be used only for data.

Diskette is not a backup diskette

RESTORE. The diskette was not created by BACKUP. The first file on a backup diskette is always BACKUPID.@@@. Rerun with the correct diskette.

Divide overflow

DOS. A program attempted to divide a number by zero, or the program had a logic error that caused an internal malfunction. The system simulates CTRL BREAK processing, halting program execution.

Do you see the leftmost 9? (Y/N)

MODE. ,R,T was specified. Respond **Y** or **N**. This prompt is repeated until you respond **Y**.

Do you wish to use the entire Fixed Disk for DOS (Y/N)......?[d]

FDISK. When the "Create DOS Partition" option is used on the current Fixed Disk and the Fixed Disk has never been set up, this question is asked. If you enter **Y**, the entire current Fixed Disk will be used for DOS. If you enter **N**, you will be asked to enter the limits of the DOS partition you want to create.

Duplicate filename or file not found

RENAME. You tried to rename a file to a file name that already exists on the diskette, or the file to be renamed could not be found on the specified (or default) drive.

E

Enter the number of the partition you want to make active...............:[ ]

FDISK. The "Change Active Partition" option is requesting that you enter the number of the partition you want to make active. Enter this number on the current Fixed Disk. (Valid partition numbers are above the prompt).

Enter partition size.............:[dddd]

FDISK. The "Create DOS Partition" option requests that you enter the size of the partition you wish to create. The number shown in the brackets is the partition size that will be used if you respond with the ENTER key.

Enter starting cylinder number....:[ddd]

FDISK. The "Create DOS Partition" option is requesting that you enter the starting cylinder number for the DOS partition that you are creating. The value in the brackets is the default value. It is the starting cylinder of the largest piece of free space on the current Fixed Disk. Type a number and press ENTER, or just press ENTER to use the default value.

Entry error

EDLIN. There is a syntax error in the last command.

Entry has a bad attribute (or size or link)

CHKDSK. This message may begin with one or two periods, indicating which entry in the sub-directory was in error. CHKDSK will attempt to correct the error if the /F parameter was specified.

Error found, F parameter not specified
Corrections will not be written to disk

CHKDSK. You are running CHKDSK without the /F option, and it has detected an error in the file structure of the disk you are checking. CHKDSK will report this error and any others it finds but will not correct the errors.

Error in EXE file

DOS. An error was detected in the relocation information placed in the file by the LINK program. This may be due to a modification to the file.

Error loading operating system

Booting. A disk error occurred while you were attempting to load your operating system from Fixed Disk. If the situation persists after several attempts to restart the system, you should start DOS from your DOS diskette and use the SYS command to transfer a new copy of DOS to your Fixed Disk.

Error reading Fixed Disk

FDISK. The FDISK program was unable to read the start-up record of the current Fixed Disk after five tries. Try the FDISK program again. If after several tries you are unable to proceed, consult the "Problem Determination" section in the *Guide to Operations* manual and see your IBM Personal Computer dealer.

Error writing to device

Commands. DOS was unable to write the requested number of bytes to the device. This indicates that you tried to send more data to the device than the device was expecting.

Errors on list device indicate that it may be off-line. Please check.

PRINT. The device being used for background printing is off-line. This message only appears when the device is off-line and you enter a new PRINT command.

EXEC failure

Commands. An error was encountered while a command was being read from disk, or the FILES= command in the configuration file (CONFIG.SYS) does not specify a large enough value. You should increase that value and restart DOS.

F

File allocation table bad, drive x
Abort, Retry, Ignore?

DOS. See the message **Disk error reading drive** x. If this error persists, the disk is unusable and should be formatted again.

File canceled by operator

PRINT. This message appears on the printer after you cancel the printing of a file to serve as a reminder that the printout is incomplete.

File cannot be copied onto itself

DOS. A request was made to use the COPY command to copy a file and place the copy (with the same name) in the same directory on the same disk as the original. You should change the name given to the copy, put it in a different directory, or put it on another disk.

File creation error

DOS and commands. An unsuccessful attempt was made to add a new filename to the directory or to replace a file that was already there. If the file was already there, it was marked read-only and therefore could not be replaced. Otherwise, run CHKDSK to determine whether the directory is full or whether some other condition caused the error.

File is cross-linked:
on cluster xx

CHKDISK. This message will appear twice for each cross-linked cluster number, naming the two files in error. The same data block is allocated to both files. No corrective action is taken automatically, so you must correct the problem. For example, you can

- Make copies of both files (use the COPY command)
- Delete the original file (use the ERASE command)
- Review the files for validity and edit as necessary.

File is currently being printed
File is in queue

PRINT. These messages appear together when you issue a PRINT command with no parameters, or individually when you queue the first or a subsequent file for printing. These messages are provided solely for your information.

File not found

DOS and commands. A file name in a command parameter does not exist in the current or specified directory on the default or specified drive.

This error may also occur if you try to use a file created under an earlier version of DOS, whose name contains characters that have special meanings in the current version of DOS.

Files were backed up $xx/xx/xxxx$

RESTORE. The files on the backup diskette were backed up on the indicated date.

First cluster number is invalid, entry truncated

CHKDSK. The file whose name precedes this message contains an invalid pointer to the data area. The file is truncated to a zero-length file if the /F parameter was specified.

Fixed Disk already has a DOS partition

FDISK. You chose the "Create DOS Partition" option and the current Fixed Disk already has a DOS partition.

FOR cannot be nested

Batch. More than one FOR subcommand was found on one command line in the batch file. Only one FOR subcommand is allowed per command line.

Format failure

FORMAT. A disk error was encountered while the target diskette was being created. The diskette is unusable.

Formatting while copying

DISKCOPY. The target diskette was found to contain unformatted tracks or to have a different format than the source diskette. DISKCOPY will format the remainder of the target diskette as it copies data. If this message is followed by the message "Incompatible drive types", you have tried to copy a double-sided diskette to a drive that does not have double-sided capability. Processing will end, and the target diskette will not contain any useful data.

I

Illegal device name

MODE. The specified printer must be **LPT1:**, **LPT2:**, or **LPT3:**; the specified Asynchronous Communications Adapter must exist and be **COM1:** or **COM2:**.

Incompatible drive types

DISKCOPY. The source diskette and drive are double-sided, but the target drive has only single-sided capability. The target diskette contains no useful data.

Incompatible system size

SYS. The target diskette contains a copy of DOS that is smaller than the one being copied. The system transfer does not take place. A possible solution might be to format a blank diskette (use the FORMAT /S command) and then copy any files to the new diskette.

Incorrect DOS version

Commands. The command you just entered requires a different version of DOS than the one you are running.

Insert backup diskette xx in drive x:
Strike any key when ready

RESTORE. Insert the next backup diskette in sequence. RESTORE will continue when you press a key.

Insert backup diskette xx in drive x:
Warning! Diskette files will be erased
Strike any key when ready

BACKUP. Insert the next diskette to be used for the backup.

Use DOS formatted diskettes only. BACKUP will continue when you press a key.

Insert COMMAND.COM disk in drive x:
and strike any key when ready

DOS. DOS is attempting to reload the command processor, but COMMAND.COM is not on the drive that DOS was booted from. Insert the DOS diskette in the indicated drive and press any key.

Insert disk to be recovered into drive x:
and press any key when ready

RECOVER. Insert the diskette to be recovered in the indicated drive and press any key.

Insert disk with batch file
and strike any key when ready

Batch. The batch processor is trying to find the next command in the file, and the diskette that contained the batch file being processed was removed. Processing will continue when you insert the diskette in the appropriate drive and press a key.

Insert DOS disk in drive x:
and strike any key when ready

SYS and FORMAT. FORMAT or SYS is trying to read DOS, but the indicated drive x: does not contain a DOS diskette.

Insert DOS diskette in drive A:
Press any key when ready...

FDISK. You have successfully created the DOS partition on the current Fixed Disk. Insert the DOS diskette into drive A: and press any key. This will restart your IBM Personal Computer. The current Fixed Disk will be assigned a drive name and can now be formatted with the FORMAT command.

Insert source diskette in drive x
Insert target diskette in drive x

DISKCOPY. Insert the appropriate diskette into the indicated drive, and press any key when prompted. The copying process will continue.

Insufficient disk space

DOS and commands. The disk does not contain enough free space to hold the file being written. Run CHKDSK to determine the status of the disk.

Insufficient memory

Commands. The amount of available memory is too small to allow these commands to function. You should change the BUFFERS= parameter in the CONFIG.SYS file to a smaller value (if you have specified BUFFERS=), restart the system, and try the command again. If the message still appears, then your system does not have enough memory to execute the command.

Insufficient room in root directory
Erase files from root and repeat CHKDSK

CHKDSK. You are running CHKDSK with the /F option. CHKDSK wants to retrieve some "lost" data space and put it in a file, but the root directory is full. CHKDSK continues running but does not retrieve the lost space. After CHKDSK has finished, copy some files out of the root directory, delete them, and run CHKDSK again to retrieve the lost data space.

Intermediate file error during pipe

DOS. DOS was unable to create an intermediate file because the default drive's root directory is full, DOS is unable to locate the piping files, or the disk does not have enough free space to hold the data being piped. You should erase some files from the default drive's root or some files from the directory and reissue the command that failed. If it still fails, one of the programs in the command line has erased a piping file. You should correct the program and reissue the command.

Invalid baud rate specified

MODE. The baud rate you specify must be 110, 150, 300, 600, 1200, 2400, 4800, or 9600 (or the first two characters of the number).

Invalid characters in volume label

FORMAT. One or more of the characters you entered in the volume label is not a valid filename character, or the name contained a period (volume labels contain 1 to 11 valid characters without a period).

Invalid COMMAND.COM in drive n

DOS. While trying to reload the command processor, DOS found the copy of COMMAND.COM on the disk to be an incorrect version. You are prompted to insert the correct DOS diskette and press any key to continue.

Invalid date

DATE. An invalid date or delimiter was entered. Enter the date in the format *mm-dd-yy*, where *mm* is the month (0 to 12), *dd* is the day (1 to 31), and *yy* is the last two digits of the year.

Invalid device

CTTY. The device name you specified is an invalid name to DOS.

Invalid directory

DOS and commands. One of the directories in the specified path does not exist.

Invalid drive in search path

DOS. An invalid drive specifier was found in one of the paths specified in the PATH command. This message appears when DOS attempts to locate a command or batch file, not at the time you issue the erroneous PATH command.

Invalid drive specification

DOS and commands. You are trying to use a disk drive that your PC does not know exists. This error may be caused by incorrect settings of switches in the System Unit if you have just reset the switches or installed a disk. If you are trying to use a Fixed Disk, this error may be caused by running the wrong version of DOS or by trying to use a Fixed Disk that has no DOS partition.

Invalid number of parameters

Commands. You have specified too few or too many parameters for the command you issued.

Invalid parameter

DOS and commands. One or more parameters or options in a command is invalid. If the command expects a drive name, be sure to enter a colon after the name.

Invalid parameters

MODE. No parameters were entered; or the first parameter was not valid; or the display adapter that the parameter refers to is not present in the machine.

Invalid partition table

Booting. While you were attempting to start DOS from your Fixed Disk, the start-up procedures detected invalid information in the disk's partition table. You should start DOS from diskette and use the FDISK command to examine and correct the Fixed Disk partition information.

Invalid path

TREE. TREE was unable to use a directory whose name was found in another directory. You should run CHKDSK to determine what is wrong with the directory structure.

Invalid path, not directory or directory not empty

RMDIR. The specified directory was not removed because one of the names you specified in the path was not a valid directory name, or the directory you specified still contains entries for files or other sub-directories. You cannot remove a directory unless it is empty of everything except the "." and ".." entries.

Invalid path or file name

COPY. You specified a directory or file name that does not exist.

Invalid sub-directory

CHKDSK. Invalid information was detected in the sub-directory whose name precedes this message. CHKDSK will attempt to correct the error. For more specific information about the nature of the error, run CHKDSK with the /V parameter.

Invalid time

TIME. An invalid time or delimiter was entered. Enter the time in the format *hh:mm* or *hh:mm:ss*, where *hh* is a number from 0 to 23, *mm* is a number from 00 to 59, and *ss* is a number from 00 to 59.

L

Label not found

Batch. A GOTO command named a label that does not exist in the batch file.

Line too long

EDLIN. In a Replace command, the replacement caused the line to expand beyond the 253-character limit. The Replace command is ended abnormally.

Split the long line into shorter lines, and then issue the Replace command again.

List output is not assigned to device

PRINT. The device you named to be the PRINT list device is not recognized as a valid device. You should reissue the PRINT command and reply with a valid list device name when prompted.

LPT*m*: not redirected

MODE. The parallel printer will now receive its own output, even if this printer's output had previously been redirected to a serial device. This indicates cancellation of any previous redirection that may have been in effect, because you have set the printer width or vertical spacing.

LPT*m*: redirected to COM*n*:

MODE. Any request that would normally have gone to the parallel printer LPT*m* (*m* = 1, 2, or 3) is sent instead to the serial device COM*n* (*n* = 1 or 2).

LPT*m*: set for 80/132

MODE. You have used the form of MODE that causes the IBM Graphic Matrix Printer to print 80 characters per line (with normal characters) or 132 characters per line (with compressed characters). Note that this form of MODE automatically directs printed output to the specified printer.

M

Maximum available space is *xxxx* cylinders at cylinder *xxxx*

FDISK. The "Create DOS Partition" option displays the largest available space on the current Fixed Disk. These numbers are also used as the defaults for the two prompts that will follow.

Memory allocation error
Cannot load COMMAND, system halted.

DOS. A program has destroyed the area in which DOS keeps track of available memory. You should restart DOS.

Missing file name

RENAME. The second of the two required filenames is not specified.

Missing operating system

Booting. While you were attempting to start DOS from the Fixed Disk, the start-up procedures determined that the DOS partition is marked as being "bootable" (startable), but that it does not contain a copy of DOS. You should start DOS from diskette and use

FORMAT with the /S parameter to place a copy of DOS on the Fixed Disk. You might want to back up your files before doing the format procedure.

—More—

MORE. The screen is full and there is more data waiting to be displayed. Press any character to see the next screenful.

Must specify destination line number

EDLIN. A MOVE or COPY command was entered without a destination line number. Reenter the command with a valid destination line number.

N

No DOS partition to delete

FDISK. You chose the "Delete DOS Partition" option when there was no DOS partition on the current Fixed Disk to be deleted.

Name of list device [PRN]:

PRINT. This message appears the first time you start printing after DOS has been started. Reply with the device name that is to receive the printed output, or press ENTER if the first parallel printer [PRN] is to be used.

No free file handles
Cannot start COMMAND, exiting

DOS. An attempt to load a second copy of the command processor has failed because there are currently too many files open. You should increase the number in the FILES= command in the configuration file (CONFIG.SYS) and restart DOS.

No Fixed Disks present

FDISK. The FDISK program was run on an IBM Personal Computer that does not have a Fixed Disk, has a Fixed Disk in the System Expansion Unit, but the Expansion Unit is not powered on; or has a Fixed Disk that is not properly installed.

No paper error reading/writing *device*
Abort, Retry, Ignore?

DOS and commands. DOS has received a "paper out" signal from the indicated *device* (normally a parallel interface printer). Load more paper and put the printer back on-line. Then enter **R** to retry the operation.

No partitions to make active

FDISK. You chose the "Change Active Partition" option when there were no partitions on the current Fixed Disk to be made active. You can use the "Create DOS partition" option to create a partition and then the "Change Active Partition" option to make it the active partition.

No path

PATH. There is currently no alternate path for DOS to search to find commands and batch files if it does not find them in the specified (or default) directory.

No room for system on destination disk

SYS. The destination diskette did not have the required reserved space for DOS; therefore, the system cannot be transferred. A possible solution would be to format a blank diskette (use the FORMAT /S command), and then copy other required files to the new diskette.

No room in directory for file

EDLIN. The directory on the specified disk is full. Your editing changes are lost. You should delete some files from the directory and run EDLIN again.

No space for an $xxxx$ cylinder partition

FDISK. You entered a partition size that is larger than the largest area of free space on the disk. Enter a smaller number.

No space for an $xxxx$ cylinder partition at cylinder $xxxx$

FDISK. You requested a partition to be created at a place on the current Fixed Disk, but the disk does not have space at that place to create a DOS partition.

No space to create a DOS partition

FDISK. You chose the "Create DOS Partition" option on the current Fixed Disk, which has no space to create a DOS partition.

No sub-directories exist

TREE. The specified drive contains only a root directory. There is, therefore, no directory path to display.

Non-system disk or disk error
Replace and strike any key when ready

Booting. The PC is trying to boot from a disk that is not bootable—that is, from a disk that was not created by running FORMAT with /S or by copying a bootable disk with DISKCOPY.

Put a bootable diskette in drive A and reboot.

Non-DOS disk error reading/writing *device*
Abort, Retry, Ignore?

DOS and commands. DOS has detected a disk on the indicated *device* that is apparently not a DOS disk. Enter **A** to return to the DOS command line prompt. You will need to run FORMAT before you can use this disk.

Not enough room to merge the entire file

EDLIN. A Transfer command was unable to merge the entire contents of the specified file because of insufficient memory. Part of the file was merged.

Not found

EDLIN. Either the specified range of lines does not contain the string being searched for by the Replace or Search commands; or if a search is resumed by an **N** reply to the OK? prompt, no further occurrences of the string were found.

Not ready error reading/writing *device*
Abort, Retry, Ignore?

DOS and commands. The indicated *device* is not ready for use. For example, if it is a diskette drive, its door may be open. Make the device ready for use and enter **R** to make DOS retry the operation.

O

Out of environment space

DOS. DOS was unable to accept the SET command you just issued because it was unable to expand the area in which the environment information is kept. This normally occurs when you try to add to the environment after loading a program that makes itself resident (PRINT, MODE, or GRAPHICS, for example).

P

Parameters not compatible

FORMAT. You attempted to use two parameters that are not compatible with each other (/B and /V, for example).

Parameter not compatible with Fixed Disk

FORMAT. You specified the /1 or /8 parameter while formatting a Fixed Disk. Neither of these parameters is valid for a Fixed Disk.

Press any key to begin formatting x:

FORMAT. The Fixed Disk (drive x) is about to be formatted. Formatting will erase all previously existing data on the disk. If you do *not* want the disk formatted, press CTRL BREAK. If you do want the disk formatted, press a character key.

Print queue is empty

PRINT. There are currently no files being processed by PRINT.

Print queue is full

PRINT. You attempted to add more than the limit of ten files to the print queue. You will have to wait until a file is printed before you can add another file to the print queue.

Printer error

MODE. The MODE command was unable to set the printer mode because of an I/O error, out-of-paper (or POWER OFF), or time-out (not ready) condition.

Printer lines per inch set

MODE. An attempt has been made to set the printer's vertical spacing to the specified six or eight lines per inch. If the attempt was unsuccessful, an error message will follow this message on the screen.

Probable non-DOS disk.
Continue (Y/N)?

CHKDSK. The format of the disk you are checking is so unlike a DOS disk that CHKDSK believes the disk is a non-DOS disk rather than a corrupted DOS disk. To make CHKDSK abandon its attempt to check the disk, press **N**. To make CHKDSK continue, enter **Y**.

Processing cannot continue

CHKDSK. This message will be followed by another message that explains why CHKDSK cannot continue. Normally, this condition is caused by insufficient memory.

Program too big to fit in memory

DOS. The file containing the external command cannot be loaded because it is larger than the amount of free memory available. You should reduce the number in the BUFFERS= parameter in your CONFIG.SYS file (provided you have specified BUFFERS=), restart your system, and reissue the command. If the message reappears, your system does not have enough memory to execute the command.

R

Read fault error reading *device*
Abort, Retry, Ignore?

DOS and commands. DOS cannot read data on the indicated *device*. When this occurs on a disk drive, it usually means that a bad spot has developed on a disk or a failure has occurred in a disk drive or disk drive adapter card. *Do not change disks until you have resolved the problem.* See "Dealing with Diskette Errors" in Chapter 18, "Operations and Procedures," for further instructions.

Resident part of PRINT installed

PRINT. The message appears the first time you use the PRINT command. A program has been loaded into memory to handle subsequent PRINT commands. Available memory for your applications has been reduced by approximately 3200 bytes.

Resident portion of MODE loaded

MODE. The message appears the first time you use MODE for a non-screen-setting function. A program has been loaded into memory to perform the requested function. Available memory for your applications is reduced by approximately 450 bytes.

***Restoring files from diskette *xx* ***

RESTORE. This message will be followed by a list of files that are being restored from the indicated diskette.

S

Sector not found error reading/writing *device*
Abort, Retry, Ignore?

DOS and commands. DOS cannot find a sector of data on the indicated *device*. This usually means that a bad spot has developed on a disk or a failure has occurred in a disk drive or disk drive adapter card. *Do not change disks until you have resolved the problem.* See "Dealing with Diskette Errors" in Chapter 18, "Operations and Procedures," for further instructions.

Sector size too large in file *filename*

Booting. The device driver named in *filename* specifies a device sector size larger than the devices previously defined to DOS.

Seek error reading/writing *device*
Abort, Retry, Ignore?

DOS and commands. DOS cannot find a track of data on the indicated *device.* This usually means that a bad spot has developed on a disk or a failure has occurred in a disk drive or disk drive adapter card. *Do not change disks until you have resolved the problem.* See "Dealing with Diskette Errors" in Chapter 18, "Operations and Procedures," for further instructions.

Syntax error

DOS. You have entered a command in an invalid manner. Check the rules for entering this command and reenter it.

T

Target diskette may be unusable

DISKCOPY. This message follows an unrecoverable read, write, or verify error message. The copy on the target diskette may be incomplete because of the unrecoverable I/O error.

Target diskette write protected
Correct, then strike any key

DISKCOPY. You are trying to produce a copy on a diskette that is write-protected.

Terminate batch job (Y/N)?

DOS. This message appears when you press CTRL BREAK while DOS is processing a batch file. Press **Y** to stop processing the batch file. Pressing **N** only ends the command that was executing when CTRL BREAK was pressed; processing resumes with the next command in the batch file.

The current active partition is x

FDISK. The "Change Active Partition" option displays the active partition on the current Fixed Disk.

The last file was not restored

RESTORE. You stopped RESTORE before it completely restored the last file listed, or there was not enough room on the Fixed Disk. RESTORE then deleted the partially restored file.

Total disk space is $xxxx$ cylinders

FDISK. The total space on the current Fixed Disk is displayed.

Track 0 bad — disk unusable

FORMAT. Track 0 is where the boot record, file allocation table, and directory must reside. The disk is unusable.

Track *xx*, side *x*

DISKCOPY. Four unsuccessful attempts were made to read the data from the source diskette. DISKCOPY continues copying, but the copy may contain incomplete data.

Tree past this point not processed

CHKDSK. CHKDSK is unable to continue processing the directory path currently being examined because track 0 is bad.

U

Unable to create directory

MDKIR. The directory you wish to create already exists, one of the directory path names you specified could not be found, or you attempted to add a directory to the root directory and it is full.

Unable to write BOOT

FORMAT. The first track of the diskette or DOS partition is bad. The boot record could not be written on it. The diskette or DOS partition is not usable.

Unrecognized command in CONFIG.SYS

Boot. An invalid command was detected in the configuration file CONFIG.SYS. You should edit the file, correct the invalid command, and restart DOS.

Unrecoverable format error on target
Target diskette unusable

DISKCOPY. An unrecoverable error was encountered while formatting the target diskette. The diskette contains no usable data.

Unrecoverable verify error on target
Track *xx*, side *x*

DISKCOPY. Four unsuccessful attempts were made to verify the write operation to the target diskette. DISKCOPY continues copying, but the copy may contain incomplete data.

Unrecoverable write error on target
Track *xx*, side *x*

DISKCOPY. Four unsuccessful attempts were made to write the data to the target diskette. DISKCOPY continues copying, but the copy may contain incomplete data.

Volume label (11 characters, ENTER for none)?

FORMAT. You are requested to enter a 1- to 11-character volume label, which will be written on the disk being formatted. If you do not want a volume label on the disk, press ENTER.

W

Warning! All data in the DOS partition will be DESTROYED.
Do you wish to continue...?[*d*]

FDISK. The "Delete DOS Partition" option is warning you that if you continue, all data in the DOS partition on the current Fixed Disk will be destroyed. If you press ENTER, the DOS partition will *not* be destroyed. If you do wish to delete the DOS partition, type **Y** and press ENTER.

Warning — directory full

RECOVER. There is insufficient directory space to recover more files. You should copy some of the files to a sub-directory or another disk, erase them from this disk, and run RECOVER again.

Warning! Diskette is out of sequence
Replace the diskette or continue
Strike any key when ready

RESTORE. The backup diskette is not the next one in sequence. Replace the diskette unless you are sure no files on the diskette(s) you skipped would be restored. RESTORE will continue when you press a key. This message will be repeated if you try to skip a diskette that contains part of a file being restored.

Warning! File xx is a read-only file
Replace the file (Y/N)?

RESTORE. The indicated file is read-only. Enter **Y** if you want to replace it or **N** if you do not. RESTORE will continue after you press ENTER. You will see this message only if you specified the /P option.

Warning! File xx was changed after it was backed up
Replace the file (Y/N)?

RESTORE. The indicated file on the Fixed Disk has a later date and time than the corresponding file on the backup diskette. Enter **Y** if you want to replace it with the backed up version or **N** if you do not. RESTORE will continue after you press ENTER. You will see this message only if you specified the /P option.

Warning! No files were found to back up

BACKUP. No Fixed Disk files were found that matched the backup file specification.

Warning! No files were found to restore

RESTORE. No backup diskette files were found that matched the restore file specification.

Write fault error writing *device*
Abort, Retry, Ignore?

DOS and commands. DOS cannot write data on the indicated *device*. When this error occurs on a disk drive, it means that a bad spot has developed on a disk or a failure has occurred in a disk drive or disk drive adapter card. *Do not change disks until you have resolved the problem.* See "Dealing with Diskette Errors" in Chapter 18, "Operations and Procedures," for further instructions.

Write protect error writing *device*
Abort, Retry, Ignore?

DOS and commands. DOS cannot write data on the indicated *device* because the device is write-protected. This usually means that a diskette's write-protect notch is covered, or a hard disk drive has a "protect" control and the control is set to "on."

If you want to write to this disk, uncover the write-protect notch or turn off the protection control; then respond **R** to retry the operation. *Do not change disks until you have resolved the problem.* See Chapter 18, "Operations and Procedures," for further instructions.

X

x is not a choice. Enter a choice

FDISK. You entered *x*, which is not a choice for this question.

x is not a choice. Enter Y or N.

FDISK. You entered *x*, which is not a choice for this question. Enter **Y** or **N**.

xxxxxxxxx bytes disk space freed

CHKDSK. Diskette space marked as allocated was not associated with any file. Therefore, the space was freed for allocation to new files.

xxxx error on file *yyyy*

PRINT. This message appears on the printer. While attempting to read data from file *yyyy* for printing, a disk error of type *xxxx* was encountered. Printing of that file is stopped.

xxx lost clusters found in *yyy* chains

CHKDSK. CHKDSK located *xxx* blocks of the data area that were marked as allocated but were not associated with a file. These clusters are assumed to contain "lost" data, and CHKDSK will ask whether you wish to free them or to recover each chain into a separate file.

Different Versions of DOS

From time to time, IBM releases new versions of DOS that offer more features and correct errors that have been found in earlier versions.

To date, four versions of DOS have been released. Their most prominent features are shown in Table A-1.

About Version Numbers

Each version of DOS is identified by a version number like 1.10 or 2.00. A change in the first digit indicates a major set of enhancements. A change in the second digit indicates a more limited set of enhancements. A change in the last digit indicates correction of errors with no significant enhancements.

When the last digit is zero, it is customarily omitted. For example, throughout this book we refer to DOS version 2.00 as "DOS 2.0."

It is a common practice to put an *X* in a release number to indicate "a release number with any digit in this position." Thus, versions 1.00, 1.05, and 1.10 could be referred to together as "version 1.XX."

Version	Released	New disk and other features	New file features	Enhanced commands	New commands
1.00	August 1981			First release of DOS	
1.05	Late 1981?		No significant new features; several errors corrected		
1.10	May 1982	Double-sided diskettes		FORMAT, DIR, DISKCOMP, DISKCOPY, MODE	
2.00	March 1983	Fixed Disk; 9-sector/track diskettes; CONFIG.SYS file	Sub-directories; redirected I/O; filters and pipes	CHKDSK, COMP, DIR, EDLIN, DISKCOPY, DISKCOMP	ASSIGN, BACKUP, BREAK, CHDIR, CLS, ECHO, FDISK, FOR, GOTO, GRAPHICS, IF, MKDIR, PATH, PRINT, PROMPT, RECOVER, RMDIR, RESTORE, SET, SHIFT, TREE, VERIFY, VOL

Table A-1.
Important Differences Among Versions of DOS

Versions 1.00 and 1.05

Version 1.00 is the first version of DOS, which was released when the PC was first introduced. Version 1.05 was released soon after to correct some serious errors that were found in version 1.00 after its release. Version 1.05 appears never to have been sold commercially, but it was offered as a "fix" to users who complained of errors in version 1.00.

These versions of DOS are now rarely used, and this book does not address them.

Version 1.10

The most notable enhancement in version 1.10 of DOS was support for double-sided disk drives.

As this book goes to press, version 1.10 remains the most widely used version of DOS, although later versions may be expected to supersede it in time. This book distinguishes between version 1.10 and version 2.00 with the notation "DOS 2.0 Only" for those features that are not found in version 1.10.

The significant enhancements in version 1.10 are

- Support for both single- and double-sided diskettes, increasing the PC's data capacity per disk from 160K to 320K. The FORMAT, DISKCOMP, and DISKCOPY commands are enhanced to support both single- and double-sided diskette formats.
- The DIR command lists the creation date and time of each file. Version 1.0X's DIR command listed the creation date only.
- TIME and DATE are internal commands. Version 1.0X's TIME and DATE were external commands (COM files).
- The MODE command is enhanced to permit the user to reassign devices and reconfigure a serial interface.

Version 1.1 requires about 250 more bytes of RAM than 1.0X. BASIC and BASICA require about 200 more bytes of RAM. These differences slightly reduce the data capacity of some BASIC programs and in a few cases prevent programs from running unless more RAM is added to the PC.

Version 2.00

DOS version 2.00 was released simultaneously with the PC XT. It is the first version of DOS that supports the PC XT's Fixed Disk. The significant enhancements in version 2.00 are

- Fixed Disk support. The FORMAT command is enhanced to support the Fixed Disk. The commands entitled FDISK, BACKUP, and RESTORE are added.
- Support for diskettes with nine sectors per track, increasing the PC's storage capacity per diskette from 320K to 360K. FORMAT and DISKCOPY are enhanced to support nine-sector diskettes and to offer the user a choice between the eight- and nine-sector formats.

  Under version 2.00, the nine-sector track format is standard. Thus an older version of DOS cannot use a diskette formatted under version 2.00 unless the diskette is intentionally formatted with eight-sector tracks.
- Several new disk and file features: sub-directories, I/O redirection, pipes, and filters. The TREE, MKDIR, RMDIR, CHDIR, and PATH commands are added to support the new features.

  Using the new disk and file features requires entering the following characters in command lines: the less-than sign ($<$), the greater-than sign ($>$), the straight bar ($|$), and the backslash ($\backslash$). Thus these characters may not be used in filenames, although earlier versions allowed them.
- Volume labels. The FORMAT command lets you assign an 11-character volume label to a disk when you format it. The VOL command is added to display the label. The DIR command also displays the label along with directory information.
- Repairing data on corrupted disks. The CHKDSK command is enhanced to offer more facilities for repairing the data on corrupted disks and to give you the option of repairing a corrupted disk or just analyzing it. The RECOVER command is added.

- System configuration. Support for the CONFIG.SYS file is added. CONFIG.SYS contains configuration commands that can change operating characteristics of DOS. DOS reads this file from the root directory of the boot disk (if it is there) when you boot.
- Several new commands that control various aspects of DOS's operation: ASSIGN, BREAK, PROMPT, SET, and VERIFY.
- Support for as many as three parallel interface devices (LPT or LPT1, LPT2, and LPT3) and two serial interface devices (COM or COM1, and COM2).
- The GRAPHICS command, which lets you print a graphics display presented by the Color/Graphics Monitor Adapter on the IBM Graphic Matrix Printer.
- Several new commands for use in batch files: CLS, ECHO, FOR, IF, SHIFT, and GOTO.
- The PRINT command, which can queue a program's printed output and then print it while you run other programs.
- Several new features in EDLIN. The COPY and MOVE commands are added. SEARCH and REPLACE begin their search at the line after the current line instead of at the current line itself, making it easy to search for several consecutive occurrences of a string. Line numbers can be specified in relative form (for example, "two lines after the current line").
- Several new features have been added to BASICA. Among these features are some that enhance its mathematical capabilities and others that support DOS 2.0's added file features, redirection capability, and sub-directories.

In addition to the features discussed above, version 2.0 contains numerous enhancements for the benefit of programmers. These enhancements will not affect you directly, but they will make it possible for software developers to offer you new and improved products.

Version 2.0 requires substantially more RAM than version 1.XX. Some programs will not run unless more RAM is added to the PC.

Effects of Release Changes
On Application Programs

Many application programs that run well under one version of DOS do not run well (or do not run at all) under another. There are several different reasons that this may happen. A program may

- Use a feature of a later version of DOS that is not supported in an earlier one.
- Take advantage of a characteristic of an earlier version of DOS that is absent in a later one. (An example of this would be a program that took advantage of the fact that DATE and TIME were external commands in DOS version 1.0X.)
- Run afoul of errors in DOS itself that occur in one version but not in another.
- Make unauthorized assumptions about DOS; that is, take advantage of characteristics of DOS that in fact change from release to release. A program may do this because of careless design or because that is the only way to achieve an important result (such as support for hard disks under DOS 1.10).

In view of these potential problems, you should always be cautious when changing from one version of DOS to another or when buying a new application program. Ask your dealer whether there are any known or likely problems with running the intended application under the intended version of DOS. You may choose to stick with the old version of DOS or of an application program for a few months after a new version has been released in order to give the supplier(s) a chance to resolve any compatibility problems that occur.

For detailed information about the effects that different releases of DOS will have on application programs distributed by IBM, consult the appendixes to IBM's *Disk Operating System* manual.

Index of Suppliers

Alloy Computer Products
12 Mercer Rd.
Natick, MA 01760   617-655-3900

Amdek Corp.
2201 Lively Blvd.
Elk Grove Village, IL 60007   312-364-1180

Anadex Inc.
9825 De Soto Ave.
Chatsworth, CA 91311   213-998-8010

Anchor Pad International Inc.
3224 Thatcher Ave.   800-235-7972;
Marina Del Rey, CA 90291   in CA 213-306-3881

Apparat Inc.
4401 S. Tamarac Pkwy.
Denver, CO 80257   800-525-7674

Applied Software Technology
170 Knowles Dr.
Los Gatos, CA 95030   408-370-2662

Ashton-Tate
9929 Jefferson Blvd.
Culver City, CA 90230   213-204-5570

Aspen Software Co.
Box 339
Tijeras, NM 87059   505-281-3371

AST Research Inc.
2372 Morse Ave.
Irvine, CA 92714   714-540-1333

Automated Business Machines
23362 Peralta Dr.
Laguna Hills, CA 92653   714-859-6531

Basic Business Software Inc.
Box 26311
Las Vegas, NV 89126   702-876-9493

BRS Inc.
1200 Route 7
Latham, NY 12110   800-833-4707

Bruce & James Program Publishers Inc.
4500 Tuller Rd.
Dublin, OH 43017   614-766-0110

Byad Inc.
101 Lions Dr.
Barrington, IL 60010   312-381-2330

C-Systems
Box 3253
Fullerton, CA 92634   714-637-5362

C. Itoh Electronics Inc.
5301 Beethoven St.
Los Angeles, CA 90066   213-306-6700

Camwil Inc.
875 Waimanu St.
Honolulu, HI 96813   808-533-6051

Central Point Software Inc.
Box 19730-203
Portland, OR 97219   503-244-5782

Centronics Data Computer Corp.
attn: R. Lorigan
Hudson, NH 03051   603-883-0111

Chang Laboratories Inc.
5300 Stevens Creek Blvd. Suite 200
San Jose, CA 95129   408-246-8020

Checks To-Go   800-854-2750;
8384 Hercules St.   in CA 800-552-8817
La Mesa, CA 92041   or 619-460-4975

Colby Computer
2 Palo Alto Sq.
Palo Alto, CA 94304   415-493-7788

Columbia Data Products Inc.
8990 Route 108
Columbia, MD 21045   301-992-3400

Columbia National General Agency
88 E. Broad St.   800-848-3469;
Columbus, OH 43215   in OH 800-848-2112

COMPAQ Computer Corp.
20333 FM149
Houston, TX 77070   713-370-7040

CompuServe
5000 Arlington Blvd.   800-848-8990;
Columbus, OH 43220   in OH 614-457-8600

Computer Innovations Inc.
10 Mechanic St. Suite J
Red Bank, NJ 07701   201-530-0995

Computer Mate Inc.
1006 Hampshire Ln.
Richardson, TX 75080

Computer Technology Innovations
1037 N. Fair Oaks Ave.
Sunnyvale, CA 94086   408-745-0180

Computerworld
Box 880
Framingham, MA 01701   617-879-0700

Comsen Inc.
20-A Erford Rd. #103
Lemoyne, PA 17043   717-737-2049

Condor Computer Corp.
2051 S. State St.
Ann Arbor, MI 48104   313-769-3988

Context Management Systems
23868 Hawthorne Blvd. Suite 101
Torrance, CA 90505   213-378-8277

Continental Software
11223 Hindry
Los Angeles, CA 90045   213-417-8031

Control Systems
2855 Anthony Ln.
Minneapolis, MN 55418   612-789-2421

Control Technology Inc.
8200 N. Classen Blvd. #101
Oklahoma City, OK 73114   405-840-3163

Corona Data Systems Inc.
31324 Via Colinas
Westlake Village, CA 91361   213-706-1505

Corvus Systems
2029 O'Toole Ave.
San Jose, CA 95131   408-946-7700

CP Aids
1061 Fraternity Circle Dr.
Kent, OH 44240   216-678-9015

Cuesta Systems Inc.
3440 Roberto Ct.
San Luis Obispo, CA 93401   805-541-4160

Curtis Manufacturing Company Inc.
Grove Street
Peterborough, NH 03458   603-924-7803

DataSource Systems Corp.
1660 S. Hwy 100   800-328-2260;
Minneapolis, MN 55416   in MN 612-544-3615

Datamac Computer Systems
595 Pastoria Ave.
Sunnyvale, CA 94086   408-735-0323

Davong Systems Inc.
217 Humboldt Ct.
Sunnyvale, CA 94089   408-734-4900

Dennison Monarch Systems Inc.
Box 4081   800-431-4958;
New Windsor, NY 12550   in NY 914-562-3100

Dennison National Co.
Box 791
Holyoke, MA 01041   413-539-9811

Diablo Systems Inc.
24500 Industrial Blvd.
Hayward, CA 94545   415-786-5000

Dialog Information Services Inc.
3460 Hillview Ave.
Palo Alto, CA 94304

800-227-1927;
in CA 800-982-5838

Digital Marketing Corp.
2363 Boulevard Circle
Walnut Creek, CA 94595

800-826-2222;
in CA 415-947-1000

Digital Research
160 Central Ave.
Pacific Grove, CA 93950

408-649-3896

Dow Jones News/Retrieval
Box 300
Princeton, NJ 08540

800-257-5114;
in NJ 609-452-1511

Dranetz Engineering Laboratories Inc.
1000 New Durham Road
Edison, NJ 08818

201-287-3680

Dynalogic Info-Tech Corp.
8 Colonnade Rd.
Ottawa, Ontario
Canada K2E 7M6

613-226-7013

Dynamic Microprocessor Associates Inc.
545 5th Ave.
New York, NY 10017

212-687-7115

Dynax Inc.
5698 Bandini Blvd.
Bell, CA 90201

Dysan Corp.
5440 Patrick Henry Dr.
Santa Clara, CA 95050

800-538-8133

Eagle Software Publishing Inc.
993 Old Eagle School Rd. Suite 409
Wayne, PA 19087

215-964-8660

Ecosoft Inc.
Box 68602
Indianapolis, IN 46268

317-255-6476

Elgar Corp.
8225 Mercury Ct.
San Diego, CA 92111

800-854-2213;
in CA 714-565-1155

Enter Computer Inc.
6867 Nancy Ridge Dr.
San Diego, CA 92121

800-227-4371;
in CA 800-227-4375

Epson America Inc.
3415 Kashiwa St.
Torrance, CA 90505

213-539-9140

Financier Inc.
Box 670
Westboro, MA 01581

617-366-0950

Flagstaff Engineering
2820 W. Darleen
Flagstaff, AZ 86001

602-774-3588

FLC Financial Services
14724 Ventura Blvd. Suite 918
Sherman Oaks, CA 91403

213-981-1700

Fox & Geller Inc.
604 Market St.
Elmwood Park, NJ 07407

201-794-8883

Freeware—The Headlands Press Inc.
Box 862
Tiburon, CA 94920

FTG Data Systems
Box 615-D
Stanton, CA 90680

714-995-3900

Genie Computer Corp.
31131 Via Colinas #607
Westlake Village, CA 91362

213-991-6210

Giltronix
3780 Fabian Way
Palo Alto, CA 94303

415-493-1300

Gould Inc.
Power Conversion Division
2727 Kurtz St.
San Diego, CA 92110

800-854-2658;
in CA 619-291-4211

Hayes Microcomputer Products Inc.
5923 Peachtree Industrial Blvd.
Norcross, GA 30092

404-449-8791

Hercules Computer Technology
2550 Ninth St. Suite 210
Berkeley, CA 94710   415-654-2476

Hewlett-Packard Co.
Marketing Communications Support Group
1820 Embarcadero Rd.
Palo Alto, CA 94303

Houston Instrument Division
Bausch & Lomb
Box 15720
Austin, TX 78761   512-835-0900

I-Bus Systems
8863 Balboa Ave.   800-382-4229;
San Diego, CA 92123   in CA 619-569-0646

IBM Corp.—SPD   800-447-4700;
Box 1328   Alaska and Hawaii
Boca Raton, FL 33432   call 800-447-0890

ICO-Ralley Corp.
2575 E. Bayshore Rd.
Palo Alto, CA 94303

IE Systems Inc.
Box 359
Newmarket, NH 03857   603-659-5891

Independent Computer
Consultants Association
Box 27412
St. Louis, MO 63141   314-567-9708

Info-Pros Inc.
2102 Business Center Dr. Suite 132
Irvine, CA 92715   714-851-8975

Information Unlimited Software Inc.
2401 Marinship Way
Sausalito, CA 94965   415-331-6700

InfoWorld
530 Lytton Ave.
Palo Alto, CA 94301   415-328-4602

Inmac
2465 Augustine Dr.
Santa Clara, CA 95051   408-737-7777

Innosys Inc.
2150 Shattuck Ave. Suite 901
Berkeley, CA 94704   415-843-8122

Innovative Data Technology
4060 Morena Blvd.
San Diego, CA 92117   619-270-3990

Innovative Software Inc.
9300 W. 110th St. #380
Overland Park, KS 66210   913-383-1089

Instor Corp.
175 Jefferson Dr.
Menlo Park, CA 94025   415-326-9830

Integral Data Systems Inc.
Milford, NH 03055   800-258-1386

International Software Enterprises Inc.
(ISE-USA)
35 W. Algonquin Rd. Suite 400
Arlington Heights, IL 60005   312-981-9200

International Software Marketing
University Bldg. Suite 42
120 E. Washington St.
Syracuse, NY 13202   315-474-3400

Key Tronic Corp.
Box 14687   800-262-6006;
Spokane, WA 99214   in WA 509-928-8000

Lang Systems Inc.
1010 O'Brien Dr.
Menlo Park, CA 94025   415-328-5555

Leading Edge Products Inc.
225 Turnpike St.   800-343-6833;
Canton, MA 02021   in MA 617-828-8150

Lexisoft Inc.
Box 267
Davis, CA 95616   916-758-3630

Lifeboat Associates
1651 3rd Ave.
New York, NY 10028   212-860-0300

Lifetree Software Inc.
411 Pacific St. Suite 315
Monterey, CA 93940   408-373-4718

Link Systems
1640 19th St.
Santa Monica, CA 90404   213-453-8921

LIST
Redgate Publishing Co.
3407 Ocean Dr.
Vero Beach, FL 32960   800-327-1300

Lotus Development Corp.
The Lotus Building
161 First St.   800-248-8002;
Cambridge, MA 02142   in MA 617-492-7171

Mark of the Unicorn
Box 423
Arlington, MA 02174   617-576-2760

Maxell Corporation of America
Computer Products Division
60 Oxford Dr.
Moonachie, NJ 07074   201-440-8020

Maynard Electronics
400 Semoran Blvd. Suite 207
Casselberry, FL 32707   305-331-6402

Memorex Corp.—CFI Division
1401 E. Orangethorpe
Fullerton, CA 92631   714-738-6100

Metasoft Corp.
711 E. Cottonwood Ln. Suite E
Casa Grande, AZ 85222   602-961-0003

Micro Applications Group
20201 Sherman Way #205
Canoga Park, CA 91306   213-700-1426

Micro Display Systems Inc.
Box 455   800-328-9524;
Hastings, MN 55033   in MN 612-437-2233

Micro-AP Inc.
7033 Village Pkwy. #206
Dublin, CA 94566   415-828-6697

MICROCOM Inc.
1400A Providence Hwy.
Norwood, MA 02062   617-762-9310

Microlog Inc.
222 Route 59
Suffern, NY 10901   914-368-0353

MicroPro International Corp.
33 San Pablo Ave.
San Rafael, CA 94903   415-499-1200

Microsoft Corp.
10700 Northup Way
Bellevue, WA 98004   206-828-8080

Microstuf Inc.
1845 The Exchange Suite 140
Atlanta, GA 30339   404-952-0267

Microware
Box 79
Kingston, MA 02364   617-746-7341

Misco Inc.
404 Timber Lane
Marlboro, NJ 07746

Moore Business Center Division
Moore Business Forms
Box 20   800-323-6230;
Wheeling, IL   in IL 312-459-0210

Nagy Systems
4411 Geary Blvd.
San Francisco, CA 94118   415-751-2233

Nebs Computer Forms
78 Hollis St.   800-225-9550;
Groton, MA 01471   in MA 800-922-8560

NEC Home Electronics Inc.
1401 Estes Ave.
Elk Grove Village, IL 60007   312-228-5900

NewsNet
945 Haverford Rd.
Bryn Mawr, PA 19010

800-345-1301;
in PA 215-527-8030

Northwest Analytical Inc.
1532 SW Morrison St.
Portland, OR 97205

503-224-7727

Norton, Mr. Peter
2210 Wilshire Blvd.
Santa Monica, CA 90403

213-399-3948

Novation
18664 Oxnard St.
Tarzana, CA 91356

800-423-5419;
in CA 213-996-5060

Oasis Systems
3692 Midway Dr.
San Diego, CA 92110

619-222-1153

Okidata Corp.
111 Gaither Dr.
Mt. Laurel, NJ 08054

609-235-2600

Olivetti Corp.
155 White Plains Rd.
Tarrytown, NY 10591

914-631-8100

Orchid Technology
47790 Westinghouse Dr.
Fremont, CA 94539

408-942-8660

Osborne/McGraw-Hill
2600 Tenth St.
Berkeley, CA 94710

415-490-8586

Panamax Corp.
150 Mitchell Blvd.
San Rafael, CA 94903

800-472-5555;
in CA 415-472-5547

Paradise Systems Inc.
150 North Hill Dr.
Brisbane, CA 94005

415-468-5320

PC Clearinghouse Inc.
11781 Lee Jackson Hwy.
Fairfax, VA 22033

PC World
555 De Haro St.
San Francisco, CA 94107

415-861-3861

PC—Ziff-Davis Publishing Co.
1 Park Ave.
New York, NY 10016   212-725-4694

Peachtree Software Inc.
3445 Peachtree Rd. NE
Atlanta, GA 30326   404-239-3000

PEARLSOFT Division/
Relational Systems International Corp.
Box 13850
Salem, OR 97302   503-390-6880

Percom Data Company Inc.
11220 Pagemill Rd.
Dallas, TX 75243   214-340-7081

Perfect Software Inc.
702 Harrison St.
Berkeley, CA 94710   415-527-2626

Personal Computer Insurance   408-723-8107

Phase One Systems Inc.
7700 Edgewater Dr. #830
Oakland, CA 94621   415-562-8085

Plantronics Inc.
Box 502
Frederick, MD 21701   800-638-6211

Princeton Graphic Systems
1101-I State Rd.   800-221-1490;
Princeton, NJ 08540   in NJ 609-683-1660

Professional Software Inc.
51 Fremont St.   800-343-4074;
Needham, MA 02194   in MA 617-444-5224

Quadram Corp.
4357 Park Dr.
Norcross, GA 30093   404-923-6666

Quantum Software Systems Inc.
7219 Shea Ct.
San Jose, CA 95139   408-629-9402

Qubie' Distributing
4809 Calle Alto   800-821-4479;
Camarillo, CA 93010   in CA 805-482-9829

Que Corp.
7960 Castleway Dr.
Indianapolis, IN 46250   800-428-5331

Qume Corp.
2350 Qume Dr.
San Jose, CA 95131   408-942-4000

RCA Service Co.
Route 38 (Bldg. 204-2)
Cherry Hill, NJ 08358   609-338-6568

RCS Inc.
2116A Walsh Ave.
Santa Clara, CA 95050   408-727-7548

Rediform Office Products
W-53 Century Rd.
Paramus, NJ 07652   201-265-5515

Renaissance Technology Corp.
1070 Shary Circle
Concord, CA 94518   415-676-5757

Rent-a-Computer Inc.
2471 E. Bayshore Rd. Suite 515
Palo Alto, CA 94303   415-493-2310

RKS Industries Inc.
4865 Scotts Valley Dr.   800-892-1342;
Scotts Valley, CA 95066   in CA 408-438-5760

Ryan-McFarland Corp.
9057 Soquel Dr.
Aptos, CA 95003   408-662-2522

SAFT America Inc.
931 N. Vandalia St.
St. Paul, MN 55114   612-645-8531

Santa Clara Systems
1860 Hartog Dr.
San Jose, CA 95131   408-287-4640

Sanyo Electric Inc.
1200 W. Artesia
Compton, CA 90220   213-537-5830

Scion Corp.
12310 Pinecrest Rd.
Reston, VA 22091   703-476-6100

SCM Corp.
65 Locust Ave.
New Canaan, CT 06840   203-972-1471

Seattle Computer Products Inc.
1114 Industry Dr.   800-426-8936;
Seattle, WA 98188   in WA 206-575-1830

Select Information Systems
919 Sir Francis Drake Blvd.
Kentfield, CA 94904   415-459-4003

Semidisk Systems
Box GG
Beaverton, OR 97075   503-642-3100

SGL Waber Electric
300 Harvard Ave.
Westville, NJ 08093   609-456-5400

Sofstar Inc.
13935 U.S. 1—Juno Sq.
Juno Beach, FL 33408   305-627-5511

Softalk For the IBM Personal Computer
Box 60
North Hollywood, CA 91603   213-980-5074

Software Arts Inc.
27 Mica Lane
Wellesley, MA 02180   617-237-4000

Software Arts Inc./SATN
Box 99
Newton Lower Falls, MA 02162   617-237-4000

Software Publishing Corp.
420 Aldo
Santa Clara, CA 95050

Sola Electric
1717 Busse Rd.
Elk Grove Village, IL 60007   312-439-2800

Sorbus Service Division
Management Assistance Inc.
50 E. Swedesford Rd.   800-423-2797;
Frazer, PA 19355   in CA 213-841-1973

Telecon Systems
1155 Meridian Ave. Suite 218
San Jose, CA 95125   408-275-1659

3COM Corp.
1390 Shorebird Way
Mountain View, CA 94043   415-961-9602

3M Data Recording Product Division
3M Center Bldg. 223-5N
St. Paul, MN 55144   612-736-9625

Tominy Inc.
4221 Malsbary Rd. Bldg. 1
Cincinnati, OH 45242   513-984-6605

Uarco Inc.
121 N. Ninth St.   800-435-0713;
DeKalb, IL 60115   in IL 815-756-8471

United States Data Systems
2988 Campus Dr.
San Mateo, CA 94403   415-572-6600

United States Instrument Rentals Inc.
2988 Campus Dr.
San Mateo, CA 94403   415-572-6600

USI International
71 Park Lane
Brisbane, CA 94005   415-468-4900

Ven-Tel Inc.
2342 Walsh Ave.   800-538-5121;
Santa Clara, CA 95051   in CA 408-727-5721

Verbatim Corp.
323 Soquel Way   800-538-1793;
Sunnyvale, CA 94086   in CA 408-737-7771

Vertex Systems
7950 W. 4th St.
Los Angeles, CA 90048   213-938-0857

VisiCorp
2895 Zanker Rd.
San Jose, CA 95134   408-496-9000

Williams and Foltz
1816 Fourth St.
Berkeley, CA 94710   415-644-2022

Wright Line Inc.
160 Gold Star Blvd.   800-225-7348;
Worcester, MA 01606   in MA 800-922-8349

XCOMP
7566 Trade St.
San Diego, CA 92121   619-271-8730

Glossary

Acoustic coupler: A type of modem that communicates with the telephone system by transmitting sound through a telephone's handset.

Active partition: The partition of a Fixed Disk that the PC boots from.

Adapter card: A printed circuit card that gives your PC more memory, enables it to control a new device, or gives it some other new capability. You plug it into one of the system expansion slots in the System Unit or System Expansion Unit.

ALT key: A key on the PC's keyboard labeled "Alt". It is pronounced "alt" (one syllable) or "alternate." Some application programs let you perform control functions by holding down the ALT key and pressing a typing key. Note that the ALT key is *not* equivalent to the CTRL key or the ESC key.

Application program: Any computer program that performs a task such as editing a letter, calculating your company's payroll, or keeping your appointment book. *See* "Operating system."

ASCII: A standard way of using numbers to represent character data. It is used to store character data on most computers, including the PC. ASCII is an acronym for "American Standard Code for Information Interchange."

ASCII file: A file that consists of printable data in ASCII notation. *See* "Text file."

Assembler language: A low-level programming language. It is actually just a convenient notation for writing programs in machine language.

Asynchronous: Describes a type of data transmission used for communication between computer devices through modems. Asynchronous transmission is most often used between small computers or between a terminal or small computer and a time-sharing system.

AUTOEXEC file: A file named AUTOEXEC.BAT, which contains DOS commands. When DOS is booted, it looks for an AUTOEXEC file in the root directory of the DOS disk. If it finds such a file, it runs the file as a batch file instead of prompting you for the date and time.

Backup: A copy of a file or diskette that is kept in a safe place in case the original is damaged or lost. *See also* "Full backup," "Partial backup."

Batch file: A file of commands that DOS can run as if you had entered them from the keyboard. A batch file must have the file-name extension BAT. You run it by entering its filename as if it were a command.

Baud: A unit of measure for how fast data is transferred between a computer and a peripheral. To convert a baud rate to an approximate number of characters per second, divide it by 10. For example, a 300 baud modem will transmit and receive about 30 characters per second.

Boot: To start a computer's operating system. The term "boot" comes from the notion of a computer "pulling itself up by its bootstraps," because a small portion of the operating system that is stored in ROM loads the rest of the operating system from disk.

Byte: The unit of storage (in RAM, ROM, or disk) that can hold one character of data. The capacity of a storage device is often measured in bytes. *See* "RAM," "ROM," "K," and "M."

Carrier tone: An audio signal generated by a modem. The modem transmits data by modulating the tone, much as a radio station transmits sound by modulating a radio signal.

Centronics interface: A kind of parallel interface used by many peripherals and computers, including the PC. Properly called a "Centronics-compatible interface," since it is a *de facto* standard first used by the Centronics Corporation. The terms "Centronics interface" and "parallel interface" are often used interchangeably, although a Centronics interface is really a specific type of parallel interface.

Co-processor card: An adapter card containing a CPU. It can enable your PC to run programs designed to use a CPU other than the PC's built-in Intel 8088.

Command: A keystroke or a line of input that you enter to make an operating system or application program do work for you. For example, DIR is a DOS command that lists the contents of a disk's directory. A word processing program would accept commands that did things like delete a word, insert a block of text, or start a new page. *See also* "External command," "Internal command."

Compiler: A program that reads a source program you have written and translates it into your PC's machine language. Such a program is ultimately translated into a COM or EXE file and is run like a command.

Composite video interface: A kind of interface used between a computer and monitor that combines all of the image and color information in a single signal. *See also* "RGB interface."

Console: A keyboard and display. Taken together, these devices make up the main interface between you and your computer.

Continuous forms: *see* "Pin-feed paper."

Control character: A character entered by holding down the CTRL key and pressing a typing key. Many application programs allow you to enter control characters for such functions as moving the cursor and manipulating data. Control characters generally are not used as data in text files, and they do not represent displayable characters in the ASCII character set. When they must be represented in writing, they are prefixed with a caret (^) or with the word CTRL.

Control key: *see* "CTRL key."

Copy-protection: The practice of making a diskette uncopyable by storing data on it in a nonstandard way. Software vendors often copy-protect their distribution diskettes to prevent a purchaser from copying the diskettes and reselling the copies.

Correspondence-quality printer: A dot-matrix printer that prints characters composed of a fine pattern of dots, giving quality comparable to the output of a typewriter with a fabric ribbon.

Corruption: What happens to data on a disk that has been scrambled by an I/O error, user error, or other problem. Symptoms of corrupted data include data that disappears from a text file; "foreign" data that spontaneously appears in a text file; an unrunnable program file; or a directory with nonsensical or missing file names or both.

CPU: An integrated circuit chip containing the part of a computer that actually does computing. Other chips in a computer perform support functions like storing data and controlling peripherals. CPU stands for "central processing unit." The PC's CPU is a model 8088 made by Intel Corporation.

Crossed cable: *see* "Null modem cable."

CTRL key: A key on the PC's keyboard labeled "Ctrl." It is pronounced "control." Many application programs let you enter program commands by holding down the CTRL key and pressing a typing key.

Current directory: The directory that DOS refers to when a file specification or a drive name is entered with no directory name. At any time, the disk on each disk drive has its own current directory. When DOS is started or a new disk is mounted, the disk's root directory is made the current directory.

Cursor: A symbol on a computer's display that marks the place where the next thing you type will appear. The PC's cursor looks like a blinking underscore.

Cursor control keys: *see* "Numeric keypad."

Customer support: All the services that you get from a dealer before and after purchasing hardware or software. Customer support includes advice on what to buy, expert help in installing a product and adapting it to your needs, training, and repair.

Cylinder: The part of a disk that can be read from and written to with the disk drive's read/write head(s) in one position. The number of tracks per cylinder depends on the number of recording surfaces a disk has. A diskette has one or two tracks per cylinder; a hard disk may have more, since it may consist of a stack of platters on a single spindle, each platter having its own pair of read/write heads.

Data base management system (DBMS): An application program that processes information organized as a set of records, each record consisting of fields of data. A DBMS can display and print reports derived from a data base and can perform various kinds of processing, such as sorting records, totaling fields from groups of records, and selecting records on the basis of the values of fields.

Default drive: The disk drive that DOS or a command uses to read from or write to a file when the drive name has been omitted from a file specification. The name of the current default drive is displayed in the standard DOS command line prompt.

Default value: A value (for example, for a parameter) that DOS or a command assumes when no value is given.

Device: A computer accessory that is used for input or output, such as a disk drive, a printer, or a keyboard. Also called an "I/O device."

Device name: A name used by DOS to identify a peripheral device like a serial interface or a console. It always ends with a colon. For example, in the command **copy con: b:example.txt{ENTER}**, "con:" is a device name that refers to the console.

Diagnostic programs: Programs for diagnosing hardware problems in the PC. They are on a diskette supplied with the PC. You run such programs by booting from the diskette (that is, by placing the diagnostic diskette in drive A and starting the PC) and making choices from the menus that the program presents to you. *See also* "Power-on diagnostics."

Direct-connect modem: A type of modem that connects to the telephone system by plugging directly into a modular wall jack.

Directory: An area on a disk that records the names and locations of the files on the disk. *See also* "Root directory," "Sub-directory," "Current directory."

Disk: A medium used for recording computer data. A disk rotates past a read/write head, which records (writes) and reads information under the computer's control. *See also* "Disk drive," "Hard disk drive," and "Diskette."

Disk drive: A device that reads and writes data on a magnetic disk, much as a tape recorder reads and writes sound recordings on magnetic tape. *See* "Diskette drive" and "Hard disk drive."

Disk Operating System: *see* "DOS."

Diskette: A flexible or "floppy" disk, 5 1/4 inches in diameter. Diskettes are one of the PC's standard media for file storage and backup.

Diskette drive: A type of disk drive that uses a diskette.

Distribution diskette: The diskette on which a software vendor sells a software product.

DOS: An acronym for "Disk Operating System." The term "DOS" generically refers to many different operating systems on different computers. In references to the IBM PC, DOS customarily refers to PCDOS, the PC's most widely used operating system.

Dot-matrix printer: A kind of printer whose print head contains a vertical row of pins that point at the paper through an inked ribbon. The printer forms printed characters by striking the paper with the wires through the ribbon as the print head moves across the paper.

Drive name: Formally known as a "drive specifier," a drive name is the name of a disk drive, used alone or as a prefix to a file specification. For example, in the command **copy b:example.txt a:{ENTER}**, "b" and "a" are drive names.

Drive specifier: *see* "Drive name."

Electronic mail: A service that lets you send a message to another person by signing onto an information utility, naming the addressee, and typing in the message. When the addressee signs on, the utility displays a message that mail is waiting and displays the **text** of each message on request.

ENTER key: The key on the PC's keyboard that is labeled ↵. It is also called the "return key," since its function resembles that of a typewriter's carriage return key.

Environment: In DOS 2.0, an area in RAM reserved for data that DOS and application programs use to decide how they should function. Examples of the sort of information that can be stored in the environment are what path a program should use to find a group of files; whether to display detailed or brief error messages; and what the DOS command line prompt should look like.

Environment string: A string of text in the environment that contains a piece of information for a particular program.

Ergonomics: The study of how the properties of the human body and mind affect the design of tools and equipment used in work.

Error level: In DOS 2.0, a value set by an external command to indicate whether the command ended normally or with an error. An IF command can test the error level and take different courses of action, depending on whether or not a preceding command ran successfully.

ESC key: A key on the PC's keyboard labeled "Esc." It is pronounced "escape." Many application programs let you use ESC to escape from an error condition or to change the program from one mode of operation to another.

Expansion Unit: *see* "System Expansion Unit."

External command: A DOS command that is stored in a disk file with the filename extension COM or EXE and that is loaded into RAM when it is to be run.

File: A collection of similar data that is stored on a disk and that may be referred to by name.

Filename: The first part of a file's name, which describes the contents of the file. In the name EXAMPLE.TXT, "EXAMPLE" is the filename.

Filename extension: The second part of a file's name, which describes the type of data in the file. In the name EXAMPLE.TXT, "TXT" is the filename extension.

File's name: The name used to identify a file. It is formally called a "file specification." It is different from the "filename," which is the part of a file's name that describes the contents of the file.

File specification: *see* "File's name."

Filter: A program that copies data from one text file to another, making some type of systematic change in the data as it copies. An example is a program that copies from a file only those lines of text that contain a certain sequence of characters. DOS 2.0 has three filter commands: SORT, FIND, and MORE.

Fixed Disk: The hard disk and hard disk drive sold by IBM for the IBM PC and installed in the PC XT.

Flexible disk: A disk made of flexible plastic material that is coated with a magnetic recording surface and protected by a square plastic jacket. *See also* "Diskette."

Floating point: A method of storing numeric data that enables a computer to represent noninteger values like 1.25, 3.1415926, and 0.0000001.

Floppy disk: An informal name for a flexible disk or diskette.

Form feed: A printer operation that advances the printer's paper to the top of a new sheet (if the paper is correctly positioned). The control character a computer sends to a printer to make it do a form feed is also called a "form feed" or a "form feed character."

Formatting: The process of writing a special pattern of data over the recording surface of a disk. You must format a disk before you can use it to store data. In DOS, you use the FORMAT command to format disks.

Fragmentation: The splitting of a disk file into two or more non-contiguous pieces as a side effect of creating and deleting files.

Excessive fragmentation can slow down disk I/O operations significantly.

Full backup: A backup of all the files on a disk. *See also* "Partial backup."

Global filename character: A symbol that can be used in a file's name to represent one or more characters. DOS recognizes two global filename characters: ? represents any one character, and * represents any number of characters.

Graphics: The technique of forming a picture from a pattern of dots or lines on a computer output device, such as a display or a printer.

Hard disk drive: A type of disk drive that uses a rigid (hard) disk. The hard disk is usually permanently sealed into the drive to protect it from contamination by dust. Hard disk drives tend to have greater capacity, speed, and reliability than diskette drives, and also tend to be more expensive.

Hidden file: A file that is stored on a disk but that does not appear in a directory listing of the disk. A bootable DOS disk holds two hidden files, which contain parts of DOS that are kept in RAM whenever the PC is running.

High-level language: A programming language in which you write programs in a notation that is close to your natural way of expressing the problem you want to solve. *See also* "Low-level language."

I/O: An abbreviation for "input/output," the two basic operations that a computer performs on its peripherals.

I/O device: *see* "Device."

I/O error: Any error associated with an I/O operation. One example of an I/O error is a disk error, which occurs when the PC is trying to read or write data on a disk.

Information utility: A business that uses a large computer to offer information and information-based services to the public.

Interface: A set of rules defining how two computer devices may communicate with each other.

Internal command: A command that is part of DOS and is therefore kept in RAM whenever DOS is running. *See also* "External command."

Interpreter: A program that reads a program you have written and performs the actions that the program's statements denote.

Joystick: An input device with a lever mounted on a universal joint. You can indicate motion (usually cursor motion) by moving the lever in any direction.

K: A unit used to measure the capacity of a computer's memory. 1K equals 1024 bytes.

Keystroke: The amount of data that you enter through a keyboard by pressing one typing key.

Label: A name given to a point in a file. In DOS 2.0, you can put a label on a line of a batch file and use the GOTO command to make DOS "go to" the label.

LAN: An acronym for "local area network." A LAN is a combination of hardware and software that connects two or more computers, enabling them to exchange data very rapidly and to share peripherals.

Letter-quality printer: A printer that forms characters by striking a raised type element against the paper through a ribbon. Letter-quality printers produce high-quality output but operate at low to moderate speeds.

Light pen: A pen-shaped device that is used with a monitor for computer input. The PC can sense when the pen touches the monitor's screen through a switch in the tip of the pen. If the monitor is displaying anything at the point of contact, the PC can determine the pen's approximate position.

Line editing: A feature of DOS that lets you edit lines with the program function keys and the INS and DEL keys. The line editing feature may be used in DOS commands, in EDLIN, and in many application programs.

Line number: A number that identifies a line in a text file.

Local area network: *see* "LAN."

Low-level language: A programming language in which you write programs in a notation that is close to the steps the computer must perform to run the program. *See also* "High-level language."

M: A unit used to measure the capacity of a computer's memory. 1M equals 1024K, or 1,048,576 bytes.

Machine language: The only type of programming language that a computer can understand directly. A program written in machine language consists of a string of numbers and is very difficult for humans to understand. Thus compilers, interpreters, and assemblers are used to let humans deal with programs in a more legible form.

Memory: Any hardware that a computer uses to store data. *See* "RAM," "ROM," and "Disk drive."

Menu: A list of things a program can do next, which the program displays to prompt you for instructions. You respond by selecting one of the menu items.

Microspacing: The technique of making a printed document's right margin even by inserting equal amounts of space between all the words on a line. Microspaced output resembles typesetting in appearance. *See also* "Proportional spacing."

Modem: A device for communicating between computers through the telephone system. A modem works by converting data between the digital form used by a computer and an audio form (a "carrier tone") that can be transmitted over the telephone. "Modem" is a contraction of "modulator/demodulator."

Monitor: A device similar to a television set that a computer can use to display words or images. A monitor may display color or monochrome images. On the IBM PC, a monitor must be used with an IBM Color/Graphics Monitor Adapter or equivalent adapter card. *See also* "Monochrome Display."

Monochrome Display: A display device, similar to a monitor, that must be used with an IBM Monochrome Display Adapter or equivalent adapter card. The Monochrome Display shows a green-on-black image with better definition and less flicker than most monitors.

Mouse: An input device that you move around on a table top or a specially ruled pad. Many application programs let you use a mouse to control cursor motion.

Multifunction card: An adapter card that provides several functions, letting you add more capabilities to your PC without running out of system expansion slots.

Node: A computer connected to a local area network (LAN), seen from the LAN's point of view.

Null modem cable: An RS-232C cable in which certain pairs of wires are cross-connected. You must use a null modem cable to connect a PC serial interface to most serial-interface printers.

Numeric keypad: A group of keys near the right side of the PC's keyboard. These keys have two functions. They can be used to enter numbers, like the keyboard of a calculator. They can also be used to perform program functions such as positioning the cursor. In the latter case, they are often called "cursor control keys." You switch the keys between these two functions by pressing the NUM LOCK key, which is located immediately above the numeric keypad.

Off-line: Not ready for use; not ready to communicate with a computer. Used to describe a peripheral device such as a printer. Opposite of "On-line."

On-line: Ready for use; ready to communicate with a computer. Used to describe a peripheral device such as a printer. Opposite of "Off-line."

Operating system: A computer program that manages the technical details of running a computer, freeing application programs to do useful work. Examples of operating system tasks are reading application programs from a disk, collecting keystrokes from the keyboard, and presenting an application program's output on the display.

Option: A letter preceded by a slash that gives a DOS command extra information about what you want it to do. For example, in the command **copy example.txt b:/v{ENTER}**, the option /V tells COPY to read back the target file while writing it, in order to verify that it is written correctly. Each DOS command recognizes its own set of options and interprets them in its own way.

Option card: *see* "Adapter card."

Overlay: A part of a computer program that is stored in a file separate from the COM or EXE file containing the main part of the program. The program loads the overlay into RAM only when needed. Large programs can reduce their RAM requirements by loading several overlays into the same part of RAM, one at a time.

Overlay file: A file containing one or more overlays.

Parallel interface: A type of interface between a computer and a peripheral. It is the preferred interface for attaching a printer to the PC. *See also* "Centronics interface."

Parameter: A word on a DOS command line that follows the command name and gives the command information about what you want it to do. For example, in the command **diskcopy a: b:{ENTER}**, "a:" and "b:" are parameters. *See also* "Option."

Parameter symbol: A percent sign (%) followed by a number, used in a batch file to represent a parameter. When the batch file is run, every "%1" in the batch file is replaced by the first parameter of the command that ran the file, while every "%2" is replaced by the second parameter, and so forth. Every "%0" is replaced by the command name itself.

Parent directory: The directory in which a sub-directory is defined. A parent directory may be the disk's root directory or another sub-directory. *See* "Tree-structured directory."

Partial backup: A backup of selected files on a disk. A partial backup usually includes all files changed since the most recent full backup of the disk or all files changed since the most recent backup of any sort.

Partition: A part of a Fixed Disk that is devoted to disk storage for a particular operating system. Each partition is visible only to the operating system it is intended for.

Path: The sequence of directories leading from a disk's root directory or current directory to some other particular directory or file. *See also* "Search path."

PC I: An early version of the IBM Personal Computer that can hold up to 64K of RAM on the System Board.

PC II: A version of the IBM Personal Computer, introduced as a replacement for the earlier PC I, that can hold up to 256K of RAM on the System Board.

PC XT: A version of the IBM Personal Computer that can hold as much as 256K of RAM on the System Board and has a built-in Fixed Disk.

PCDOS: The most commonly used operating system on the PC. *See* "DOS."

Peripheral: A device that a computer uses to transfer information back and forth between itself and the outside world. Some examples of peripherals are a display screen, a disk drive, and a printer.

Pin-feed paper: Paper with a row of sprocket holes along each edge. Also called "continuous forms." It is usually sold in cartons of several thousand sheets, with the sheets joined end to end in a continuous folded strip.

Pipe: A direct connection between the output of one program and the input to another. DOS 2.0 can create a pipe between one program's display output and another program's keyboard input.

Pixel: The smallest image element in a graphics image; a dot that may be either lighted or dark. "Pixel" is a contraction of "picture element."

Plotter: An output device that draws graphics by moving a pen over a sheet of paper under computer control.

Power conditioner: A device that protects your PC and peripherals from certain types of electrical damage by filtering the line power that runs them.

Power-on diagnostics: Checkout procedures that the PC runs automatically when it is turned on. These checkout procedures verify that all of the PC's hardware is functioning properly. If the diagnostics detect problems, your PC displays error codes before (or instead of) booting DOS. The error codes can help a service person determine what is wrong with your PC.

Print wheel: The informal name for a kind of printing element used by many letter-quality printers. The print wheel resembles the hub and spokes of a wagon wheel; one printable character is embossed on the end of each "spoke." The printer positions different characters in front of the paper by rotating the wheel on its axis. *See also* "Thimble."

Program function keys (PFKs): Ten keys at the left end of the PC's keyboard. Many application programs let you use the PFKs to perform control operations. For example, a word processor might let you use them to move the cursor around, insert or delete text, and search the text for words or phrases.

Programming language: A form of notation for writing computer programs. Many different programming languages with different strengths and weaknesses are available for the PC. *See also* "High-level language" and "Low-level language."

Prompt: A message from a computer inviting you to enter some information. DOS's standard command line prompt consists of the name of the current default disk followed by the greater-than character ($>$).

Proportional spacing: A printer feature that makes some letters (like *m*) wider than others (like *i*). Proportional-spaced printing resembles typesetting in appearance. *See also* "Microspacing."

Queue: A place to keep a list of things that are waiting for something to happen. In DOS 2.0, the PRINT command queues files to be printed. While the files are printing, you can run other commands on your PC. The files are printed in the order they are queued; each file must wait for the preceding file to finish printing. The print queue is sometimes called the "spool."

RAM: An acronym for random-access memory, which is a type of memory that is used to hold a computer program and the data that the program operates on while the program is running. RAM is found on the PC's System Board and adapter cards.

RAM card: An adapter card that expands your PC's RAM capacity.

RAM disk: A program that enables DOS to use part of your PC's RAM to store files as if the RAM were a disk.

Random-access memory: *see* "RAM."

Raster graphics: The technique of constructing a picture out of a pattern of parallel scan lines. This technique is used by television sets and most computer display screens.

Read-only memory: *see* "ROM."

Read/write head: The magnetic sensor in a disk drive or tape drive that writes information on disk or tape and reads it back.

Redirection: Sending output intended for one destination to a different one, or fetching input intended to come from one origin from a different one. DOS 2.0 lets you redirect most programs' display output and keyboard input to files or devices.

Resolution: The smallest separation between points in an image that a device can represent as separate points in its output. For example, a dot matrix printer that prints 72 dots per linear inch has a resolution of 1/72 inch. Resolution is a measure of how much detail a graphics device can print or display.

Return key: *see* "ENTER key."

RF modulator: A device that adapts a television set for use as a computer display.

RGB interface: A kind of interface used between computers and certain color monitors. It uses a separate wire to send image information for each color (red, green, and blue). It tends to produce a higher quality image than a composite video interface.

ROM: An acronym for read-only memory, which is a type of memory that permanently holds data stored when the ROM is manufactured. The computer can read the data but cannot change it. ROM is · ;ed to hold some parts of the PC's operating system, the BASIC interpreter, and other fundamental operating software.

Root directory: The first directory defined on a disk. All files and sub-directories on a disk must be stored in the root directory or in sub-directories that can be traced back to the root directory.

RS-232C interface: A kind of serial interface used by many peripherals and computers, including the PC. The terms "RS-232C interface" and "serial interface" are often used interchangeably, although an RS-232C interface is actually a specific type of serial interface.

Search path: A group of one or more paths leading to directories that DOS is to search when you enter a command and DOS cannot find the command in the directory that the command line indicates.

Sector: A physical unit of recorded information on a disk track. In DOS, a diskette's sector is 512 bytes long, and each track contains either eight or nine sectors.

Semigraphics: The technique of constructing a picture out of characters, often utilizing special symbols such as boxes and triangles.

Serial interface: One type of interface between a computer and a peripheral. On the PC, it is most often used for communicating with a modem or another computer. Many printers also use serial interfaces. *See also* "RS-232C interface."

Slaving: Making an operating system copy its display output to a printer is called "slaving the printer to the display." In DOS, you slave the printer to the display by entering CTRL PRTSC.

Software: All of the computer programs that make a computer do useful tasks. Also, the set of computer programs that make a computer do a particular useful task.

Source: The "from" point in a copying or moving operation. Usually used in a phrase like "source file," "source disk," and so on.

Spooling: The process of sending text files to a queue, from which they may then be printed. *See* "Queue." The word "spool" is an acronym for "system peripheral output, on-line."

Standby power system: A device that protects a computer or other electrical device from blackouts. It is similar to an uninterruptible power supply but does not provide protection against such power disturbances as spikes and surges.

String: A sequence of characters. Many programs can search files for occurrences of a string in one manner or another. Examples are the Search command in EDLIN and the FIND command in DOS.

Sub-directory: A directory that is stored in another directory as if it were a file. DOS 2.0 allows you to define many levels of sub-directories on a disk.

Synchronous: Describes a type of data transmission used to communicate between one computer and another through modems. Synchronous transmission is most often used between two large computers, or between a terminal or small computer and the sort of large computer that many businesses operate for their own use.

System Board: The large printed circuit board inside the System Unit with many electronic components mounted on it. It contains most of the electronics at the heart of the PC's operations.

System expansion slot: A socket for holding an adapter card. The System Unit and System Expansion Unit both have system expansion slots.

System Expansion Unit: A component that attaches to the System Unit through a data cable. It provides slots for additional adapter cards and room for additional disk drives.

System Unit: The central component of the IBM PC. It contains one or more disk drives, a power supply, the System Board, and a variable number of adapter cards.

Target: The "to" point in a copying or moving operation. Usually used in a phrase like "target file," "target disk," and so on.

Template: A line of text that DOS's line editing feature uses as the basis for creating a new or modified line of text. By using the program function keys, the INS key, and the DEL key, you can copy characters from the template to the new line, skip over template characters, and insert new characters in the new line.

Text editor: A program for creating and modifying text files.

Text file: A file that contains text such as a letter, research paper, or customer list.

Thimble: The informal name for a kind of printing element used by some letter-quality printers. The thimble's printable characters are embossed on arms that rise from the edge of a flat plastic disk, so that the printing element resembles a thimble, with the arms making up the thimble's sides. The printer positions different characters in front of the paper by rotating the thimble on its axis. *See also* "Print wheel."

Time-sharing system: A large computer that can be shared by many users performing unrelated tasks. Many time-sharing systems are run as commercial services.

Time stamp: A record of the date and time that a file was created or last modified. Each DOS file's time stamp is kept in the file's directory entry.

Track: A ring of data on a disk that passes a read/write head as the disk rotates.

Tractor: A mechanism that pulls pin-feed paper through a printer. It engages the paper's sprocket holes with a pair of sprocketed wheels or belts. A tractor may be built into a printer or may be added as an accessory.

Tree-structured directory: The type of directory that DOS 2.0 uses to manage disk files. The root directory contains sub-directories ("branches") and files ("leaves"), and each sub-directory may itself contain other sub-directories and files.

Typing key: Any key on the PC's keyboard that, when pressed, enters a character.

Uninterruptible power supply (UPS): A device that protects a computer or other electrical device from all types of electric power disturbances, including blackouts. When the voltage in the power mains drops below an acceptable level, the UPS automatically provides AC power generated from a battery. Most UPSs for small computers deliver power only long enough for you to halt your work and turn off your computer in an orderly way. *See also* "Standby power system."

UPS: *see* "Uninterruptible power supply."

User group: An organization of computer users with common interests. Many user groups now exist for owners of the IBM PC.

Verification: The process of reading back disk data after writing it to be sure it was written correctly. To make the COPY command verify its output, use the /V option. To make DOS 2.0 verify all disk output, run the VERIFY command.

Volume label: A name that identifies a disk. DOS 2.0 allows you to give any disk a volume label up to 11 characters long.

Winchester disk: The type of hard disk most often used on small computers like the PC. It is sealed into a dust-proof case and permanently fixed to the disk drive.

Word processor: A text editor designed especially for editing documents like letters, memos, and manuscripts, as distinguished from data files like mailing lists and financial records.

Write-protect notch: A notch in the right edge of a diskette's plastic jacket. If the notch is covered by a piece of tape, any attempt to write to the diskette will fail.

INDEX

432